Teach Yourself
Microsoft®
Excel 97

IDG's **3-D Visual** Series

IDG BOOKS *From* **maranGraphics**

IDG Books Worldwide, Inc.
An International Data Group Company
Foster City, CA • Indianapolis • Chicago • New York

Teach Yourself Microsoft® Excel 97 VISUALLY™

Published by
IDG Books Worldwide, Inc.
An International Data Group Company
919 E. Hillsdale Blvd., Suite 400
Foster City, CA 94404

Copyright© 1998 by maranGraphics Inc.
5755 Coopers Avenue
Mississauga, Ontario, Canada
L4Z 1R9

Library of Congress Catalog Card No.: 98-75599

ISBN: 0-7645-6063-8

Printed in the United States of America
10 9 8 7 6 5

Distributed in the United States by IDG Books Worldwide, Inc.

Distributed by Transworld Publishers Limited in the United Kingdom; by IDG Norge Books for Norway; by IDG Sweden Books for Sweden; by Woodslane Pty. Ltd. for Australia; by Woodslane (NZ) Ltd. for New Zealand; by Addison Wesley Longman Singapore Pte Ltd. for Singapore, Malaysia, Thailand, Indonesia and Korea; by Norma Comunicaciones S.A. for Colombia; by Intersoft for South Africa; by International Thomson Publishing for Germany, Austria and Switzerland; by Toppan Company Ltd. for Japan; by Distribuidora Cuspide for Argentina; by Livraria Cultura for Brazil; by Ediciencia S.A. for Ecuador; by Ediciones ZETA S.C.R. Ltda. for Peru; by WS Computer Publishing Corporation, Inc., for the Philippines; by Unalis Corporation for Taiwan; by Contemporanea de Ediciones for Venezuela; by Computer Book & Magazine Store for Puerto Rico; by Express Computer Distributors for the Caribbean and West Indies. Authorized Sales Agent: Anthony Rudkin Associates for the Middle East and North Africa.

For corporate orders, please call maranGraphics at 800-469-6616.

For general information on IDG Books Worldwide's books in the U.S., please call our Consumer Customer Service department at 800-762-2974.

For reseller information, including discounts and premium sales, please call our Reseller Customer Service department at 800-434-3422.

For information on where to purchase IDG Books Worldwide's books outside the U.S., please contact our International Sales department at 650-655-3200 or fax 650-655-3297.

For information on foreign language translations, please contact our Foreign & Subsidiary Rights department at 650-655-3021 or fax 650-655-3281.

For sales inquiries and special prices for bulk quantities, please contact our Sales department at 650-655-3200.

For information on using IDG Books Worldwide's books in the classroom or for ordering examination copies, please contact our Educational Sales department at 800-434-2086 or fax 317-596-5499.

For press review copies, author interviews, or other publicity information, please contact our Public Relations department at 650-655-3000 or fax 650-655-3299.

For authorization to photocopy items for corporate, personal, or educational use, please contact maranGraphics at 800-469-6616.

Trademark Acknowledgments

Permissions

©1998 maranGraphics, Inc.

The 3-D illustrations are the copyright of maranGraphics, Inc.

U.S. Corporate Sales	**U.S. Trade Sales**
Contact maranGraphics at (800) 469-6616 or Fax (905) 890-9434.	Contact IDG Books at (800) 434-3422 or (650) 655-3000.

Welcome to the world of IDG Books Worldwide.

IDG Books Worldwide, Inc., is a subsidiary of International Data Group, the world's largest publisher of computer-related information and the leading global provider of information services on information technology. IDG was founded more than 25 years ago and now employs more than 8,500 people worldwide. IDG publishes more than 270 computer publications in over 75 countries (see listing below). More than 90 million people read one or more IDG publications each month.

Launched in 1990, IDG Books Worldwide is today the #1 publisher of best-selling computer books in the United States. We are proud to have received eight awards from the Computer Press Association in recognition of editorial excellence and three from Computer Currents' First Annual Readers' Choice Awards. Our best-selling ...For Dummies® series has more than 25 million copies in print with translations in 30 languages. IDG Books Worldwide, through a joint venture with IDG's Hi-Tech Beijing, became the first U.S. publisher to publish a computer book in the People's Republic of China. In record time, IDG Books Worldwide has become the first choice for millions of readers around the world who want to learn how to better manage their businesses.

Our mission is simple: Every one of our books is designed to bring extra value and skill-building instructions to the reader. Our books are written by experts who understand and care about our readers. The knowledge base of our editorial staff comes from years of experience in publishing, education, and journalism - experience which we use to produce books for the '90s. In short, we care about books, so we attract the best people. We devote special attention to details such as audience, interior design, use of icons, and illustrations. And because we use an efficient process of authoring, editing, and desktop publishing our books electronically, we can spend more time ensuring superior content and spend less time on the technicalities of making books.

You can count on our commitment to deliver high-quality books at competitive prices on topics you want to read about. At IDG Books Worldwide, we continue in the IDG tradition of delivering quality for more than 25 years. You'll find no better book on a subject than one from IDG Books Worldwide.

John Kilcullen
CEO
IDG Books Worldwide, Inc.

Steven Berkowitz
President and Publisher
IDG Books Worldwide, Inc.

IDG Books Worldwide, Inc., is a subsidiary of International Data Group, the world's largest publisher of computer-related information and the leading global provider of information services on information technology. International Data Group publishes over 276 computer publications in over 75 countries. Ninety million people read one or more International Data Group publications each month. International Data Group's publications include: Argentina: Annuario de Informatica, Computerworld Argentina, PC World Argentina; Australia: Australian Macworld, Client/Server Journal, Computer Living, Computerworld, Computerworld 100, Digital News, IT Casebook, Network World, On-line World Australia, PC World, Publishing Essentials, Reseller, WebMaster; Austria: Computerwelt Österreich, Networks Austria, PC Tip; Belarus: PC World Belarus; Belgium: Data News; Brazil: Annuário de Informática, Computerworld Brazil, Connections, Super Game Power, Macworld, PC Player, PC World Brazil, Publish Brazil, Reseller News; Bulgaria: Computerworld Bulgaria, Networkworld/Bulgaria, PC & MacWorld Bulgaria; Canada: CIO Canada, Client/Server World, ComputerWorld Canada, InfoCanada, Network World Canada; Chile: Computerworld Chile, PC World Chile; Colombia: Computerworld Colombia, PC World Colombia; Costa Rica: PC World Centro America; The Czech and Slovak Republics: Computerworld Czechoslovakia, Elektronika Czechoslovakia, Macworld Czech Republic, PC World Czechoslovakia; Denmark: Communications World, Computerworld Danmark, Macworld Danmark, PC Privat Danmark, PC World Danmark, PC World Danmark Supplements, TECH World; Dominican Republic: PC World Republica Dominicana; Ecuador: PC World Ecuador; Egypt: Computerworld Middle East, PC World Middle East; El Salvador: PC World Centro America; Finland: MikroPC, Tietoverkko, Tietoviikko; France: Distributique, Golden, Hebdo-Distributique, Info PC, Le Guide du Monde Informatique, Le Monde Informatique, Reseaux & Telecoms; Germany: Computer Partner, Computerwoche, Computerwoche Extra, Computerwoche Focus, I/M Information Management, Macwelt, PC Welt; Greece: GamePro, Multimedia World; Guatemala: PC World Centro America; Honduras: PC World Centro America; Hong Kong: Computerworld Hong Kong, PCWorld Hong Kong, Publish in Asia; Hungary: ABCD CD-ROM, Computerworld Szamitastechnika, PC & Mac World Hungary, PC-X Magazine; Iceland: Tolvuheimur/PC World Island; India: Information Systems Computerworld, PC World India, Publish in Asia; Indonesia: InfoKomputer PC World, Komputek Computerworld, Publish in Asia; Ireland: ComputerScope, PC Live!; Israel: People & Computers; Italy: Computerworld Italia, Computerworld Italia Special Editions, Macworld Italia, Networking Italia, PC Shopping, PC World Italia, PC World/Walt Disney; Japan: DTP World, HP Open World Japan, Macworld Japan, Nikkei Personal Computing, Open World Japan, OS/2 World Japan, SunWorld Japan, Windows World Japan; Kenya: East African Computer News; Korea: Hi-Tech Information/Computerworld, Macworld Korea, PC World Korea; Macedonia: PC World Macedonia; Malaysia: Computerworld Malaysia, PC World Malaysia, Publish in Asia; Mexico: Computerworld Mexico, Macworld, PC World Mexico; Myanmar: PC World Myanmar; Netherlands: Computer! Totaal, LAN Magazine, LanWorld Buyers Guide, Net Magazine, Totaal! Beurskrant; New Zealand: Absolute Beginner's Guide, Computer Buyer, Computer Industry Directory, Computerworld New Zealand, MTB, Network World, PC World New Zealand; Nicaragua: PC World Centro America; Nigeria: PC World Nigeria; Norway: Computerworld Norge, Computerworld Privat (Datamagasinet), CW Rapport Norge, IDG's KURSGUIDE, Macworld Norge, Multimediaworld, PC World Ekspress, PC World Nettverk, PC World Norge, PC World's Produktguide, Windows World Spesial; Pakistan: Computerworld Pakistan, PC World Pakistan; Panama: PC World Panama; P. R. of China: China Computer Users, China Computerworld, China Infoworld, China Telecom World Weekly, Computer & Communication, Electronic Design China, Electronics Today, Electronics Weekly, Game Camp, Game Soft, Network World China, PC World China, Popular Computer Weekly, Software Weekly, Software World, Telecom World; Peru: Computerworld Peru, PC World Profesional Peru, PC World Peru; Poland: Computerworld Poland, Computerworld Special Report, Macworld, Networld, PC World Komputer; Philippines: Computerworld Philippines, PC World Philippines, Publish in Asia, Portugal: Cerebro/PC World, Computerworld/Correio Informático, Dealer World Portugal, Mac*In/PC*In, Multimedia World Portugal; Puerto Rico: PC World Puerto Rico; Romania: Computerworld Romania, PC World Romania, Telecom Romania; Russia: Computerworld Russia, Mir PK, Sety; Singapore: Computerworld Singapore, PC World Singapore, Publish in Asia; Slovenia: MONITOR; South Africa: Computing S.A., InfoWorld S.A., Network World S.A., Software World; Spain: Computerworld Espa-a, COMUNICACIONES WORLD, Dealer World, Macworld Espa-a, PC World Espa-a; Sweden: CAP&Design, Computer Sweden, Corporate Computing, Macworld, Maxi Data, MikroDatorn, Nätverk & Kommunikation, PC/Aktiv, PC World, Windows World; Switzerland: Computerworld Schweiz, Macworld Schweiz, PCtip; Taiwan: Computerworld Taiwan, Macworld Taiwan, PC World Taiwan, Publish Taiwan, Windows World; Thailand: Thai Computerworld, Publish in Asia; Turkey: Computerworld Turkiye, MACWORLD Turkiye, PC WORLD Turkiye; Ukraine: Computerworld Kiev, Computers & Software, Multimedia World Ukraine, PC World Ukraine; United Kingdom: Acorn User, Amiga Action, Amiga Computing, Appletalk, Computing, GamePro, Macworld, Network News, Parents and Computers, PC Advisor, PC Home, PSX Pro UK, The WEB; United States: Cable in the Classroom, CD Review, CIO Magazine, Computerworld, Computerworld Client/Server Journal, Digital Video Magazine, DOS World, Federal Computer Week, GamePro, InfoWorld, I-Way, JavaWorld, Macworld, Multimedia World, Netscape World Online, Network World, PC Entertainment, PC World, Publish, SunWorld Online, SWATPro Magazine, Video Event, WebMaster; Uruguay: PC World Uruguay; Venezuela: Computerworld Venezuela, PC World Venezuela; and Vietnam: PC World Vietnam.

**Every maranGraphics book represents
the extraordinary vision and commitment of a unique family:
the Maran family of Toronto, Canada.**

Back Row (from left to right): *Sherry Maran, Rob Maran, Richard Maran,
Maxine Maran, Jill Maran.*
Front Row (from left to right): *Judy Maran, Ruth Maran.*

Richard Maran is the company founder and its inspirational leader. He developed maranGraphics' proprietary communication technology called "visual grammar." This book is built on that technology—empowering readers with the easiest and quickest way to learn about computers.

Ruth Maran is the Author and Architect—a role Richard established that now bears Ruth's distinctive touch. She creates the words and visual structure that are the basis for the books.

Judy Maran is the Project Manager. She works with Ruth, Richard and the highly talented maranGraphics illustrators, designers and editors to transform Ruth's material into its final form.

Rob Maran is the Technical and Production Specialist. He makes sure the state-of-the-art technology used to create these books always performs as it should.

Sherry Maran manages the Reception, Order Desk and any number of areas that require immediate attention and a helping hand.

Jill Maran is a jack-of-all-trades who works in the Accounting and Human Resources department.

Maxine Maran is the Business Manager and family sage. She maintains order in the business and family—and keeps everything running smoothly.

CREDITS

Author & Architect:
Ruth Maran

Copy Development Director:
Kelleigh Wing

Copy Developers:
Roxanne Van Damme
Jason M. Brown
Cathy Benn

Project Manager:
Judy Maran

Editing & Screen Captures:
Raquel Scott
Janice Boyer
Michelle Kirchner
James Menzies
Frances Lea
Emmet Mellow

Layout Designer:
Treena Lees

Illustrators:
Russ Marini
Jamie Bell
Peter Grecco
Sean Johannesen
Steven Schaerer

Screen Artists:
Jimmy Tam
Sean Johannesen

Indexer:
Raquel Scott

Permissions Coordinator:
Jenn Hillman

Post Production:
Robert Maran

Editorial Support:
Michael Roney

ACKNOWLEDGMENTS

Thanks to the dedicated staff of maranGraphics, including
Jamie Bell, Cathy Benn, Janice Boyer, Jason M. Brown,
Francisco Ferreira, Peter Grecco, Jenn Hillman, Sean Johannesen,
Michelle Kirchner, Wanda Lawrie, Frances Lea, Treena Lees,
Jill Maran, Judy Maran, Maxine Maran, Robert Maran,
Sherry Maran, Russ Marini, Emmet Mellow, James Menzies,
Steven Schaerer, Raquel Scott, Jimmy Tam, Roxanne Van Damme,
Paul Whitehead and Kelleigh Wing.

Finally, to Richard Maran who originated the easy-to-use
graphic format of this guide. Thank you for your
inspiration and guidance.

TABLE OF CONTENTS

Chapter 1

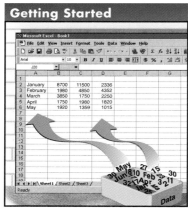

Getting Started

Chapter 2

Save and Open Your Workbooks

Chapter 3

Edit Your Worksheets

Chapter 4

Work With Formulas and Functions

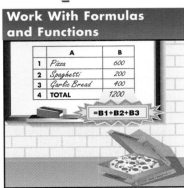

TABLE OF CONTENTS

Chapter 5

Change Your Screen Display

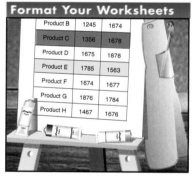

Chapter 6

Format Your Worksheets

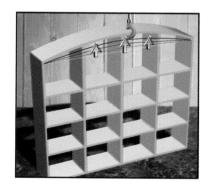

Chapter 7

Print Your Worksheets

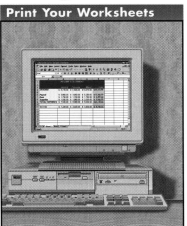

Chapter 8

Work With Multiple Worksheets

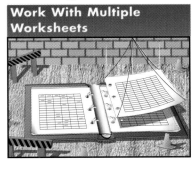

TABLE OF CONTENTS

Chapter 9

Work With Charts

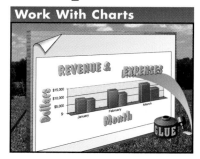

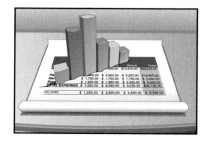

Chapter 10

Work With Graphics

Chapter 11

Create Powerful Worksheets

Chapter 12

Manage Data in a List

Chapter 13

Excel and the Internet

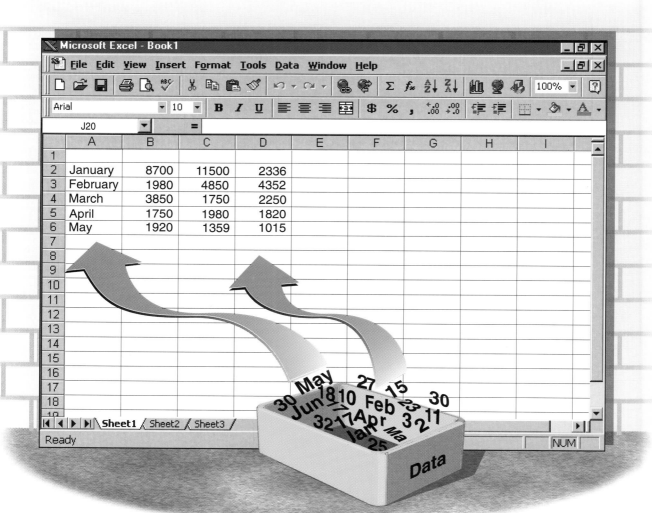

CHAPTER 1

Getting Started

Are you ready to begin using Microsoft Excel 97? This chapter will help you get started.

INTRODUCTION TO EXCEL

Excel is a spreadsheet program you can use to organize, analyze and attractively present financial data, such as a budget or sales report.

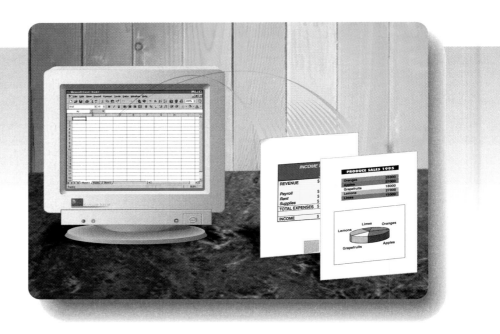

Enter and Edit Data

Excel lets you efficiently enter and edit data in your worksheets. You can move, copy and find data. You can also check for spelling mistakes and add comments to cells.

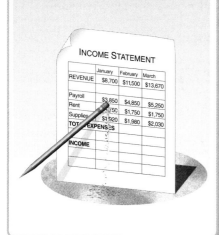

Using Formulas and Functions

You can use formulas and functions to perform calculations and analyze data in your worksheets.

Common calculations include finding the sum, average or total number of items in a list. You can also create scenarios to see how different values will affect the calculations in a worksheet.

Format Worksheets

Excel includes many formatting features that can help you change the appearance of your worksheets. You can add borders and color to the cells in a worksheet or enhance the data by changing the font, color or alignment. Changing the format of numbers in worksheets can make values easier to identify.

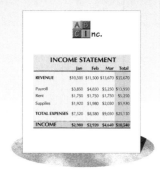

Print Worksheets

Excel allows you to preview your worksheets to
see how they will appear on a printed page. You
can adjust the margins or change the orientation
of the printed data. You can also add a header or
footer to print additional information on each page.

Create Charts

Excel helps you create colorful charts from your
worksheet data. You can move, size and print
charts. Excel also allows you to change the chart
type and format chart text. If your worksheet
contains geographical data, you can create a
map to present the data.

Add Graphics

You can add graphics to enhance the appearance
of your worksheets and illustrate important concepts.
Graphics you can add include AutoShapes, text boxes,
text effects, clip art images and pictures.

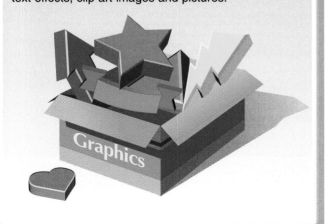

Manage Data in a List

Excel provides tools that help you manage and
analyze a large collection of data, such as a mailing
list or product list. You can edit, sort and filter a list.
You can also add subtotals to a list to summarize
the data.

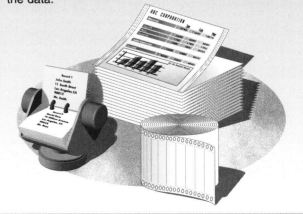

USING THE MOUSE

A mouse is a handheld device that lets you select and move items on your screen.

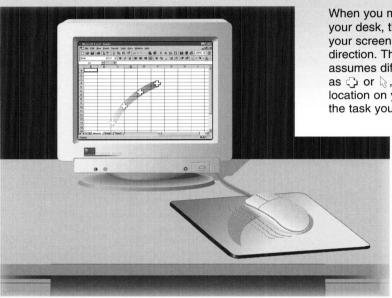

When you move the mouse on your desk, the mouse pointer on your screen moves in the same direction. The mouse pointer assumes different shapes, such as ⊕ or ▷, depending on its location on your screen and the task you are performing.

Resting your hand on the mouse, use your thumb and two rightmost fingers to move the mouse on your desk. Use your two remaining fingers to press the mouse buttons.

MOUSE ACTIONS

Click

Press and release the left mouse button.

Double-click

Quickly press and release the left mouse button twice.

Right-click

Press and release the right mouse button.

Drag

Position the mouse pointer over an object on your screen and then press and hold down the left mouse button. Still holding down the button, move the mouse to where you want to place the object and then release the button.

START EXCEL

When you start Excel, a blank worksheet appears. You can enter data into this worksheet.

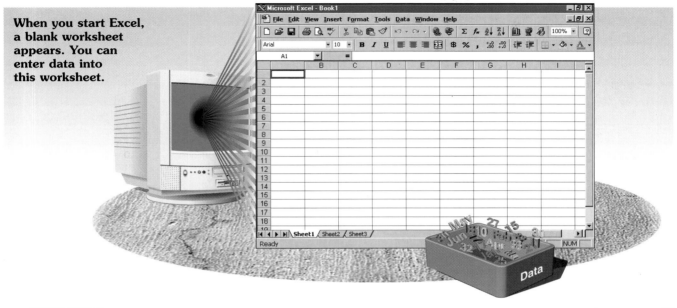

■ START EXCEL ■

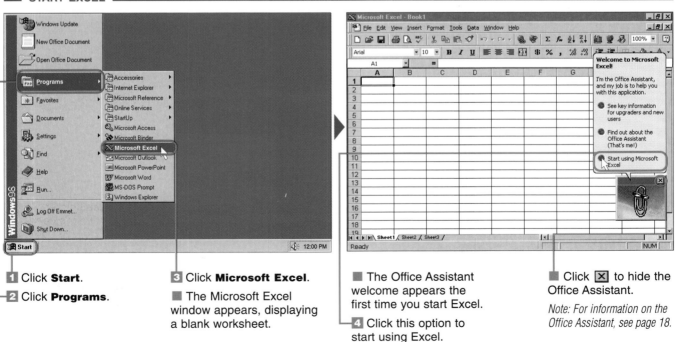

1 Click **Start**.

2 Click **Programs**.

3 Click **Microsoft Excel**.

■ The Microsoft Excel window appears, displaying a blank worksheet.

■ The Office Assistant welcome appears the first time you start Excel.

4 Click this option to start using Excel.

■ Click ☒ to hide the Office Assistant.

Note: For information on the Office Assistant, see page 18.

THE EXCEL SCREEN

The Excel screen displays a worksheet, which consists of rows and columns. The screen also displays several items to help you perform tasks efficiently.

Row

A horizontal line of cells. A number identifies each row.

Column

A vertical line of cells. A letter identifies each column.

Cell

The area where a row and column intersect.

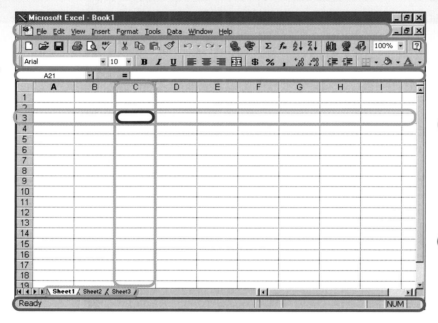

Menu Bar

Contains commands that let you perform tasks.

Toolbars

Contain buttons to help you quickly select common commands.

Formula Bar

Displays the cell reference and contents of the active cell.

Worksheet Tabs

An Excel file is called a workbook. Each workbook is divided into several worksheets. Excel displays a tab for each worksheet.

A workbook is similar to a three-ring binder that contains several sheets of paper.

Status Bar

Displays information about the task you are performing.

The active cell is the cell you are currently working with.

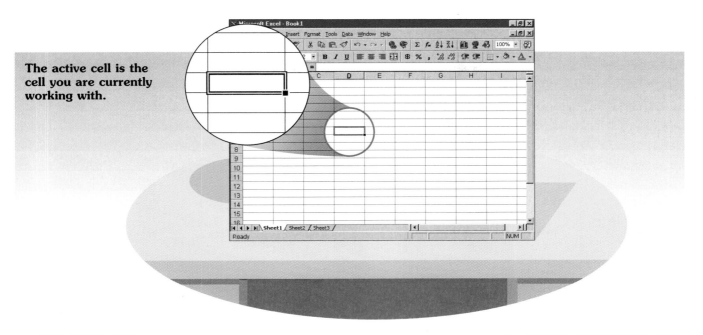

THE ACTIVE CELL

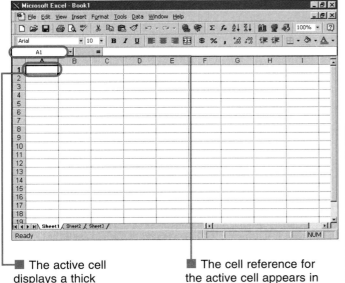

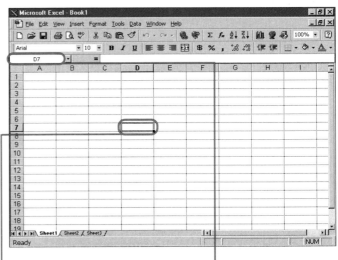

■ The active cell displays a thick border.

■ The cell reference for the active cell appears in this area. A cell reference identifies the location of each cell in a worksheet and consists of a column letter followed by a row number (example: **A1**).

CHANGE THE ACTIVE CELL

1 To make another cell the active cell, click the cell.

Note: To use your keyboard to change the active cell, press the ←, →, ↑ or ↓ key.

■ The cell reference for the new active cell appears in this area.

ENTER DATA

You can enter data into your worksheet quickly and easily.

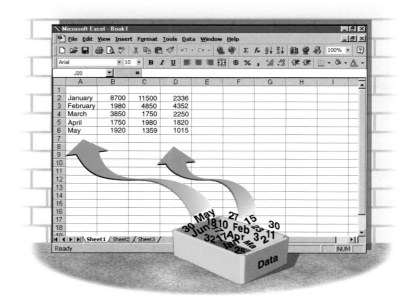

ENTER DATA

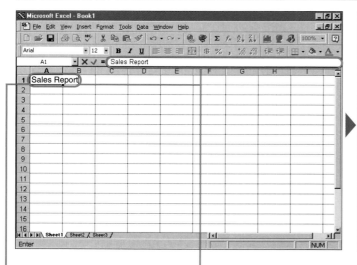

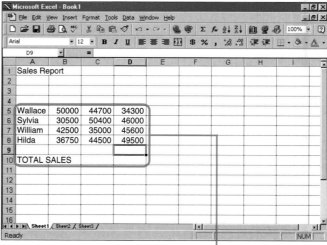

1 Click the cell where you want to enter data. Then type the data.

■ If you make a typing mistake, press the `Back Space` key to remove the incorrect data and then type the correct data.

■ The data you type appears in the active cell and in the formula bar.

Note: In this example, the size of data was changed from 10 to 12 point to make the worksheet easier to read. For information on changing the size of data, see page 121.

2 To enter the data and move down one cell, press the `Enter` key.

Note: To enter the data and move one cell in any direction, press the ←, →, ↑ *or* ↓ *key.*

3 Repeat steps **1** and **2** until you finish entering all the data.

How do I use the number keys on the right side of my keyboard?

When **NUM** appears at the bottom of your screen, you can use the number keys on the right side of your keyboard to enter numbers.

■ To turn the display of **NUM** on or off, press the `Num Lock` key.

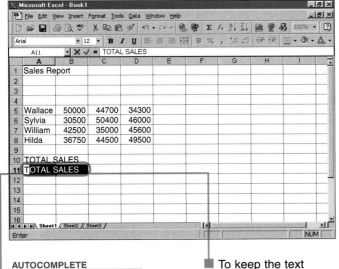

AUTOCOMPLETE

■ If the first few letters you type match another cell in the column, Excel may complete the text for you.

■ To keep the text Excel provides, press the `Enter` key.

■ To enter different text, continue typing.

4	TOTAL EXPENSES		
5			
6			

4	TOTAL EX	227	
5			
6			

Long Words

If text is too long to fit in a cell, the text will spill into the neighboring cell.

If the neighboring cell contains data, Excel will display as much of the text as the column width will allow. To change the column width, see page 116.

4	1.22E+10	
5		
6		

4	#####	
5		
6		

Long Numbers

If a number is too long to fit in a cell, Excel will display the number in scientific form or as number signs (#). To change the column width, see page 116.

COMPLETE A SERIES

Excel can save you time by completing a text or number series for you.

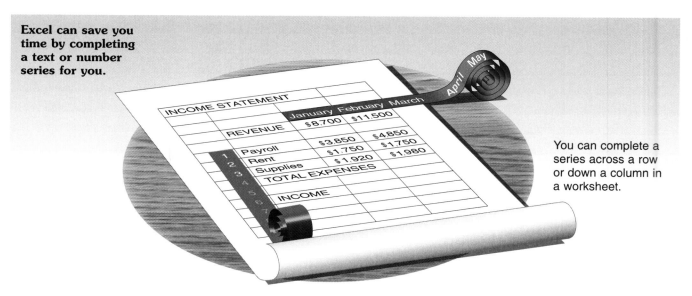

You can complete a series across a row or down a column in a worksheet.

COMPLETE A TEXT SERIES

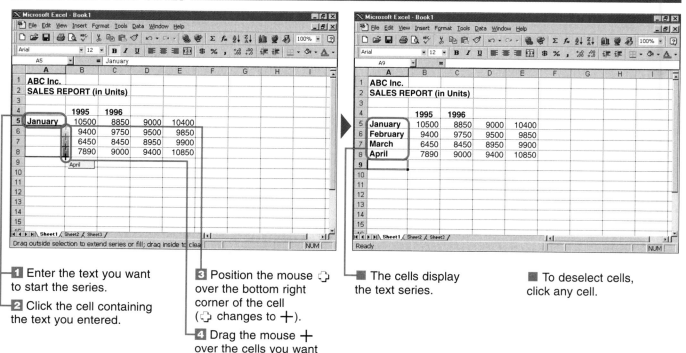

1 Enter the text you want to start the series.

2 Click the cell containing the text you entered.

3 Position the mouse ⌖ over the bottom right corner of the cell (⌖ changes to +).

4 Drag the mouse + over the cells you want to include in the series.

■ The cells display the text series.

■ To deselect cells, click any cell.

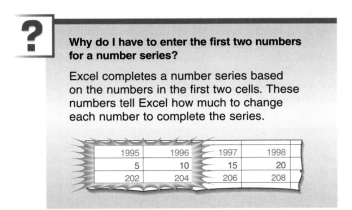

?

Why do I have to enter the first two numbers for a number series?

Excel completes a number series based on the numbers in the first two cells. These numbers tell Excel how much to change each number to complete the series.

1995	1996	1997	1998
5	10	15	20
202	204	206	208

■ COMPLETE A NUMBER SERIES ■

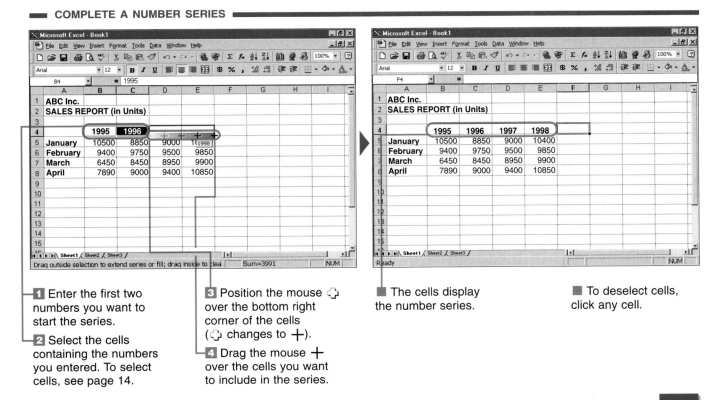

1 Enter the first two numbers you want to start the series.

2 Select the cells containing the numbers you entered. To select cells, see page 14.

3 Position the mouse ⟨⟩ over the bottom right corner of the cells (⟨⟩ changes to ╋).

4 Drag the mouse ╋ over the cells you want to include in the series.

■ The cells display the number series.

■ To deselect cells, click any cell.

SELECT CELLS

Before performing many tasks in Excel, you must select the cells you want to work with. Selected cells appear highlighted on your screen.

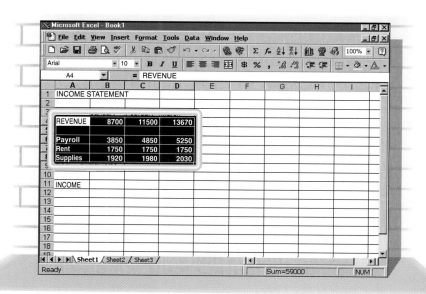

SELECT CELLS

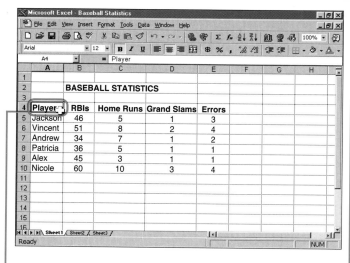

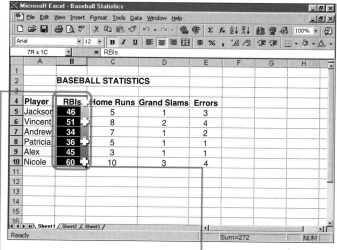

1 To select one cell, click the cell you want to select.

■ The cell becomes the active cell and displays a thick border.

■ To select multiple cells, press and hold down the **Ctrl** key as you click each cell you want to select.

Note: To deselect cells, click any cell.

SELECT A GROUP OF CELLS

1 Position the mouse 🖑 over the first cell you want to select.

2 Drag the mouse 🖑 to highlight all the cells you want to select.

■ To select multiple groups of cells, press and hold down the **Ctrl** key as you repeat steps **1** and **2** for each group.

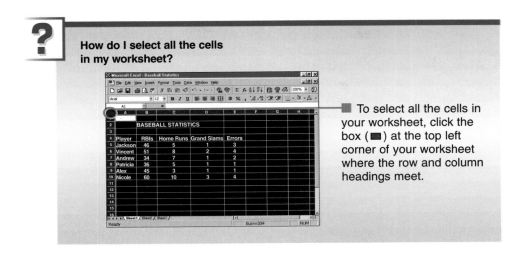

How do I select all the cells in my worksheet?

■ To select all the cells in your worksheet, click the box (■) at the top left corner of your worksheet where the row and column headings meet.

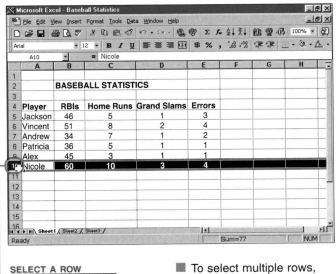

SELECT A ROW

1 Click the number of the row you want to select.

■ To select multiple rows, position the mouse ⟨⟩ over the number of the first row you want to select. Then drag the mouse ⟨⟩ to highlight all the rows you want to select.

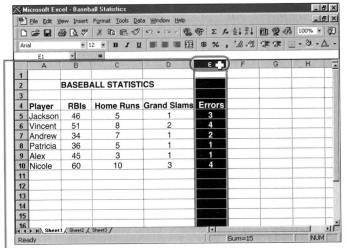

SELECT A COLUMN

1 Click the letter of the column you want to select.

■ To select multiple columns, position the mouse ⟨⟩ over the letter of the first column you want to select. Then drag the mouse ⟨⟩ to highlight all the columns you want to select.

SCROLL THROUGH A WORKSHEET

If your worksheet contains a lot of data, your computer screen may not be able to display all the data at once. You must scroll through the worksheet to view other areas.

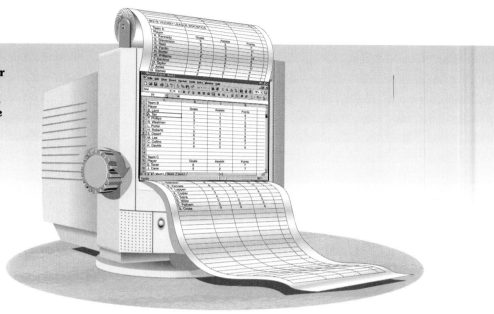

SCROLL UP OR DOWN

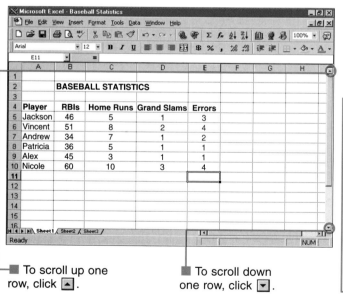

■ To scroll up one row, click ▲.

■ To scroll down one row, click ▼.

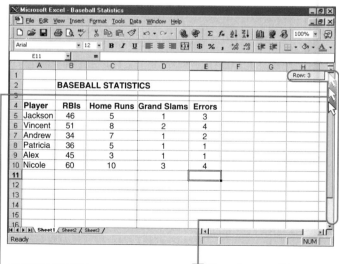

QUICKLY SCROLL

1 To quickly scroll to any row in the worksheet, position the mouse � over the scroll box.

2 Drag the scroll box up or down the scroll bar until the yellow box displays the number of the row you want to appear at the top of the worksheet.

How do I use a wheeled mouse to scroll through my worksheet?

A wheeled mouse has a wheel between the left and right mouse buttons. Moving this wheel lets you quickly scroll through your worksheet. The Microsoft IntelliMouse is a popular example of a wheeled mouse.

SCROLL LEFT OR RIGHT

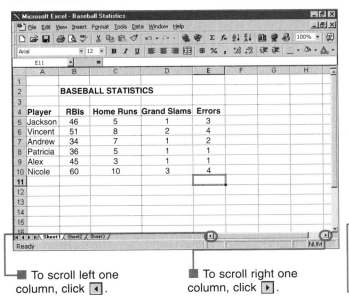

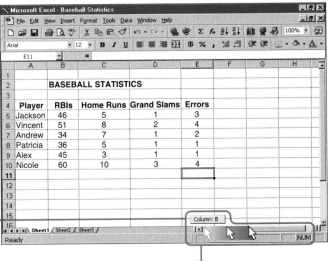

■ To scroll left one column, click ◀.

■ To scroll right one column, click ▶.

QUICKLY SCROLL

1 To quickly scroll to any column in the worksheet, position the mouse over the scroll box.

2 Drag the scroll box left or right along the scroll bar until the yellow box displays the letter of the column you want to appear at the left side of the worksheet.

GETTING HELP

If you do not know how to perform a task in Excel, you can ask the Office Assistant for help.

USING THE OFFICE ASSISTANT

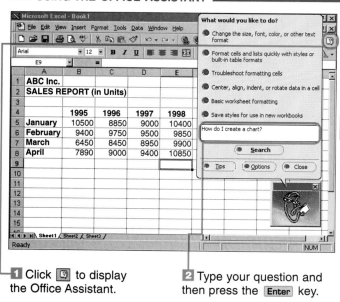

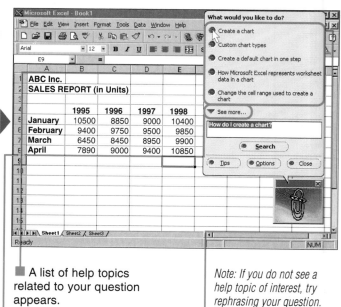

1 Click 🔲 to display the Office Assistant.

Note: If the question area does not appear, click the Office Assistant.

2 Type your question and then press the `Enter` key.

■ A list of help topics related to your question appears.

■ If more help topics exist, you can click **See more** to view the additional topics.

Note: If you do not see a help topic of interest, try rephrasing your question.

3 Click the help topic of interest.

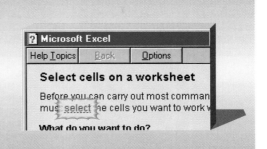

Why do some words in the help information appear in green with a dotted underline?

You can display a definition of words that appear in green with a dotted underline in the help information. To display the definition, click the word. To remove the definition, click anywhere on the screen.

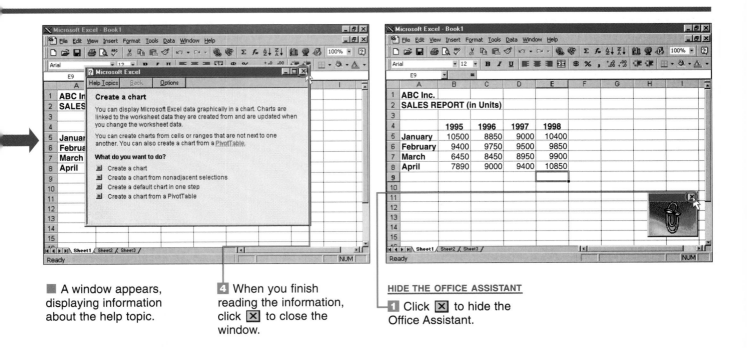

■ A window appears, displaying information about the help topic.

4 When you finish reading the information, click **X** to close the window.

HIDE THE OFFICE ASSISTANT

1 Click **X** to hide the Office Assistant.

GETTING HELP

You can use Excel's
help index to locate
topics of interest.

USING THE HELP INDEX

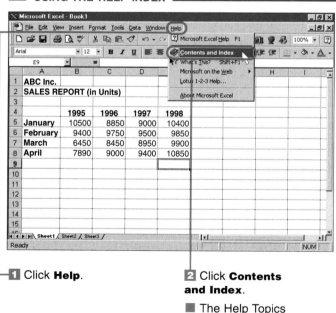

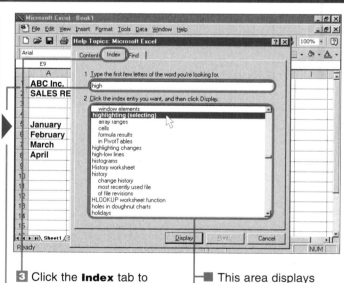

1 Click **Help**.

2 Click **Contents and Index**.

■ The Help Topics dialog box appears.

3 Click the **Index** tab to display an alphabetical list of help topics.

4 To locate a help topic of interest, click this area and then type the first few letters of the topic.

■ This area displays help topics beginning with the letters you typed.

5 Double-click the help topic you want to display information on.

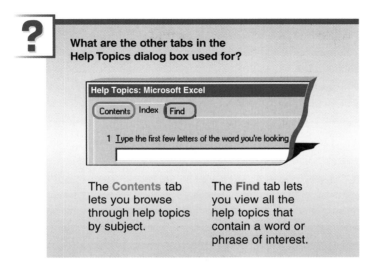

What are the other tabs in the Help Topics dialog box used for?

Help Topics: Microsoft Excel

Contents | Index | Find

1 Type the first few letters of the word you're looking

The **Contents** tab lets you browse through help topics by subject.

The **Find** tab lets you view all the help topics that contain a word or phrase of interest.

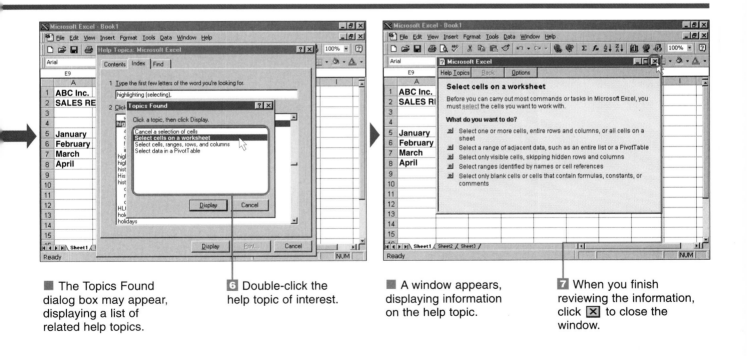

■ The Topics Found dialog box may appear, displaying a list of related help topics.

6 Double-click the help topic of interest.

■ A window appears, displaying information on the help topic.

7 When you finish reviewing the information, click ☒ to close the window.

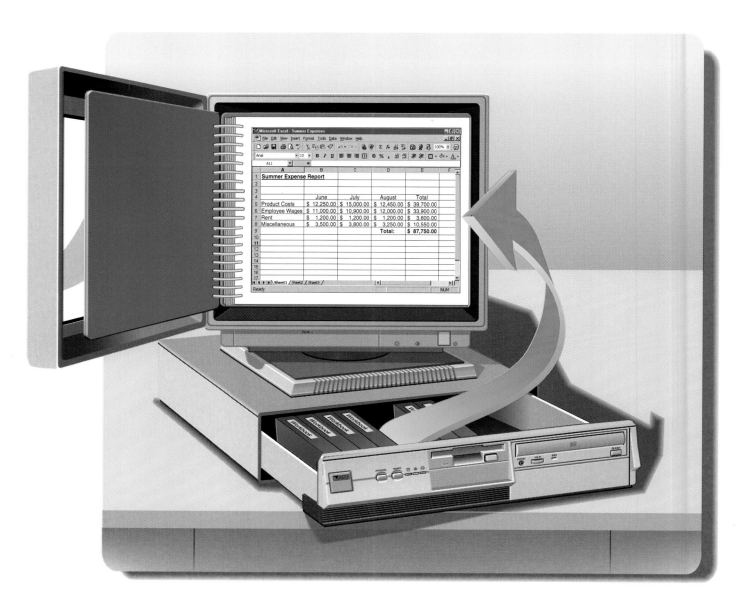

CHAPTER 2

Save and Open Your Workbooks

Are you wondering how to save, close and open an Excel workbook? Would you like to protect a workbook with a password? Learn how in this chapter.

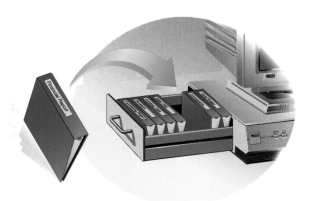

SAVE A WORKBOOK

You can save your workbook to store it for future use. This lets you later review and make changes to the workbook.

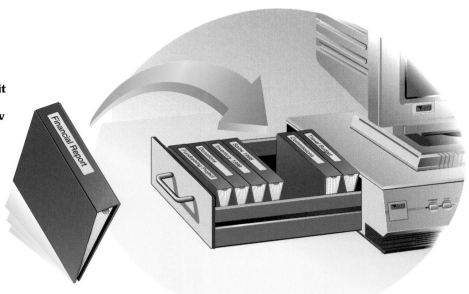

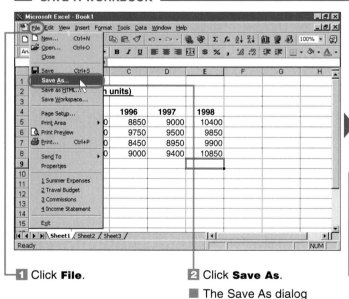

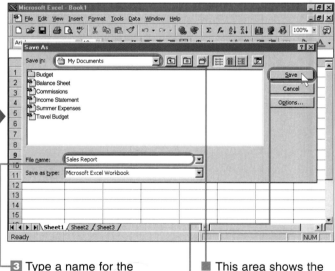

1 Click **File**.

2 Click **Save As**.

■ The Save As dialog box appears.

3 Type a name for the workbook.

Note: You can use up to 218 characters, including spaces, to name a workbook.

■ This area shows the location where Excel will save the workbook. You can click this area to change the location.

4 Click **Save** to save the workbook.

24

? I want to make changes to a workbook I saved, but I don't want to lose my original data. What should I do?

You can save your workbook again with a different name to create a copy of the workbook that you can change. Repeat steps 1 to 4 below to save your workbook with a new name.

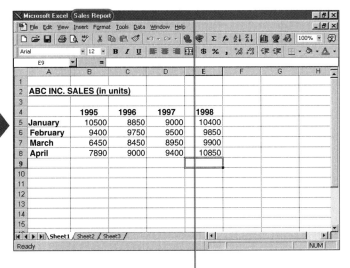

■ Excel saves the workbook.

■ The name of the workbook appears at the top of the screen.

SAVE CHANGES

You should regularly save changes you make to a workbook to avoid losing your work.

1 Click 🖫 to save your changes.

PROTECT A WORKBOOK

You can prevent other people from opening or making changes to a workbook by protecting it with a password.

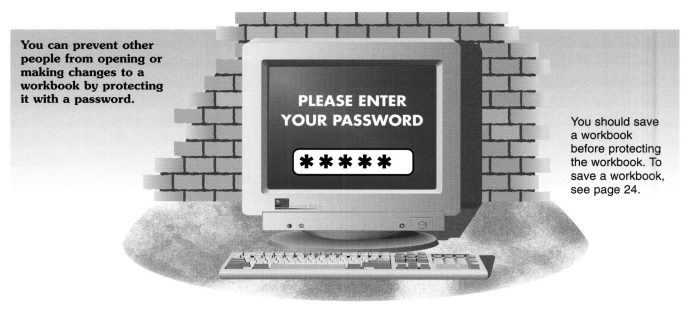

PLEASE ENTER YOUR PASSWORD

* * * * *

You should save a workbook before protecting the workbook. To save a workbook, see page 24.

PROTECT A WORKBOOK

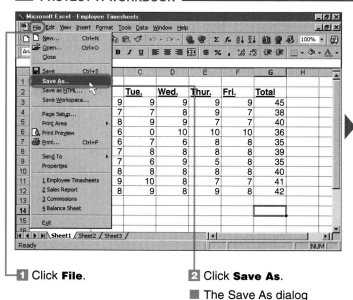

■1 Click **File**.

■2 Click **Save As**.

■ The Save As dialog box appears.

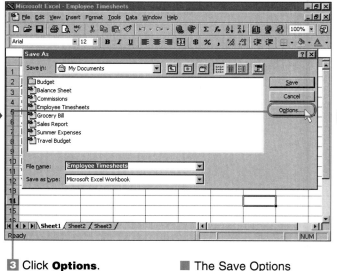

■3 Click **Options**.

■ The Save Options dialog box appears.

?

What password should I use to protect my workbook?

When choosing a password, you should not use words that people can easily associate with you, such as your name or favorite sport. The most effective passwords connect two words or numbers with a special character (example: **blue@123**). A password can contain up to 15 characters, including letters, numbers and symbols.

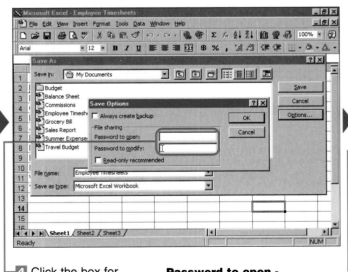

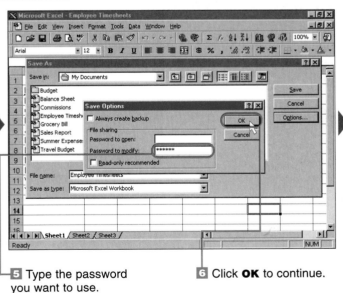

4 Click the box for the type of password you want to enter.

Password to open - Prevents people from opening the workbook without entering the correct password.

Password to modify - Prevents people from making changes to the workbook without entering the correct password.

5 Type the password you want to use.

6 Click **OK** to continue.

CONTINUED

PROTECT A WORKBOOK

After you save a
workbook with a
password, Excel will
ask you to enter the
password each time
you want to open
the workbook.

You should write down
your password and keep
it in a safe place. If you
forget the password, you
may not be able to open
the workbook.

PROTECT A WORKBOOK (CONTINUED)

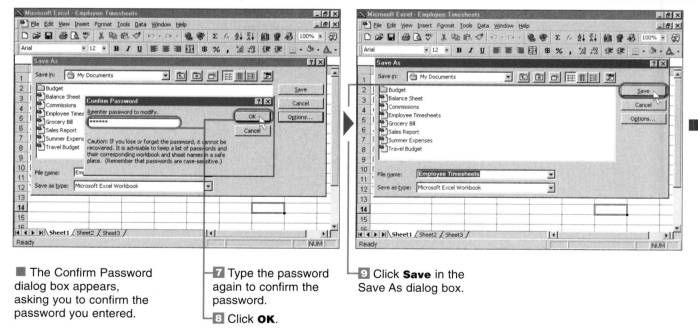

■ The Confirm Password
dialog box appears,
asking you to confirm the
password you entered.

7 Type the password
again to confirm the
password.

8 Click **OK**.

9 Click **Save** in the
Save As dialog box.

I typed the correct password, but Excel will not open my workbook. What is wrong?

Passwords in Excel are case sensitive. If you do not enter the correct uppercase and lowercase letters, Excel will not accept the password. For example, if your password is **Car**, you cannot enter **car** or **CAR** to open the workbook.

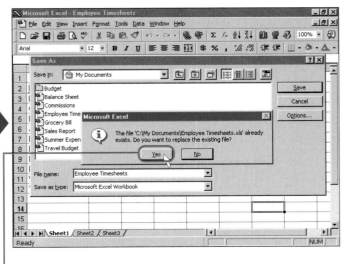

■ A dialog box appears, stating that you are about to replace the existing file.

10 Click **Yes** to replace the file and save the workbook with the password.

■ To unprotect a workbook, perform steps **1** to **6** starting on page 26, except delete the existing password in step **5**. Then perform steps **9** and **10**.

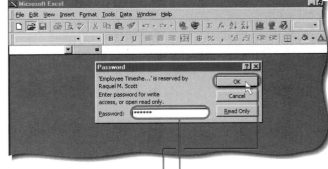

OPEN A PROTECTED WORKBOOK

■ A dialog box appears each time you open a protected workbook. To open a workbook, see page 36.

Note: The appearance of the dialog box depends on the type of password assigned to the workbook.

1 Type the correct password.

2 Click **OK**.

■ If the workbook is protected with a Password to modify password, you can click **Read Only** to open the workbook without entering a password. You will not be able to save changes you make to the workbook.

CREATE A NEW WORKBOOK

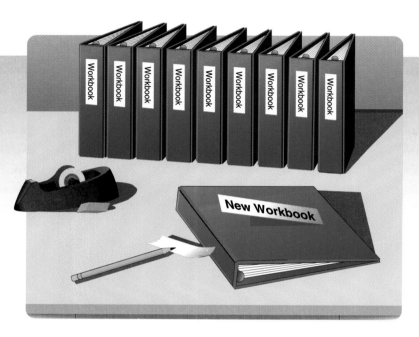

You can easily create another workbook to store new data.

CREATE A NEW WORKBOOK

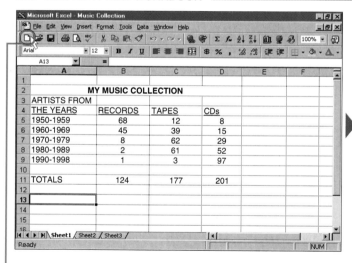

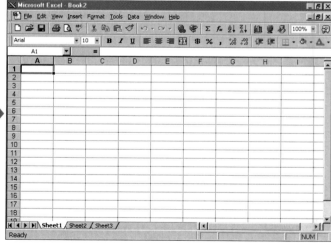

1 Click ▢ to create a new workbook.

■ A new workbook appears. The previous workbook is now hidden behind the new workbook.

SWITCH BETWEEN WORKBOOKS

Excel lets you have several workbooks open at once. You can easily switch from one open workbook to another.

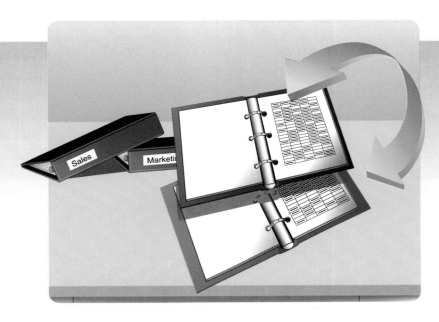

SWITCH BETWEEN WORKBOOKS

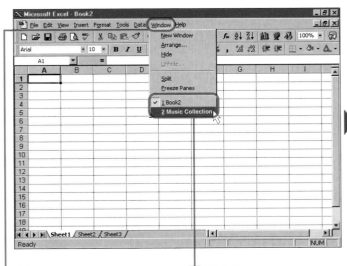

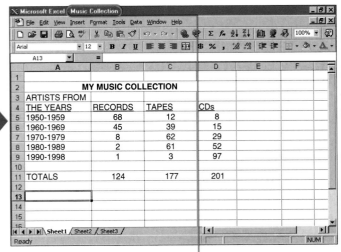

1 Click **Window** to display a list of all the workbooks you have open.

2 Click the name of the workbook you want to display.

■ The workbook appears.

■ Excel displays the name of the workbook at the top of the screen.

VIEW ALL OPEN WORKBOOKS

You can arrange open workbooks on your screen to view the contents of all the workbooks at once.

VIEW ALL OPEN WORKBOOKS

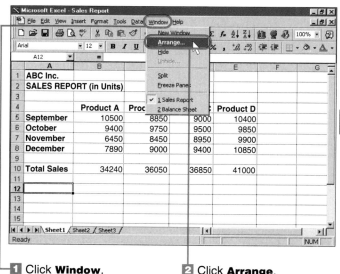

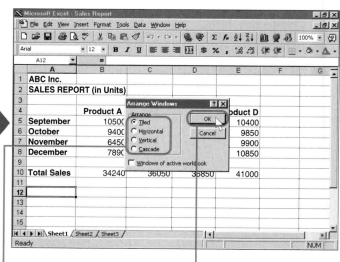

1 Click **Window**.

2 Click **Arrange**.

■ The Arrange Windows dialog box appears.

3 Click an option to select the way you want to arrange all the open workbooks (○ changes to ⊙).

4 Click **OK** to arrange the workbooks.

How can I arrange open workbooks on my screen?

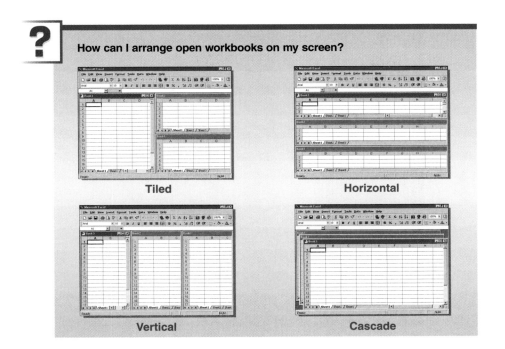

Tiled

Horizontal

Vertical

Cascade

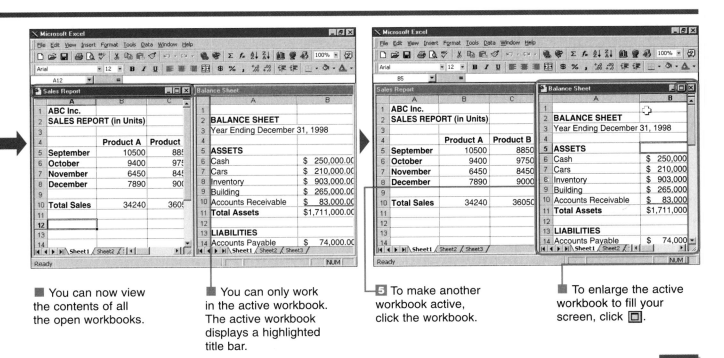

■ You can now view
the contents of all
the open workbooks.

■ You can only work
in the active workbook.
The active workbook
displays a highlighted
title bar.

5 To make another
workbook active,
click the workbook.

■ To enlarge the active
workbook to fill your
screen, click ▣.

CLOSE A WORKBOOK

When you finish using a workbook, you can close the workbook to remove it from your screen.

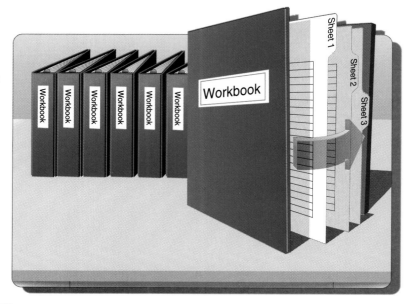

When you close a workbook, you do not exit the Excel program. You can continue to work with other workbooks.

CLOSE A WORKBOOK

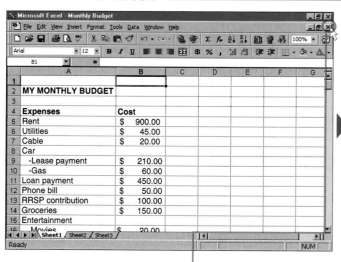

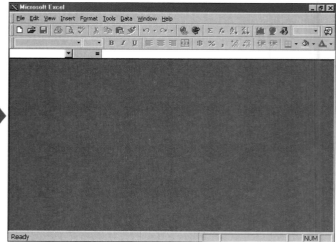

1 Save the workbook displayed on your screen before closing the workbook. To save a workbook, see page 24.

2 Click **X** to close the workbook.

■ Excel removes the workbook from your screen.

■ If you had more than one workbook open, the second last workbook you worked with would appear on the screen.

When you finish using Excel, you can exit the program.

To prevent the loss of data, you should always exit all open programs and shut down Windows before turning off your computer.

EXIT EXCEL

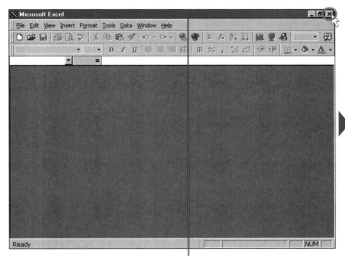

1 Save all your open workbooks before exiting Excel. To save a workbook, see page 24.

2 Click **X** to exit Excel.

■ The Microsoft Excel window disappears from the screen.

OPEN A WORKBOOK

You can open a saved workbook and display it on your screen. This lets you review and make changes to the workbook.

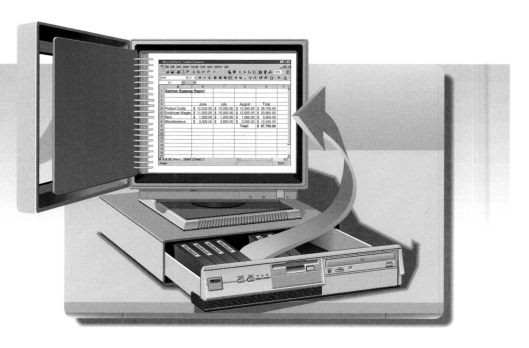

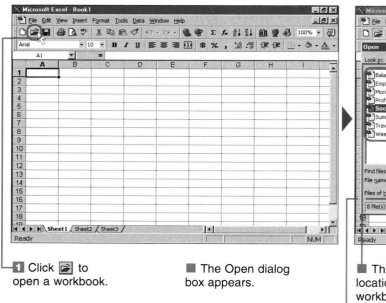

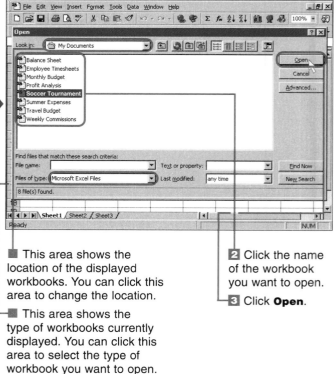

1 Click 📂 to open a workbook.

■ The Open dialog box appears.

■ This area shows the location of the displayed workbooks. You can click this area to change the location.

■ This area shows the type of workbooks currently displayed. You can click this area to select the type of workbook you want to open.

2 Click the name of the workbook you want to open.

3 Click **Open**.

?

Why would I open a different type of workbook in Excel?

Opening a different type of workbook allows you to use workbooks created by colleagues who do not use Excel 97. You can open workbooks created in programs such as Lotus 1-2-3, Quattro Pro and previous versions of Excel.

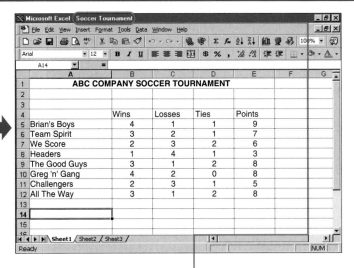

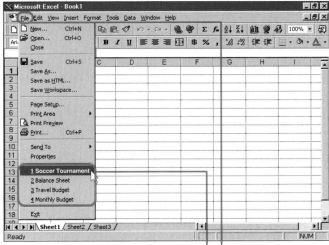

■ Excel opens the workbook and displays it on the screen. You can now review and make changes to the workbook.

■ The name of the workbook appears at the top of the screen.

QUICKLY OPEN A WORKBOOK

Excel remembers the names of the last four workbooks you used. You can quickly open one of these workbooks.

1 Click **File**.

2 Click the name of the workbook you want to open.

FIND A WORKBOOK

If you cannot locate a
workbook you want to
open, you can have Excel
search for the workbook.

FIND A WORKBOOK

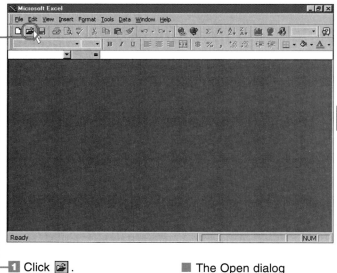

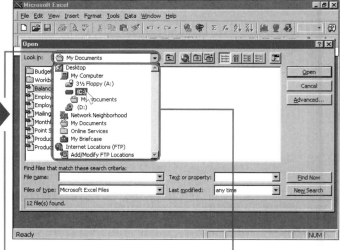

1 Click 🗁 .

■ The Open dialog
box appears.

2 To specify where you
want Excel to search
for the workbook, click
this area.

3 Click the location
you want to search.

Can Excel find a workbook if I know only part of the workbook name?

Excel will find all the workbooks with names containing the text you specify. For example, searching for **income** will find **1998 Income**, **Income Statement** and **Roxanne's Income**.

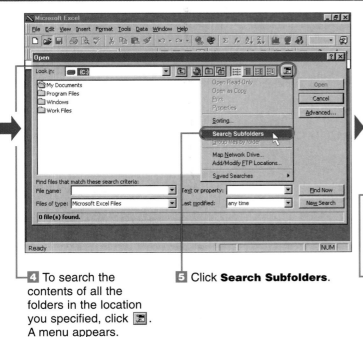

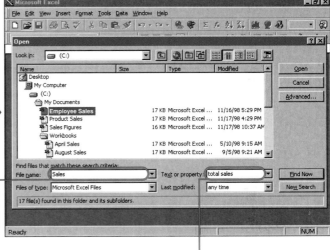

◤4 To search the contents of all the folders in the location you specified, click 🗐. A menu appears.

◤5 Click **Search Subfolders**.

◤6 If you know all or part of the name of the workbook you want to find, click this area and then type the name.

◤7 If you know a word or phrase in the workbook you want to find, click this area and then type the word or phrase.

CONTINUED ▶

FIND A WORKBOOK

When the search is complete, Excel displays the names of the workbooks it found.

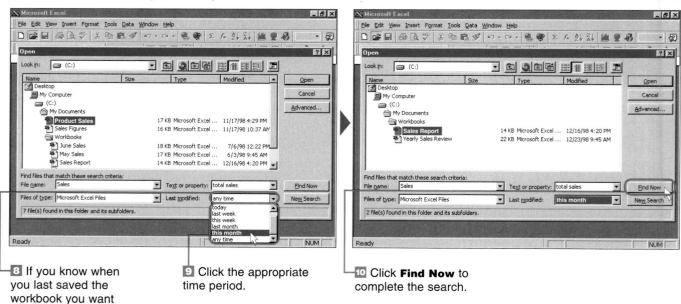

8 If you know when you last saved the workbook you want to find, click this area.

9 Click the appropriate time period.

10 Click **Find Now** to complete the search.

Excel did not find the workbook I was looking for. What can I do?

If the search did not provide the results you were expecting, you may not have provided Excel with enough information or you may have specified incorrect information.

■ Click **New Search** in the Open dialog box to clear the information you entered and begin a new search.

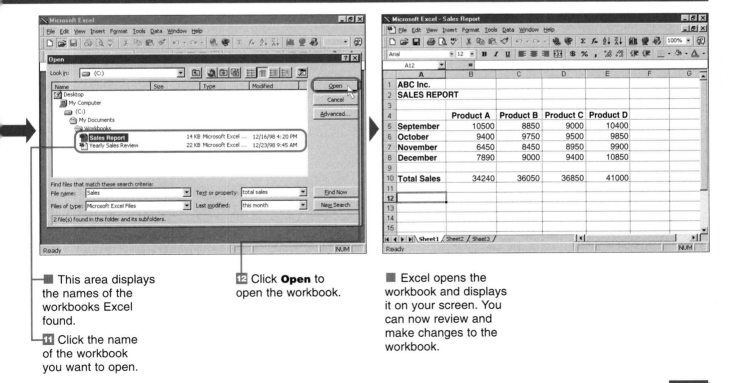

■ This area displays the names of the workbooks Excel found.

11 Click the name of the workbook you want to open.

12 Click **Open** to open the workbook.

■ Excel opens the workbook and displays it on your screen. You can now review and make changes to the workbook.

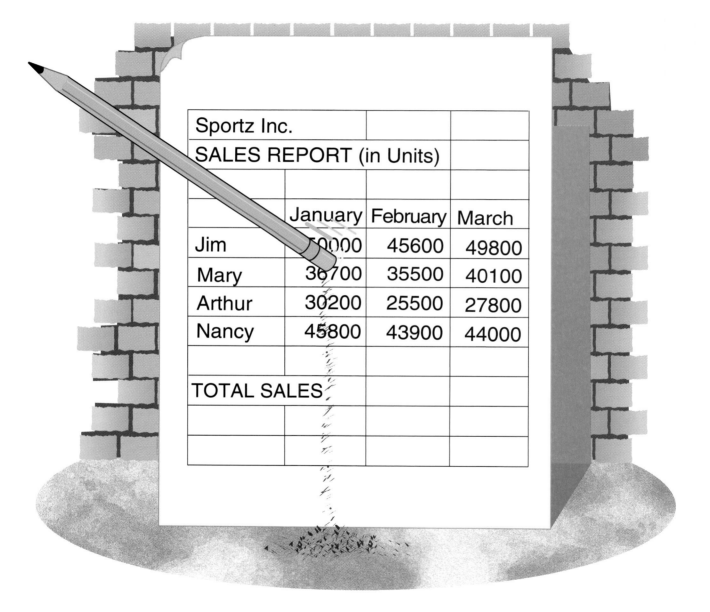

Sportz Inc.			
SALES REPORT (in Units)			
	January	February	March
Jim	50000	45600	49800
Mary	36700	35500	40100
Arthur	30200	25500	27800
Nancy	45800	43900	44000
TOTAL SALES			

CHAPTER 3

Edit Your Worksheets

Do you want to edit the data in your worksheet or check your worksheet for spelling errors? This chapter teaches you how.

EDIT DATA

You can change data in your worksheet to correct a mistake or update the data.

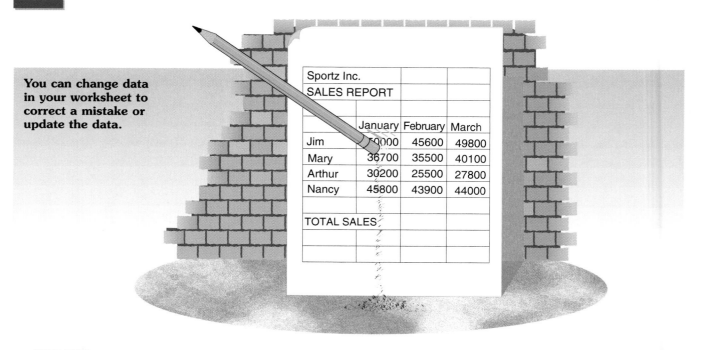

Sportz Inc.			
SALES REPORT			
	January	February	March
Jim	50000	45600	49800
Mary	36700	35500	40100
Arthur	30200	25500	27800
Nancy	45800	43900	44000
TOTAL SALES			

EDIT DATA

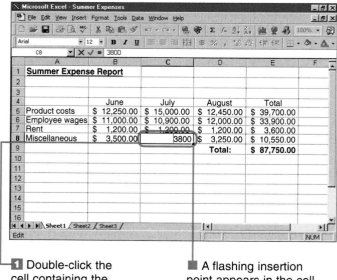

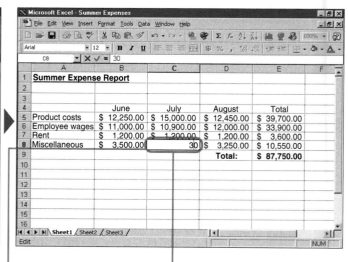

1 Double-click the cell containing the data you want to edit.

■ A flashing insertion point appears in the cell.

2 Press the ← or → key to move the insertion point to where you want to remove or insert characters.

3 To remove the character to the left of the insertion point, press the Back Space key.

■ To remove the character to the right of the insertion point, press the Delete key.

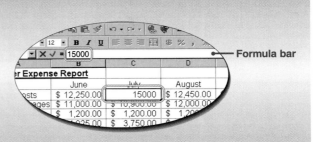

Is there another way to edit data?

When you select a cell, the data in the cell also appears in the formula bar. You can click the data in the formula bar and then edit the data as you would edit data in a cell.

— Formula bar

REPLACE DATA IN A CELL

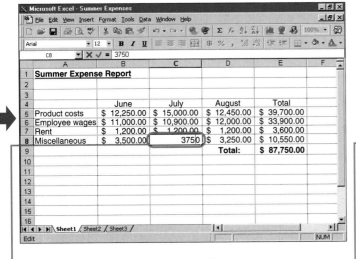

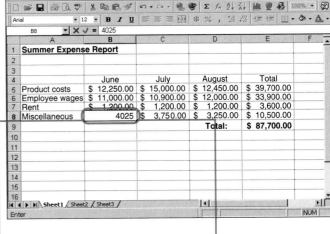

4 To insert data where the insertion point flashes on the screen, type the data.

5 When you finish making changes to the data, press the **Enter** key.

1 Click the cell containing the data you want to replace with new data.

2 Type the new data and then press the **Enter** key.

DELETE DATA

You can remove data
you no longer need
from cells in your
worksheet.

You can delete
data from a single
cell or from several
cells at once.

DELETE DATA

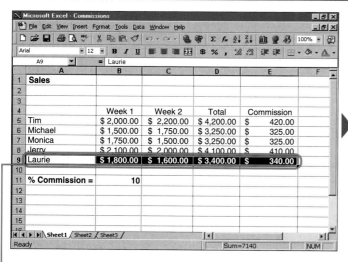

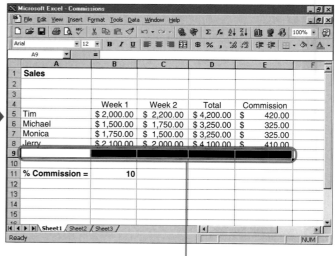

1 Select the cells
containing the data
you want to delete.
To select cells, see
page 14.

2 Press the Delete key.

■ The data in the cells
you selected disappears.

Excel remembers the last
changes you made to your
worksheet. If you regret
these changes, you
can cancel them using
the Undo feature.

UNDO LAST CHANGE

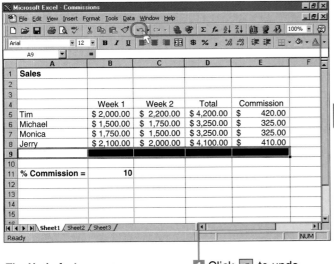

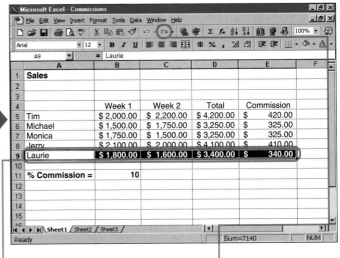

**The Undo feature can
cancel your last editing
and formatting changes.**

1 Click 🔄 to undo
your last change.

■ Excel cancels the last
change you made to the
worksheet.

■ You can repeat step **1**
to cancel previous changes
you made.

■ To reverse the
results of using the
Undo feature, click 🔄.

MOVE DATA

You can reorganize
your worksheet by
moving data from
one location to
another.

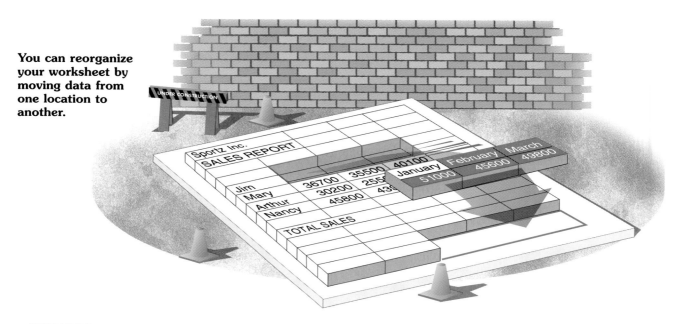

MOVE DATA

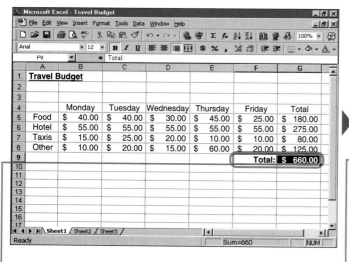

1 Select the cells
containing the data
you want to move.
To select cells, see
page 14.

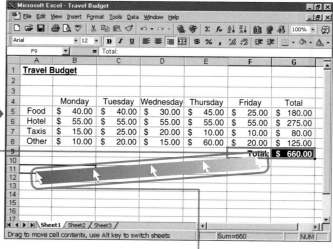

2 Position the mouse ✛
over a border of the selected
cells (✛ changes to ↘).

3 Drag the mouse ↘
to where you want to
place the data.

■ A gray box indicates
where the data will
appear.

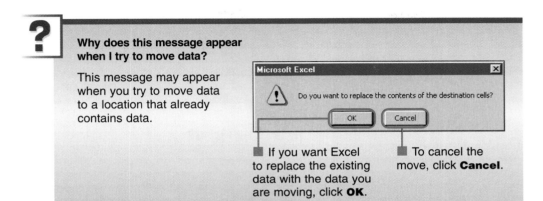

Why does this message appear when I try to move data?

This message may appear when you try to move data to a location that already contains data.

■ If you want Excel to replace the existing data with the data you are moving, click **OK**.

■ To cancel the move, click **Cancel**.

MOVE DATA USING TOOLBAR BUTTONS

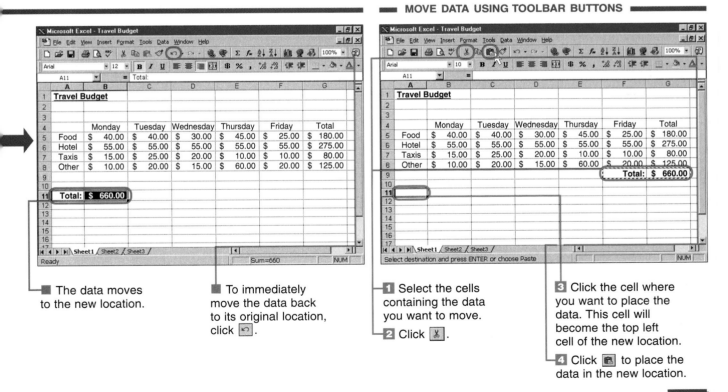

■ The data moves to the new location.

■ To immediately move the data back to its original location, click ↶.

1 Select the cells containing the data you want to move.

2 Click ✂.

3 Click the cell where you want to place the data. This cell will become the top left cell of the new location.

4 Click 📋 to place the data in the new location.

COPY DATA

You can place a copy of data in a different location in your worksheet. This saves you time since you do not have to retype the data.

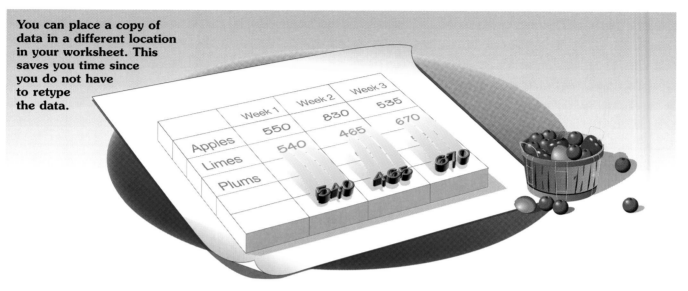

COPY DATA

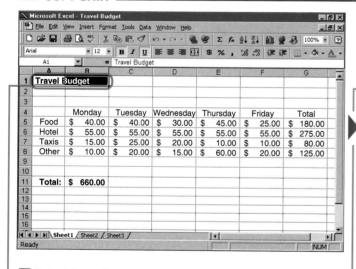

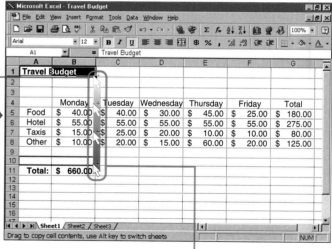

1 Select the cells containing the data you want to copy. To select cells, see page 14.

2 Position the mouse over a border of the selected cells (changes to).

3 Press and hold down the **Ctrl** key.

4 Still holding down the **Ctrl** key, drag the mouse to where you want to place the copy.

■ A gray box indicates where the copy will appear.

?

Can I copy data to several locations in my worksheet?

When you use the toolbar buttons to copy data, you can copy the data to many different locations. Perform steps **1** to **4** below. Then repeat steps **3** and **4** for each location where you want to place a copy of the data.

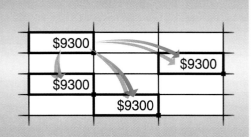

COPY DATA USING TOOLBAR BUTTONS

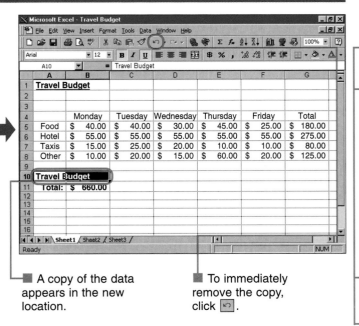

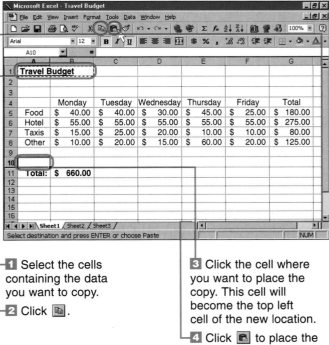

■ A copy of the data appears in the new location.

■ To immediately remove the copy, click ⟲ .

1 Select the cells containing the data you want to copy.

2 Click 📋 .

3 Click the cell where you want to place the copy. This cell will become the top left cell of the new location.

4 Click 📋 to place the copy in the new location.

LINK DATA

You can link data in one cell to another cell. When you change the data in the original cell, the linked data will also display the changes.

Linking data is useful when you want cells to always display the same information.

LINK DATA

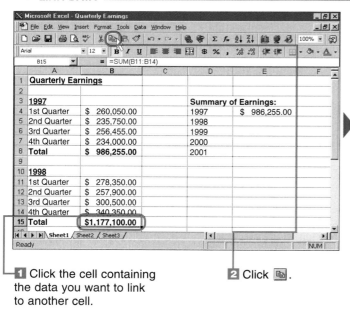

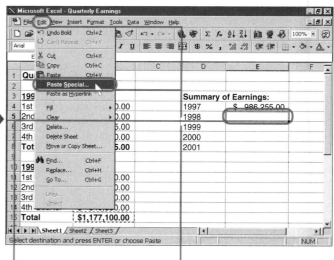

1 Click the cell containing the data you want to link to another cell.

2 Click 📋.

3 Click the cell where you want to place the linked data.

Note: You can select a cell in the same worksheet, a worksheet in the same workbook or a worksheet in another workbook.

4 Click **Edit**.

5 Click **Paste Special**.

Can I move or delete the data in the original cell without affecting the link?

When you move the data in the original cell, the link is not affected. When you delete the data in the original cell, the linked cell displays a zero (0).

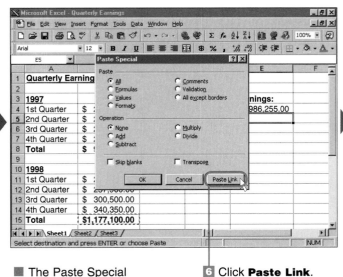

■ The Paste Special dialog box appears.

6 Click **Paste Link**.

■ The linked data appears in the cell.

■ The formula bar displays the column letter and row number of the original cell.

■ To remove the moving border around the original cell, press the **Esc** key.

■ When you change the data in the original cell, the linked data will also display the change.

CHECK SPELLING

You can find and correct all the spelling errors in your worksheet.

Excel compares every word in your worksheet to words in its dictionary. If a word in your worksheet does not exist in Excel's dictionary, Excel considers the word misspelled.

CHECK SPELLING

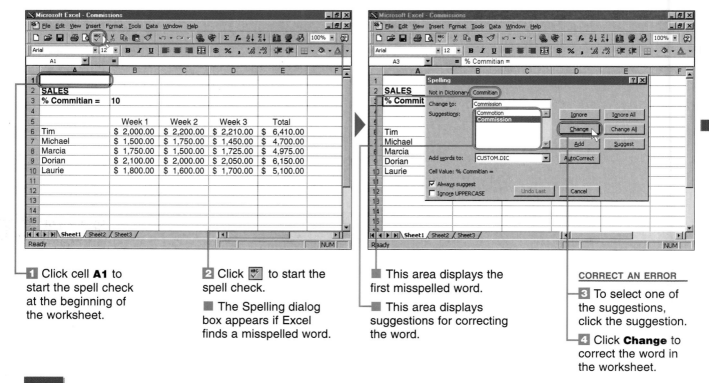

1 Click cell **A1** to start the spell check at the beginning of the worksheet.

2 Click ![ABC] to start the spell check.

■ The Spelling dialog box appears if Excel finds a misspelled word.

■ This area displays the first misspelled word.

■ This area displays suggestions for correcting the word.

CORRECT AN ERROR

3 To select one of the suggestions, click the suggestion.

4 Click **Change** to correct the word in the worksheet.

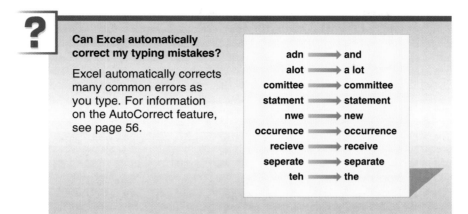

Can Excel automatically correct my typing mistakes?

Excel automatically corrects many common errors as you type. For information on the AutoCorrect feature, see page 56.

adn	⟹	and
alot	⟹	a lot
comittee	⟹	committee
statment	⟹	statement
nwe	⟹	new
occurence	⟹	occurrence
recieve	⟹	receive
seperate	⟹	separate
teh	⟹	the

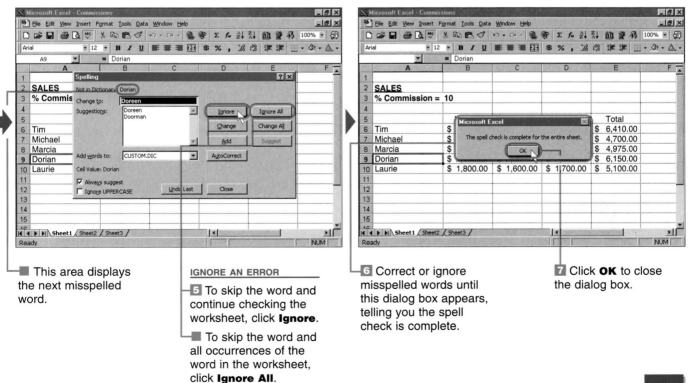

■ This area displays the next misspelled word.

IGNORE AN ERROR

5 To skip the word and continue checking the worksheet, click **Ignore**.

■ To skip the word and all occurrences of the word in the worksheet, click **Ignore All**.

6 Correct or ignore misspelled words until this dialog box appears, telling you the spell check is complete.

7 Click **OK** to close the dialog box.

USING AUTOCORRECT

Excel automatically corrects hundreds of common typing and spelling errors as you type. You can create an AutoCorrect entry to add your own words and phrases to the list.

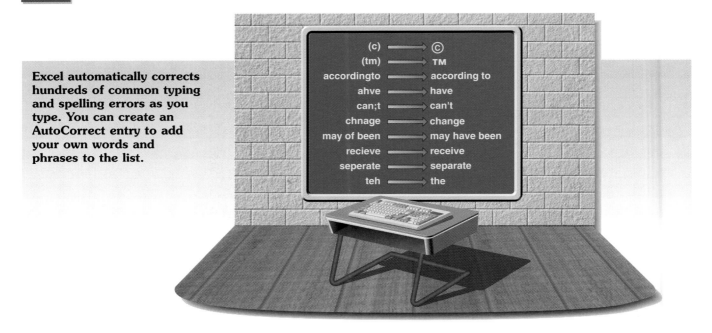

(c)	→	©
(tm)	→	TM
accordingto	→	according to
ahve	→	have
can;t	→	can't
chnage	→	change
may of been	→	may have been
recieve	→	receive
seperate	→	separate
teh	→	the

USING AUTOCORRECT

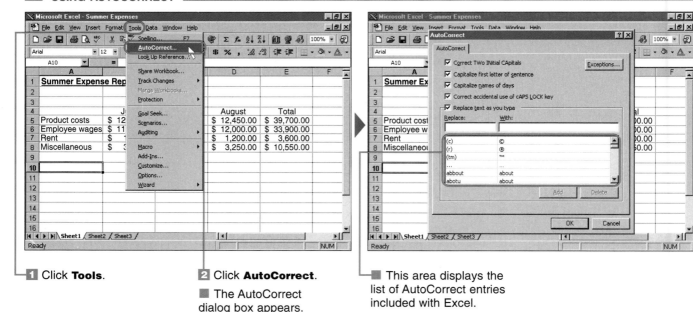

1 Click **Tools**.

2 Click **AutoCorrect**.

■ The AutoCorrect dialog box appears.

■ This area displays the list of AutoCorrect entries included with Excel.

Can I use the AutoCorrect feature to save time typing?

Yes. You can add a short form of a long word or phrase you regularly type to the list of AutoCorrect entries. For example, you can have the AutoCorrect feature replace **mfs** with **Melbourne Financial Services**. AutoCorrect will replace every instance of the short form with the longer word or phrase, so you should make sure the short form you use is not a real word.

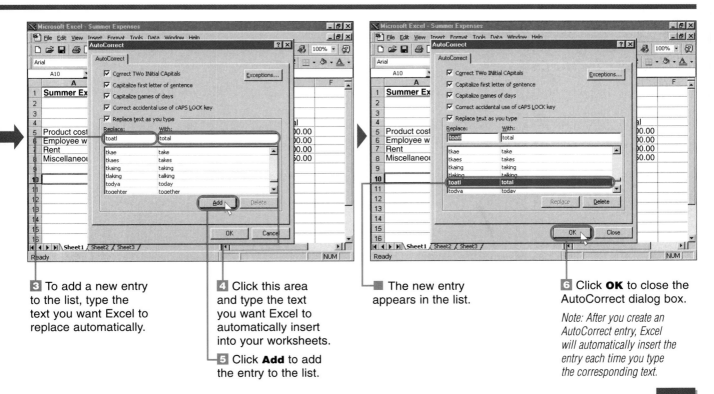

3 To add a new entry to the list, type the text you want Excel to replace automatically.

4 Click this area and type the text you want Excel to automatically insert into your worksheets.

5 Click **Add** to add the entry to the list.

■ The new entry appears in the list.

6 Click **OK** to close the AutoCorrect dialog box.

Note: After you create an AutoCorrect entry, Excel will automatically insert the entry each time you type the corresponding text.

FIND DATA

You can use the Find feature to quickly locate a word or number in the current worksheet.

FIND DATA

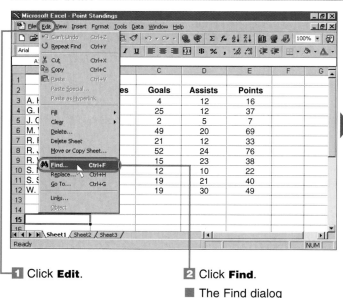

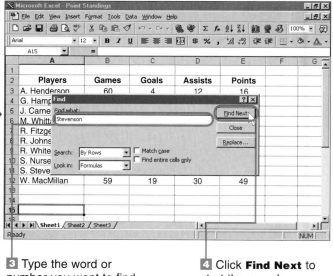

1 Click **Edit**.

2 Click **Find**.

■ The Find dialog box appears.

3 Type the word or number you want to find.

4 Click **Find Next** to start the search.

*Note: A dialog box appears if Excel cannot find the word or number you specified. Click **OK** to close the dialog box. Then skip to step 8.*

Can I search for part of a word or number?

When you search for data in your worksheet, Excel will find the data even if it is part of a larger word or number. For example, if you search for 105, Excel will also find 105.35, 2105 and 1056.

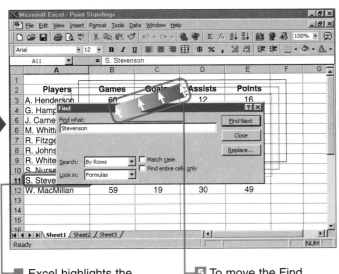

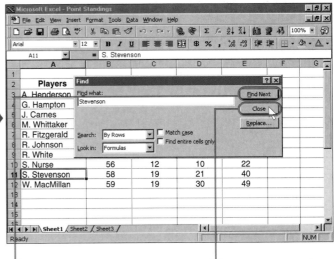

■ Excel highlights the first cell containing the word or number.

■ If the highlighted cell is hidden behind the Find dialog box, you can move the dialog box.

5 To move the Find dialog box, position the mouse over the title bar.

6 Drag the dialog box to a new location.

7 To find the next matching word or number, click **Find Next**. Repeat this step until you find all the occurrences of the word or number you are searching for.

8 Click **Close** to close the Find dialog box.

FIND AND REPLACE DATA

You can use the Replace feature to locate and replace every occurrence of a word or number in your worksheet. This is useful if you incorrectly entered data throughout the worksheet.

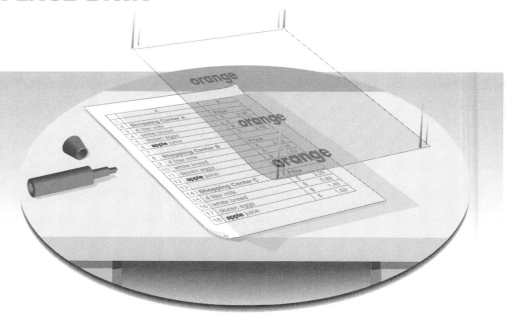

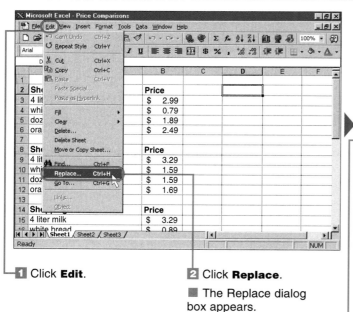

1 Click **Edit**.

2 Click **Replace**.

■ The Replace dialog box appears.

3 Type the word or number you want to replace with new data.

4 Click this area and then type the new word or number.

5 Click **Find Next** to start the search.

Note: A dialog box appears if Excel cannot find the word or number you specified. Click OK to close the dialog box. Then skip to step 8.

Can Excel find and replace a number used in my formulas?

Excel automatically searches the formulas in your worksheet for the number you specified. This is useful if you want to change a value used in several formulas. For example, if sales tax increases from 7% to 8%, you can search for all occurrences of **1.07** in your formulas and replace them with **1.08**.

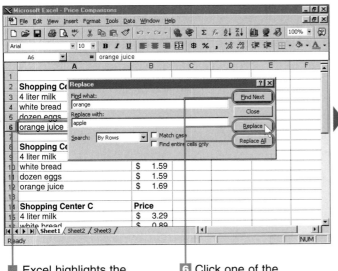

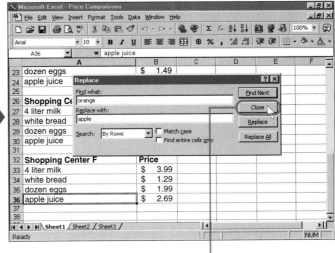

■ Excel highlights the first cell containing the word or number you specified.

6 Click one of the following options.

Find Next - Ignore word or number

Replace - Replace word or number

Replace All - Replace all occurrences of word or number in the worksheet

7 Repeat step **6** until you find all the occurrences of the word or number you want to replace.

8 Click **Close** to close the Replace dialog box.

INSERT A ROW OR COLUMN

You can add a row or column to your worksheet when you want to insert additional data.

INSERT A ROW

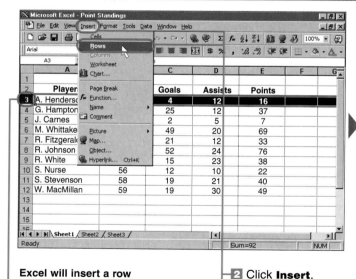

Excel will insert a row above the row you select.

1 To select a row, click the row number.

2 Click **Insert**.

3 Click **Rows**.

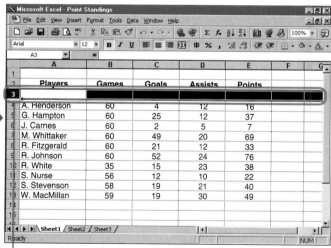

■ The new row appears and all the rows that follow shift downward.

?

How do I insert several rows or columns at once?

You can use the method shown below to insert several rows or columns at once, but you must first select the number of rows or columns you want to insert. For example, to insert three rows, select three rows before performing steps 2 and 3 on page 62.

Note: To select rows or columns, see page 15.

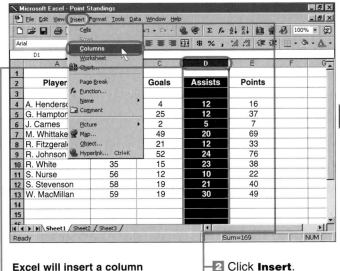

INSERT A COLUMN

Excel will insert a column to the left of the column you select.

1 To select a column, click the column letter.

2 Click **Insert**.

3 Click **Columns**.

■ The new column appears and all the columns that follow shift to the right.

DELETE A ROW OR COLUMN

You can delete a row or column from your worksheet to remove cells and data you no longer need.

DELETE A ROW

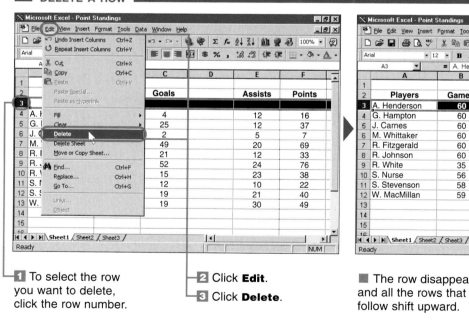

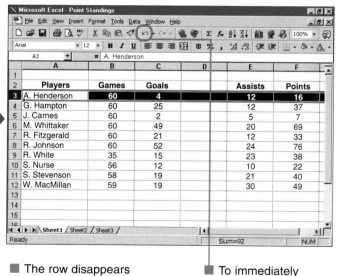

1 To select the row you want to delete, click the row number.

2 Click **Edit**.

3 Click **Delete**.

■ The row disappears and all the rows that follow shift upward.

■ To immediately return the row to the worksheet, click 🔙.

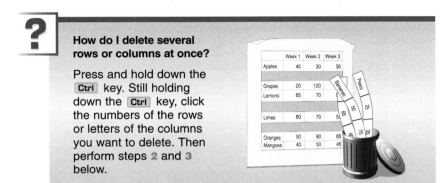

How do I delete several rows or columns at once?

Press and hold down the **Ctrl** key. Still holding down the **Ctrl** key, click the numbers of the rows or letters of the columns you want to delete. Then perform steps **2** and **3** below.

DELETE A COLUMN

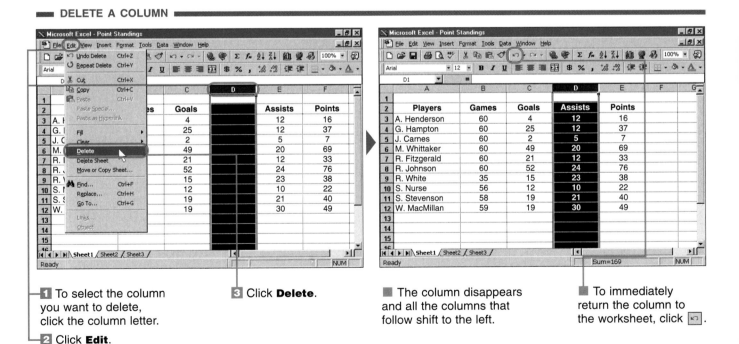

1 To select the column you want to delete, click the column letter.

2 Click **Edit**.

3 Click **Delete**.

■ The column disappears and all the columns that follow shift to the left.

■ To immediately return the column to the worksheet, click 🔄.

INSERT CELLS

If you want to add new data to the middle of existing data, you can insert cells. The surrounding cells move to make room for the new cells.

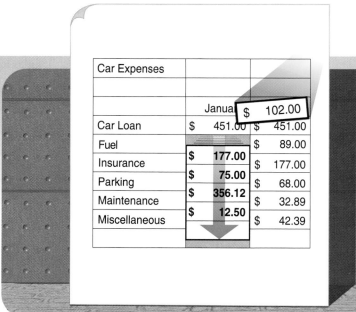

Car Expenses		
	Janua $\quad$ $ 102.00	
Car Loan	$ 451.00	$ 451.00
Fuel		$ 89.00
	$ 177.00	$ 177.00
Insurance		
Parking	$ 75.00	$ 68.00
	$ 356.12	
Maintenance		$ 32.89
Miscellaneous	$ 12.50	$ 42.39

INSERT CELLS

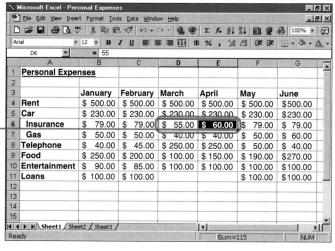

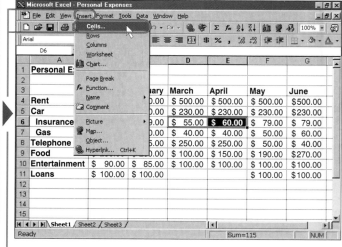

1 Select the cells where you want to insert new cells. To select cells, see page 14.

Note: Excel will insert the same number of cells as you select.

2 Click **Insert**.

3 Click **Cells**.

■ The Insert dialog box appears.

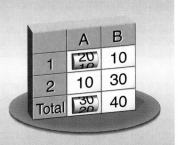

Do I need to adjust my formulas when I insert cells?

Excel automatically updates any formulas affected by the insertion, but you may want to check your formulas to verify that Excel updated the formulas properly. For information on formulas, see page 78.

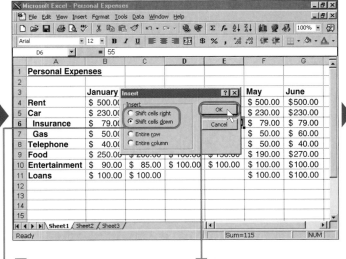

4 Click an option to shift the surrounding cells to the right or downward to make room for the new cells (O changes to ⊙).

5 Click **OK** to insert the cells.

■ Excel inserts the new cells and shifts the surrounding cells in the direction you specified.

DELETE CELLS

You can remove cells you no longer need from your worksheet. The surrounding cells move to fill the empty space.

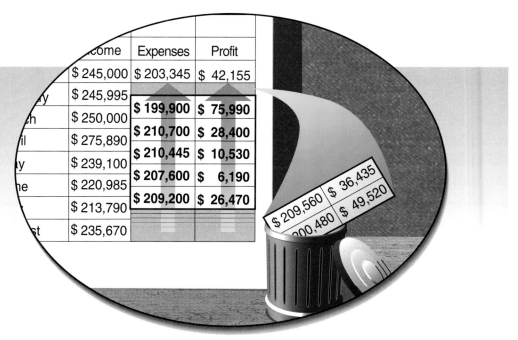

DELETE CELLS

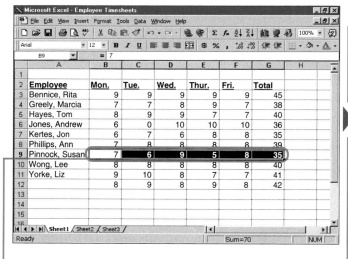

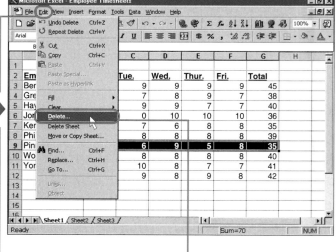

1 Select the cells you want to delete. To select cells, see page 14.

2 Click **Edit**.

3 Click **Delete**.

■ The Delete dialog box appears.

Why did #REF! appear in a cell after I deleted cells in my worksheet?

If **#REF!** appears in a cell in your worksheet, you deleted data needed to calculate a formula. For information on formulas, see page 78.

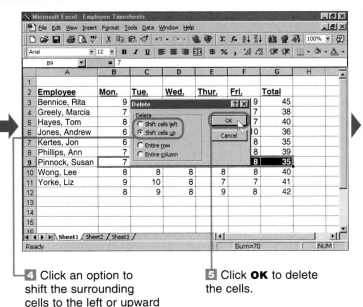

■ **4** Click an option to shift the surrounding cells to the left or upward to fill the empty space (○ changes to ⊙).

■ **5** Click **OK** to delete the cells.

■ Excel removes the cells and shifts the surrounding cells in the direction you specified.

■ To immediately return the cells to the worksheet, click 🔄.

NAME CELLS

You can give cells in your worksheet a meaningful name. Using named cells can save you time when selecting cells and entering formulas.

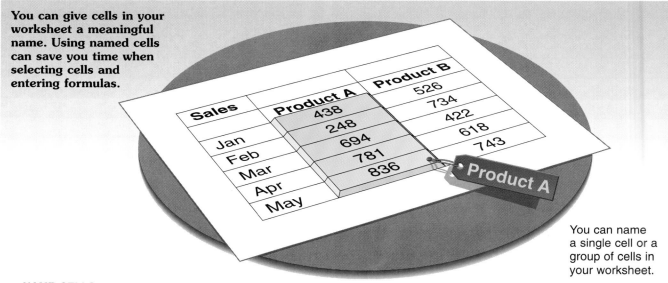

You can name a single cell or a group of cells in your worksheet.

NAME CELLS

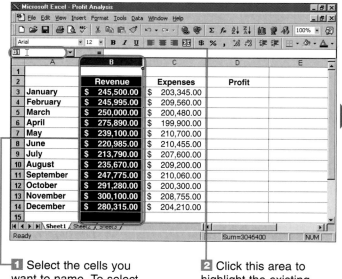

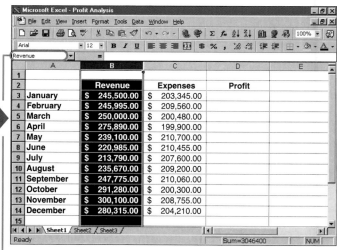

1 Select the cells you want to name. To select cells, see page 14.

2 Click this area to highlight the existing information.

3 Type the name you want to use for the cells. The name cannot start with a number or contain spaces.

4 Press the Enter key.

70

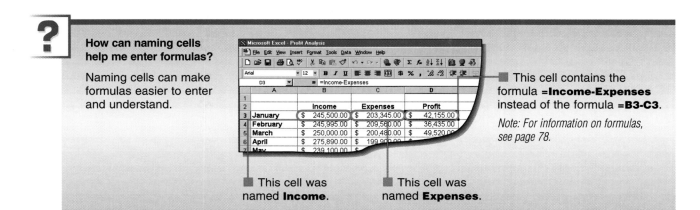

How can naming cells help me enter formulas?

Naming cells can make formulas easier to enter and understand.

■ This cell contains the formula **=Income-Expenses** instead of the formula **=B3-C3**.

Note: For information on formulas, see page 78.

■ This cell was named **Income**.

■ This cell was named **Expenses**.

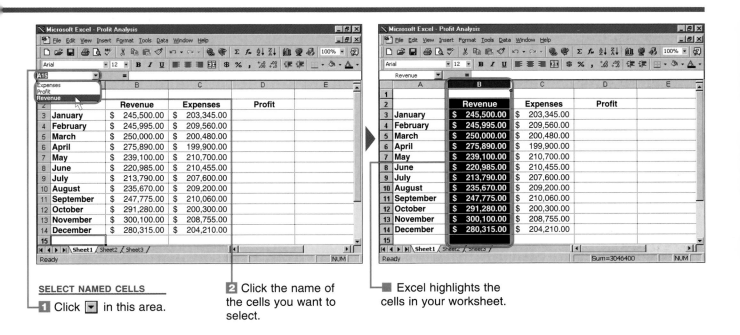

SELECT NAMED CELLS

1 Click ▾ in this area.

2 Click the name of the cells you want to select.

■ Excel highlights the cells in your worksheet.

ADD A COMMENT

You can add a comment to a cell in your worksheet. A comment can provide detailed information about data or remind you of data that needs to be verified.

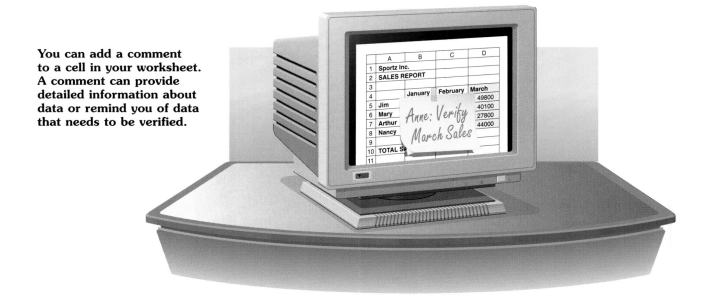

ADD A COMMENT

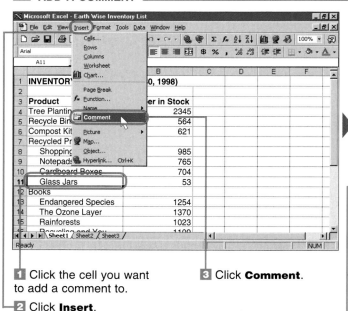

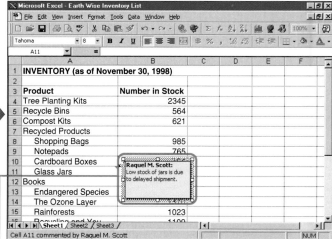

1 Click the cell you want to add a comment to.

2 Click **Insert**.

3 Click **Comment**.

■ A yellow comment box appears, displaying your name.

4 Type your comment.

5 When you finish typing your comment, click outside the comment box.

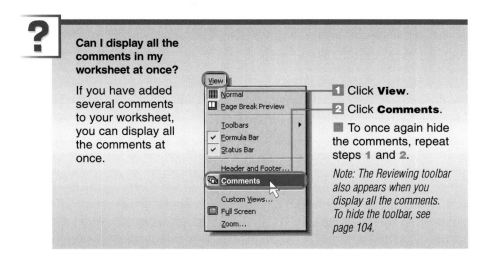

?

Can I display all the comments in my worksheet at once?

If you have added several comments to your worksheet, you can display all the comments at once.

■ Click **View**.

■ Click **Comments**.

■ To once again hide the comments, repeat steps 1 and 2.

Note: The Reviewing toolbar also appears when you display all the comments. To hide the toolbar, see page 104.

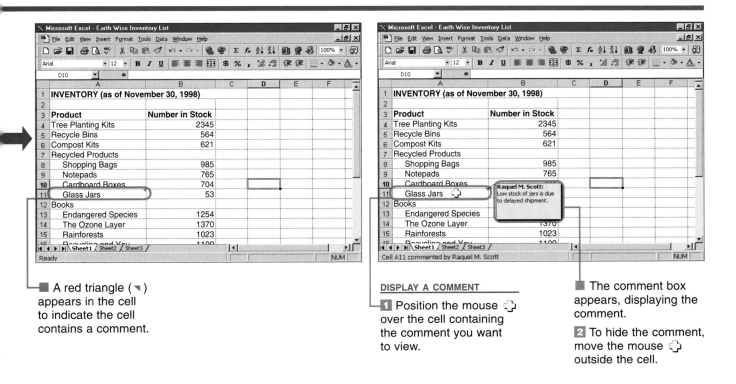

■ A red triangle (◥) appears in the cell to indicate the cell contains a comment.

DISPLAY A COMMENT

1 Position the mouse ⇩ over the cell containing the comment you want to view.

■ The comment box appears, displaying the comment.

2 To hide the comment, move the mouse ⇩ outside the cell.

ADD A COMMENT

You can edit a comment to update the information it displays. You can also delete a comment you no longer need.

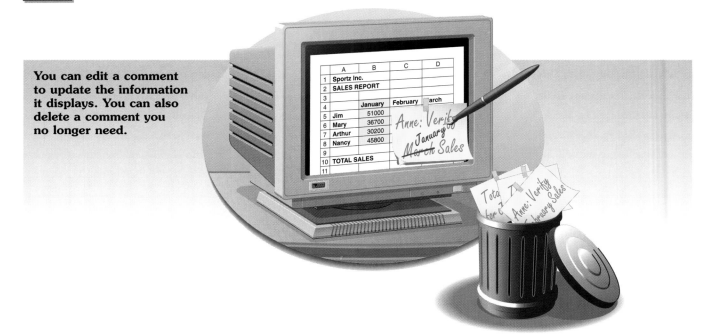

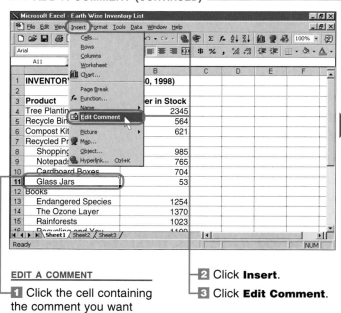

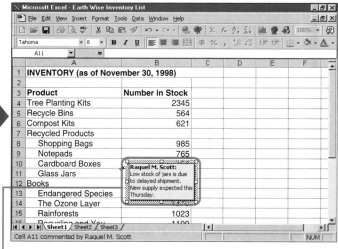

EDIT A COMMENT

1 Click the cell containing the comment you want to edit.

2 Click **Insert**.

3 Click **Edit Comment**.

■ The comment box appears. You can now edit the comment.

4 When you finish editing the comment, click outside the comment box.

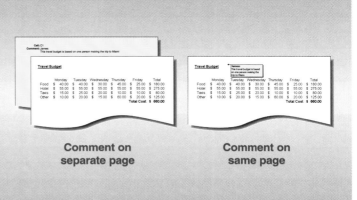

Why didn't my comments print when I printed my worksheet?

By default, Excel does not print comments. To print comments, you must change Excel's print options. For information, see page 162.

You can have Excel print the comments on a separate page or as they are displayed in the worksheet. To print the comments as they are displayed in the worksheet, you must first display all the comments. For information, see the top of page 73.

Comment on separate page

Comment on same page

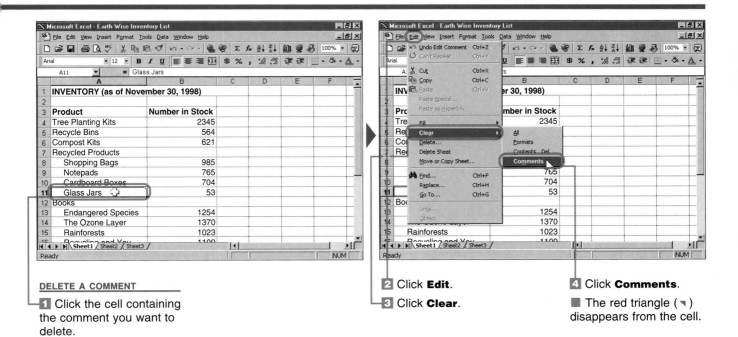

DELETE A COMMENT

1 Click the cell containing the comment you want to delete.

2 Click **Edit**.

3 Click **Clear**.

4 Click **Comments**.

■ The red triangle (▾) disappears from the cell.

TAKE-OUT ORDERS

	A	B
1	*Pizza*	*600*
2	*Spaghetti*	*200*
3	*Garlic Bread*	*400*
4	**TOTAL**	*1200*

=B1+B2+B3

CHAPTER 4

Work With Formulas and Functions

Would you like to perform calculations on the data in your worksheet? In this chapter you will learn how to work with formulas and functions.

USING FORMULAS

A formula helps you calculate and analyze data in your worksheet.

A formula always begins with an equal sign (=).

$$45 - 3 + 4 * 5 = 62$$
$$OR$$
$$45 - (3 + 4) * 5 = 10$$

Cell References

When entering formulas, use cell references instead of actual data whenever possible. For example, enter the formula **=A1+A2** instead of **=10+30**.

When you use cell references and you change a number used in a formula, Excel will automatically redo the calculations for you.

Order of Calculations

Excel performs calculations in the following order:

1 Exponents (^)

2 Multiplication (*) and Division (/)

3 Addition (+) and Subtraction (-)

You can use parentheses ( ) to change the order in which Excel performs calculations. Excel will perform the calculations inside the parentheses first.

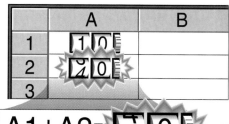

EXAMPLES OF FORMULAS

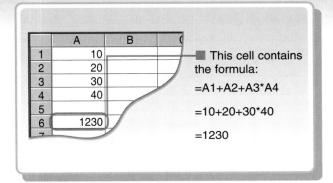

■ This cell contains the formula:

=A1+A2+A3*A4

=10+20+30*40

=1230

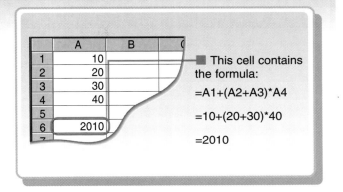

■ This cell contains the formula:

=A1+(A2+A3)*A4

=10+(20+30)*40

=2010

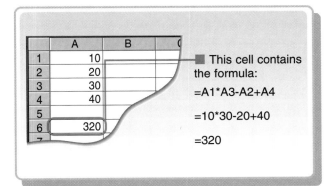

■ This cell contains the formula:

=A1*A3-A2+A4

=10*30-20+40

=320

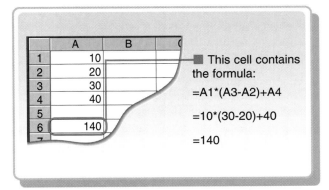

■ This cell contains the formula:

=A1*(A3-A2)+A4

=10*(30-20)+40

=140

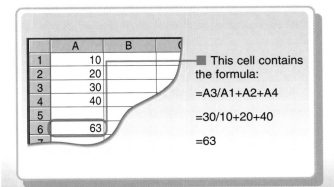

■ This cell contains the formula:

=A3/A1+A2+A4

=30/10+20+40

=63

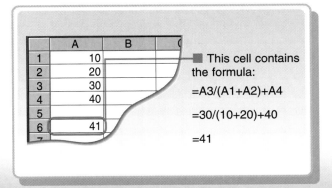

■ This cell contains the formula:

=A3/(A1+A2)+A4

=30/(10+20)+40

=41

ENTER A FORMULA

You can enter
a formula into
any cell in your
worksheet.

TAKE-OUT ORDERS

	A	B
1	*Pizza*	*600*
2	*Spaghetti*	*200*
3	*Garlic Bread*	*400*
4	**TOTAL**	*1200*

=B1+B2+B3

ENTER A FORMULA

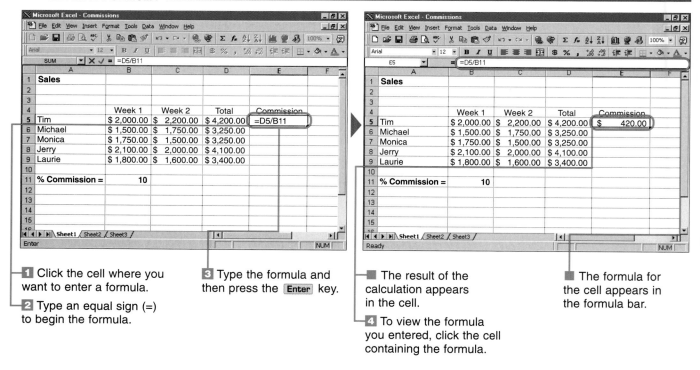

1 Click the cell where you want to enter a formula.

2 Type an equal sign (=) to begin the formula.

3 Type the formula and then press the **Enter** key.

■ The result of the calculation appears in the cell.

4 To view the formula you entered, click the cell containing the formula.

■ The formula for the cell appears in the formula bar.

? **What happens if I change a number used in a formula?**

If you change a number used in a formula, Excel will automatically calculate a new result.

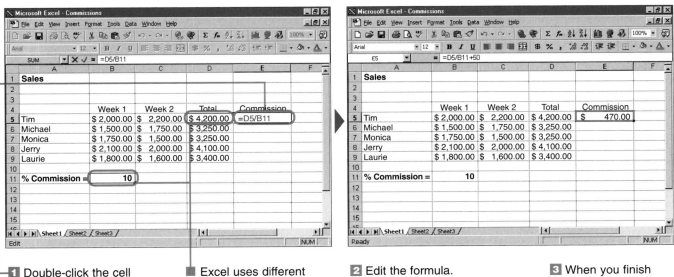

TAKE-OUT ORDERS

	A	B
1	Pizza	600
2	Spaghetti	200
3	Garlic Bread	~~400~~ 500
4	TOTAL	~~1200~~ 1300

■ EDIT A FORMULA ■

■ **Double-click the cell** containing the formula you want to change.

■ The formula appears in the cell.

■ Excel uses different colors to highlight each cell used in the formula.

2 Edit the formula. To edit data in a cell, perform steps **2** to **4** starting on page 44.

3 When you finish making changes to the formula, press the **Enter** key.

USING FUNCTIONS

A function is a ready-to-use formula that you can use to perform a calculation on the data in your worksheet.

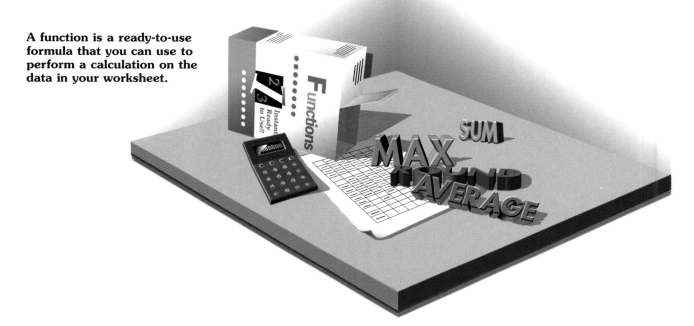

INTRODUCTION TO FUNCTIONS

■ A function always begins with an equal sign (=).

■ The data Excel will use to calculate a function is enclosed in parentheses ( ).

```
=SUM(A1,A2,A3)

=AVERAGE(C1,C2,C3)

=MAX(B7,C7,D7,E7)

=COUNT(D12,D13,D14)
```

Specify Individual Cells

When there is a comma (,) between cell references in a function, Excel uses each cell to perform the calculation.

For example, =SUM(A1,A2,A3) is the same as the formula =A1+A2+A3.

```
=SUM(A1:A3)

=AVERAGE(C1:C3)

=MAX(B7:E7)

=COUNT(D12:D14)
```

Specify Group of Cells

When there is a colon (:) between cell references in a function, Excel uses the specified cells and all cells between them to perform the calculation.

For example, =SUM(A1:A3) is the same as the formula =A1+A2+A3.

COMMON FUNCTIONS

Average

Calculates the average value
of a list of numbers.

	A	B	
1	10		
2	20		
3	30		
4	40		
5			
6	25		
7			

■ This cell contains
the function:

=AVERAGE(A1:A4)

=(A1+A2+A3+A4)/4

=(10+20+30+40)/4

=25

Count

Calculates the number
of values in a list.

	A	B	
1	10		
2	20		
3	30		
4	40		
5			
6	4		
7			

■ This cell contains
the function:

=COUNT(A1:A4)

=4

Max

Finds the largest value in a
list of numbers.

	A	B	
1	10		
2	20		
3	30		
4	40		
5			
6	40		
7			

■ This cell contains
the function:

=MAX(A1:A4)

=40

Min

Finds the smallest value
in a list of numbers.

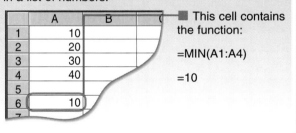

■ This cell contains
the function:

=MIN(A1:A4)

=10

Sum

Adds a list of numbers.

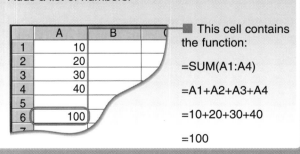

■ This cell contains
the function:

=SUM(A1:A4)

=A1+A2+A3+A4

=10+20+30+40

=100

Round

Rounds a value to a specific
number of digits.

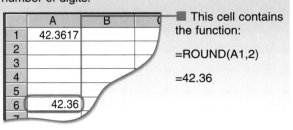

■ This cell contains
the function:

=ROUND(A1,2)

=42.36

ENTER A FUNCTION

Excel helps you
enter functions in
your worksheet. This
lets you perform
calculations without
typing long, complex
formulas.

=SUM(A1:A4)
=AVERAGE(A1:A4)
=ROUND(E4,2)
=COUNT(B1:B6)
=MAX(E1:E4)

ENTER A FUNCTION

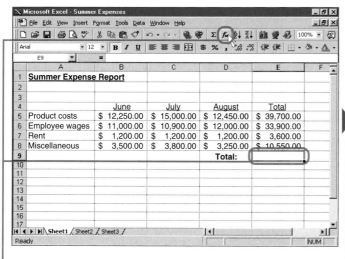

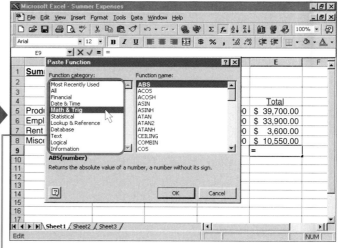

1 Click the cell where
you want to enter a
function.

2 Click ![fx].

■ The Paste Function
dialog box appears.

*Note: The first time you
display the Paste Function
dialog box, the Office Assistant
may appear. Click **No** to hide
the Office Assistant.*

3 Click the category that
contains the function you
want to use.

*Note: If you do not know
which category contains
the function you want to
use, select **All** to display
a list of all the functions.*

How many functions does Excel offer?

Excel offers over 200 functions to help you analyze data in your worksheet. There are financial functions, math and trigonometry functions, date and time functions, statistical functions and many more.

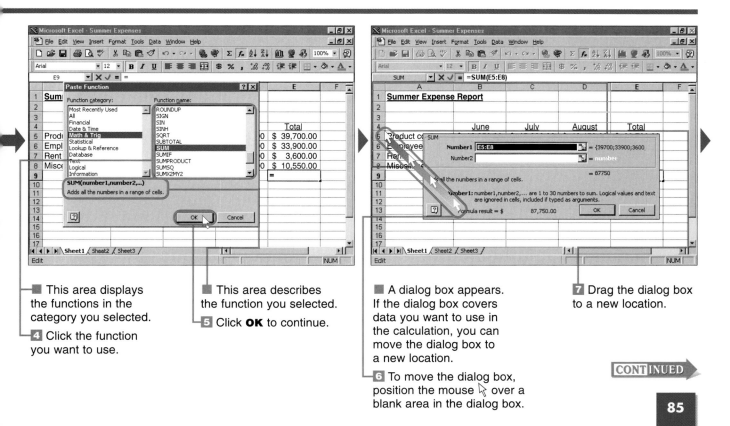

■ This area displays the functions in the category you selected.

4 Click the function you want to use.

■ This area describes the function you selected.

5 Click **OK** to continue.

■ A dialog box appears. If the dialog box covers data you want to use in the calculation, you can move the dialog box to a new location.

6 To move the dialog box, position the mouse ⌖ over a blank area in the dialog box.

7 Drag the dialog box to a new location.

CONTINUED

ENTER A FUNCTION

When entering a function, you must specify which numbers you want to use in the calculation.

=SUM(D1:D4)

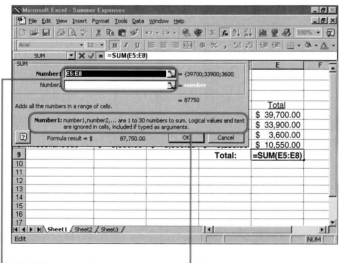

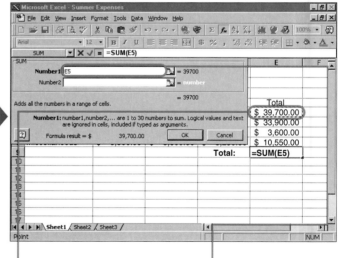

■ This area displays boxes where you enter the numbers you want to use in the calculation.

■ This area describes the number you need to enter.

8 To enter a number, click the cell that contains the number.

Note: If the number you want to enter does not appear in the worksheet, type the number.

■ The cell reference for the number appears in this area.

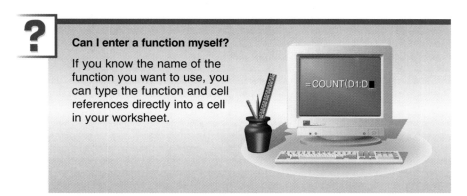

?

Can I enter a function myself?

If you know the name of the function you want to use, you can type the function and cell references directly into a cell in your worksheet.

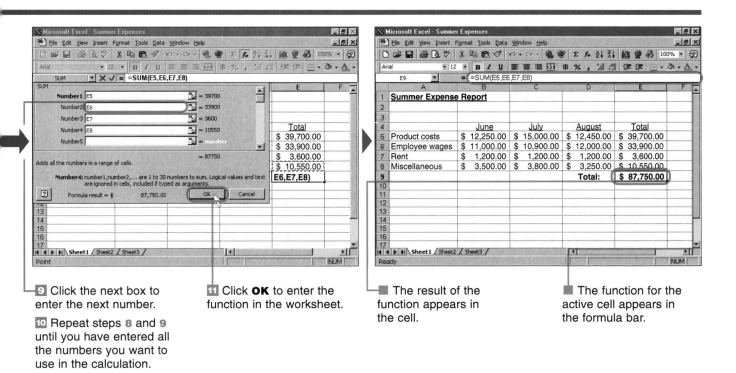

9 Click the next box to enter the next number.

10 Repeat steps **8** and **9** until you have entered all the numbers you want to use in the calculation.

11 Click **OK** to enter the function in the worksheet.

■ The result of the function appears in the cell.

■ The function for the active cell appears in the formula bar.

USING AUTOCALCULATE

You can view the
results of common
calculations without
entering a formula
into your worksheet.

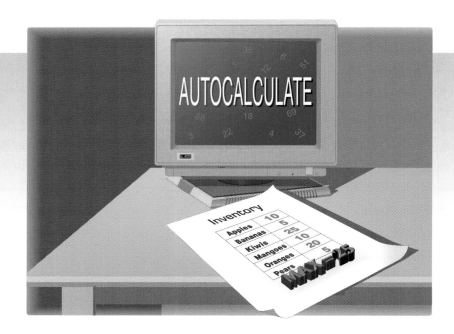

USING AUTOCALCULATE

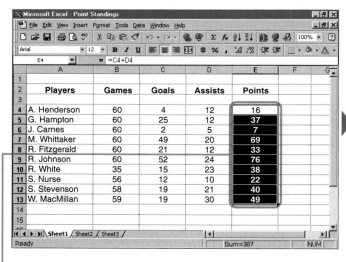

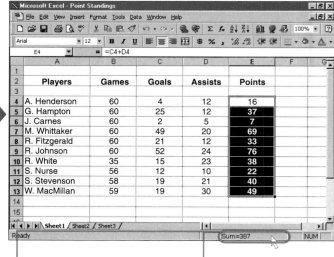

1 Select the cells you
want to include in the
calculation. To select
cells, see page 14.

■ This area displays
the sum of the cells
you selected.

2 To display the result
for a different calculation,
right-click this area.

?

What calculations can AutoCalculate perform?

Average

Calculates the average value of a list of numbers.

Count

Calculates the number of items in a list, including text.

Count Nums

Calculates the number of values in a list.

Max

Finds the largest value in a list.

Min

Finds the smallest value in a list.

Sum

Adds a list of numbers.

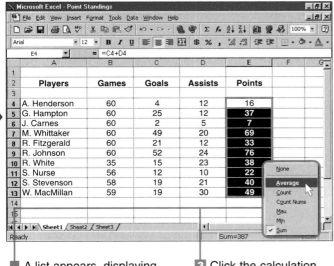

■ A list appears, displaying the calculations you can perform.

3 Click the calculation you want to perform.

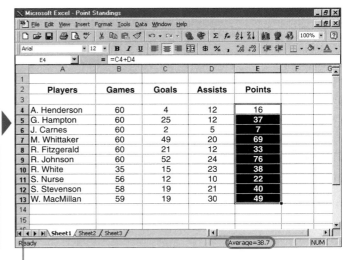

■ This area displays the result for the new calculation.

ADD NUMBERS

You can calculate the sum of a list of numbers in your worksheet.

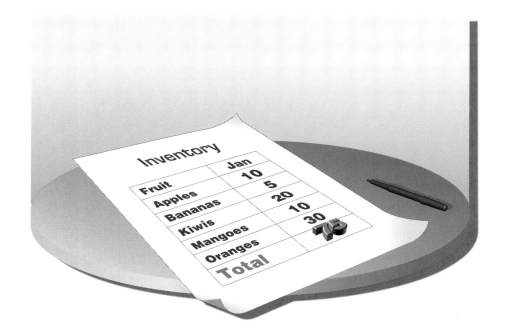

ADD NUMBERS

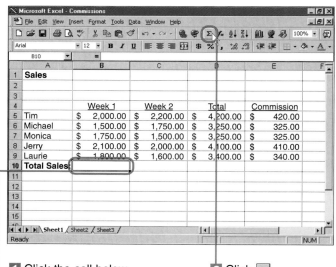

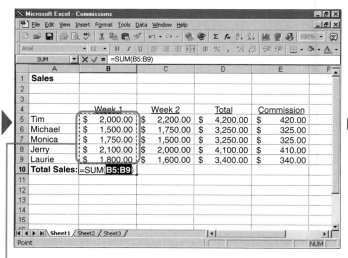

1 Click the cell below or to the right of the cells containing the numbers you want to add.

2 Click Σ.

■ Excel outlines the cells it will use in the calculation with a dotted line.

■ If Excel does not outline the correct cells, select the cells containing the numbers you want to add. To select cells, see page 14.

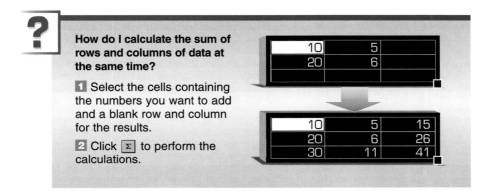

How do I calculate the sum of rows and columns of data at the same time?

■1 Select the cells containing the numbers you want to add and a blank row and column for the results.

■2 Click ∑ to perform the calculations.

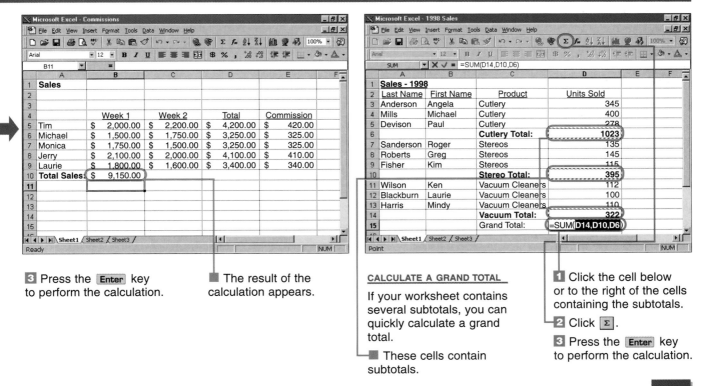

■3 Press the **Enter** key to perform the calculation.

■ The result of the calculation appears.

CALCULATE A GRAND TOTAL

If your worksheet contains several subtotals, you can quickly calculate a grand total.

■ These cells contain subtotals.

■1 Click the cell below or to the right of the cells containing the subtotals.

■2 Click ∑.

■3 Press the **Enter** key to perform the calculation.

DISPLAY FORMULAS

You can display the formulas in your worksheet instead of the results of the calculations. This is useful when you want to review or edit all the formulas in your worksheet.

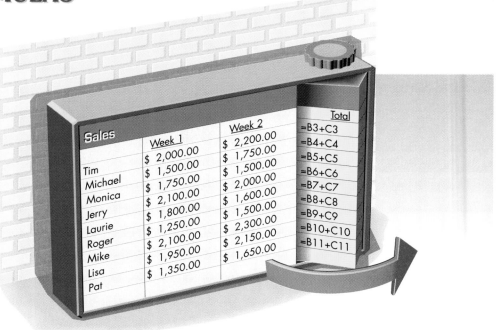

DISPLAY FORMULAS

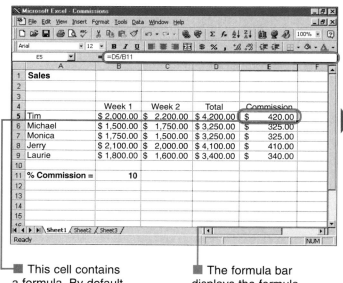

■ This cell contains a formula. By default, Excel displays formula results in the worksheet.

■ The formula bar displays the formula for the active cell.

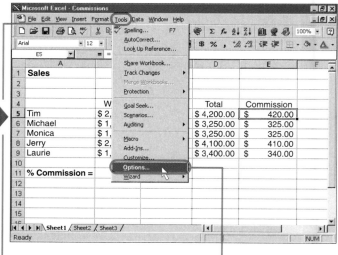

1 To display the formulas in the worksheet, click **Tools**.

2 Click **Options**.

■ The Options dialog box appears.

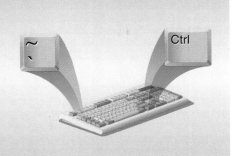

Is there another way to display the formulas in my worksheet?

You can use the keyboard to switch between the display of formulas and formula results in your worksheet. To change the display at any time, press and hold down the Ctrl key and then press the ~ key.

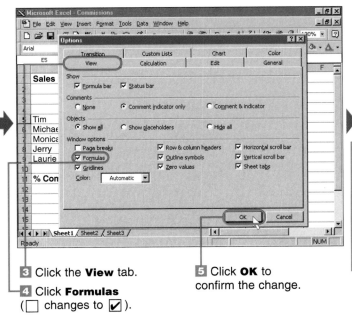

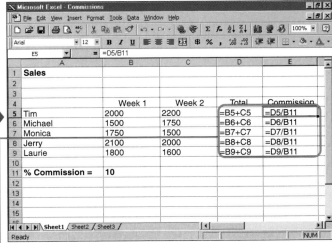

3 Click the **View** tab.

4 Click **Formulas** (☐ changes to ☑).

5 Click **OK** to confirm the change.

■ The formulas appear in the worksheet.

■ Excel automatically adjusts the widths of the columns in the worksheet to clearly display the formulas. To change the width of columns yourself, see page 116.

■ To once again show the formula results in the worksheet, repeat steps **1** to **5** (☑ changes to ☐ in step **4**).

COPY A FORMULA

If you want to use the same formula several times in your worksheet, you can save time by copying the formula.

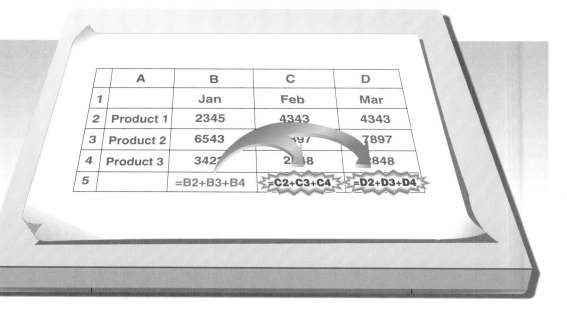

	A	B	C	D
1		Jan	Feb	Mar
2	Product 1	2345	4343	4343
3	Product 2	6543	~~97~~	7897
4	Product 3	342~~?~~	2~~?~~8	~~?~~848
5		=B2+B3+B4	=C2+C3+C4	=D2+D3+D4

COPY A FORMULA — USING RELATIVE REFERENCES

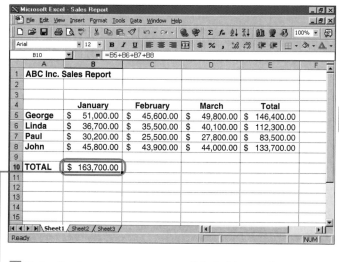

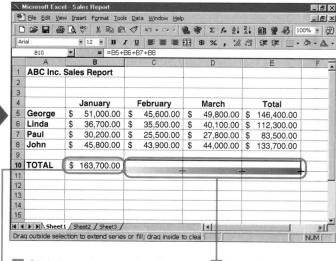

1 Enter the formula you want to copy to other cells.

*Note: In this example, cell **B10** contains the formula =B5+B6+B7+B8.*

2 Click the cell containing the formula you want to copy.

3 Position the mouse ⇩ over the bottom right corner of the cell (⇩ changes to ✛).

4 Drag the mouse ✛ over the cells you want to receive a copy of the formula.

What is a relative reference?

A relative reference is a cell reference that changes when you copy a formula.

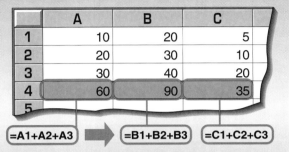

	A	B	C
1	10	20	5
2	20	30	10
3	30	40	20
4	60	90	35
5			

=A1+A2+A3 ➡ =B1+B2+B3 =C1+C2+C3

This cell contains the formula =A1+A2+A3.

If you copy the formula to other cells in the worksheet, Excel automatically changes the cell references in the new formulas.

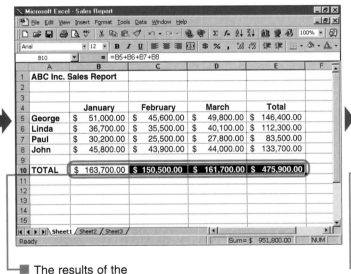

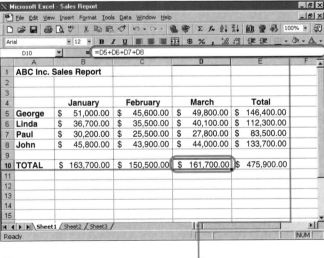

■ The results of the formulas appear.

5 To see one of the new formulas, click a cell that received a copy of the formula.

■ The formula bar displays the formula with the new cell references.

COPY A FORMULA

You can copy a formula to other cells in your worksheet to save time. If you do not want Excel to change a cell reference when you copy a formula, you can use an absolute reference.

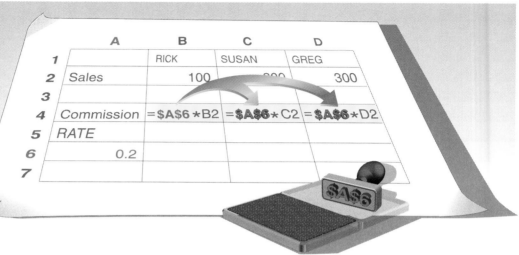

COPY A FORMULA — USING ABSOLUTE REFERENCES

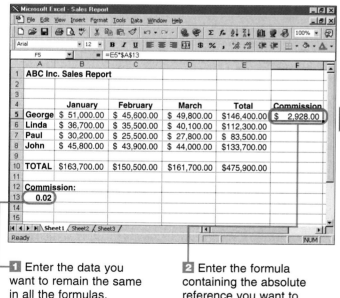

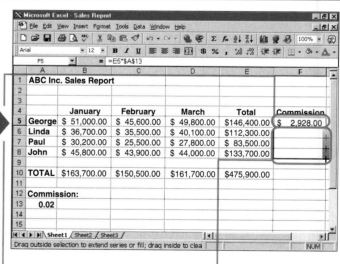

1 Enter the data you want to remain the same in all the formulas.

2 Enter the formula containing the absolute reference you want to copy to other cells.

*Note: In this example, cell **F5** contains the formula =E5*$A$13.*

3 Click the cell containing the formula you want to copy.

4 Position the mouse ⇩ over the bottom right corner of the cell (⇩ changes to ✛).

5 Drag the mouse ✛ over the cells you want to receive a copy of the formula.

What is an absolute reference?

An absolute reference is a cell reference that does not change when you copy a formula. To make a cell reference absolute, type a dollar sign ($) before both the column letter and row number (example: **$A$7**).

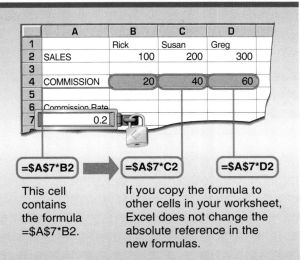

=$A$7*B2

This cell contains the formula =$A$7*B2.

=$A$7*C2

=$A$7*D2

If you copy the formula to other cells in your worksheet, Excel does not change the absolute reference in the new formulas.

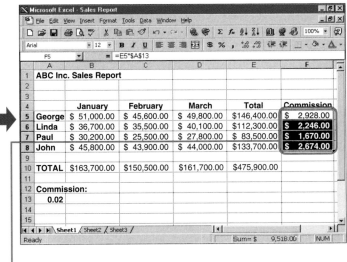

■ The results of the formulas appear.

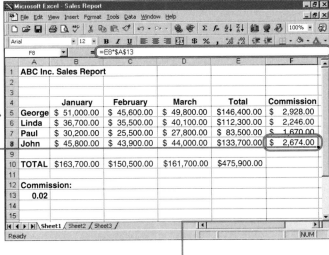

6 To see one of the new formulas, click a cell that received a copy of the formula.

■ The absolute reference (**$A$13**) in the formula did not change.

■ The relative reference (**E8**) in the formula did change.

ERRORS IN FORMULAS

An error message appears when Excel cannot properly calculate a formula.

ERROR

Errors in formulas are often the result of typing mistakes. You can correct an error by editing the data in the cell containing the error. To edit data in a cell, see page 44.

#####

The column is too narrow to display the result of the calculation. You can change the column width to display the result. To change the column width, see page 116.

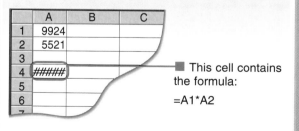

	A	B	C
1	9924		
2	5521		
3			
4	#####		
5			
6			

■ This cell contains the formula:

=A1*A2

#DIV/0!

The formula divides a number by zero (0). Excel considers a blank cell to contain a value of zero.

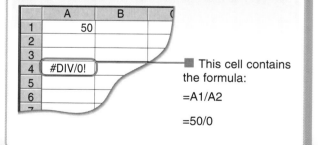

	A	B	C
1	50		
2			
3			
4	#DIV/0!		
5			
6			

■ This cell contains the formula:

=A1/A2

=50/0

#NAME?

The formula contains a function name or cell reference Excel does not recognize.

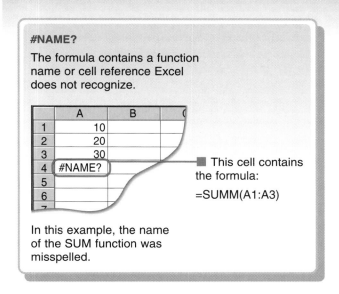

■ This cell contains the formula:

=SUMM(A1:A3)

In this example, the name of the SUM function was misspelled.

#REF!

The formula contains a cell reference for a cell that is not valid.

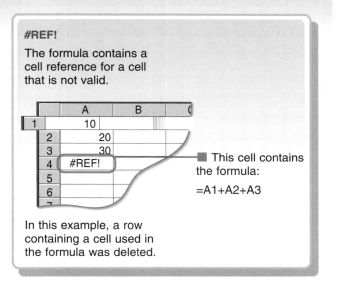

■ This cell contains the formula:

=A1+A2+A3

In this example, a row containing a cell used in the formula was deleted.

#VALUE!

The formula contains a cell reference for a cell that Excel cannot use in a calculation.

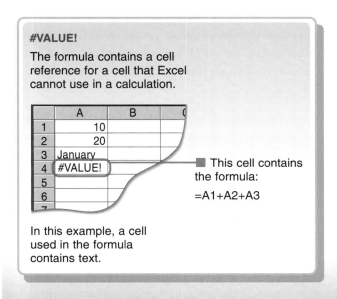

■ This cell contains the formula:

=A1+A2+A3

In this example, a cell used in the formula contains text.

Circular Reference

A warning message appears when a formula refers to the cell containing the formula. This is called a circular reference.

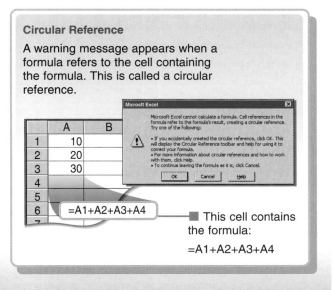

■ This cell contains the formula:

=A1+A2+A3+A4

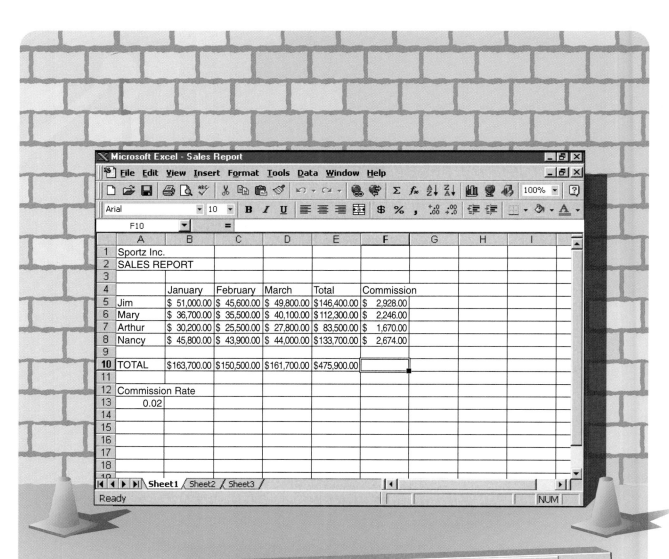

CHAPTER 5

Change Your Screen Display

Are you wondering how to change the way your worksheet appears on the screen? In this chapter you will learn how to zoom in or out, display or hide a toolbar, hide columns and more.

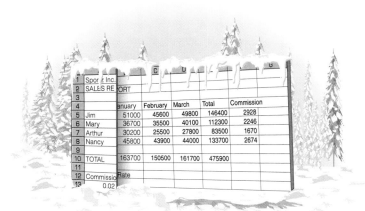

ZOOM IN OR OUT

Excel allows you to enlarge or reduce the display of data on your screen.

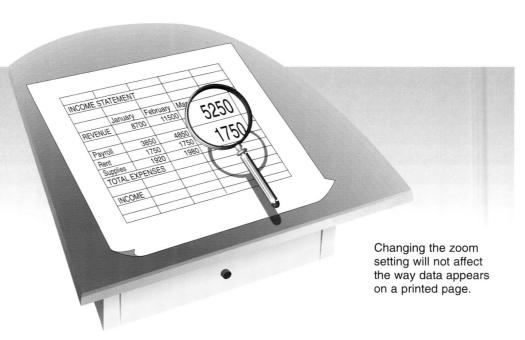

Changing the zoom setting will not affect the way data appears on a printed page.

ZOOM IN OR OUT

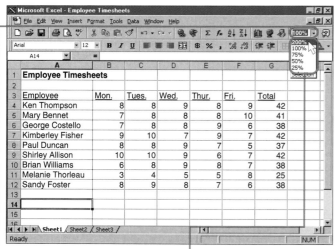

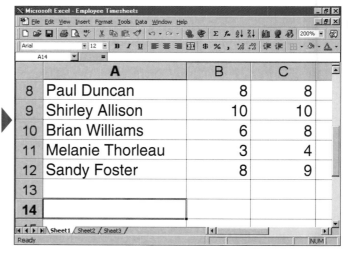

■ When you first start Excel, the worksheet appears in the 100% zoom setting.

1 Click ▼ in this area to display a list of zoom settings.

2 Click the zoom setting you want to use.

■ The worksheet appears in the new zoom setting. You can edit the worksheet as usual.

■ To return to the normal zoom setting, repeat steps **1** and **2**, except select **100%** in step **2**.

You can display a larger working area by hiding parts of the Excel screen.

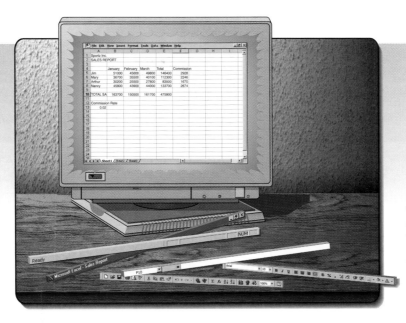

Using the full screen to view a worksheet is useful if you want to display as many cells as possible while you review and edit a large worksheet.

DISPLAY FULL SCREEN

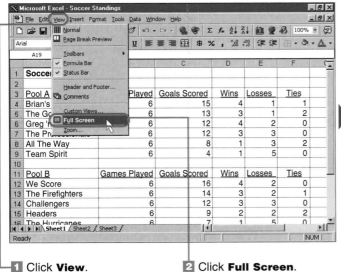

1 Click **View**.

2 Click **Full Screen**.

■ Excel hides parts of the screen to display a larger working area.

■ To redisplay the hidden parts of the screen, click **Close Full Screen**.

Note: You can also repeat steps 1 and 2 to redisplay the hidden parts of the screen.

DISPLAY OR HIDE A TOOLBAR

Excel offers several toolbars that you can display or hide at any time. Each toolbar contains buttons that help you quickly perform common tasks.

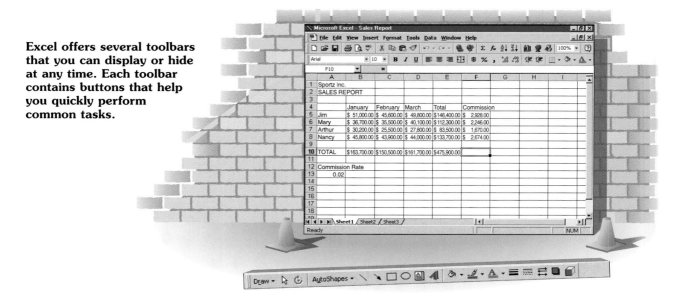

DISPLAY OR HIDE A TOOLBAR

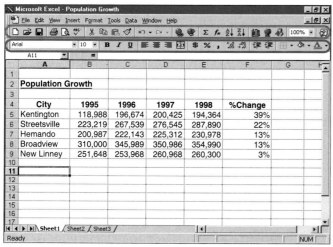

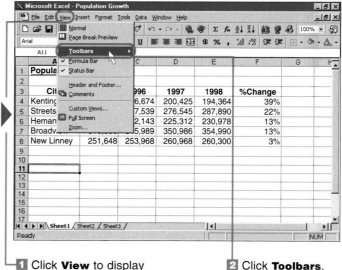

■ Excel automatically displays the following toolbars on the screen.

Standard Toolbar

Formatting Toolbar

1 Click **View** to display or hide a toolbar.

2 Click **Toolbars**.

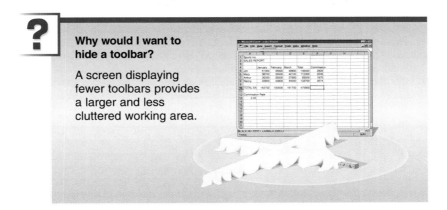

?

Why would I want to hide a toolbar?

A screen displaying fewer toolbars provides a larger and less cluttered working area.

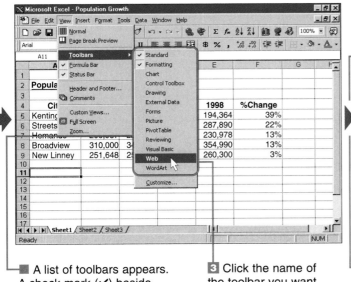

■ A list of toolbars appears. A check mark (✔) beside a toolbar name indicates the toolbar is currently displayed.

3 Click the name of the toolbar you want to display or hide.

■ Excel displays or hides the toolbar you selected.

■ To display the name of a toolbar button, position the mouse ⌖ over the button. After a few seconds, the name of the button appears.

HIDE COLUMNS

You can hide columns in your worksheet to reduce the amount of data displayed on your screen or hide confidential data.

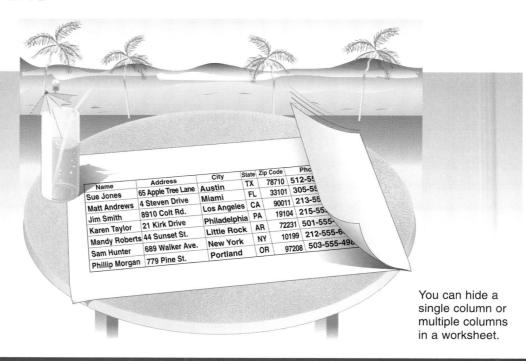

You can hide a single column or multiple columns in a worksheet.

HIDE COLUMNS

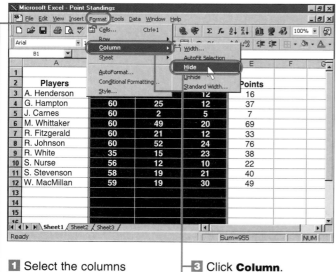

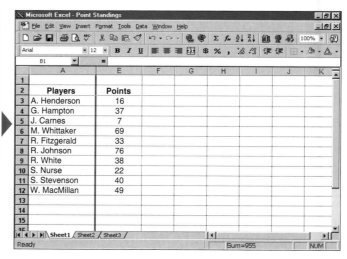

1 Select the columns you want to hide. To select columns, see page 15.

2 Click **Format**.

3 Click **Column**.

4 Click **Hide**.

■ Excel hides the columns you selected.

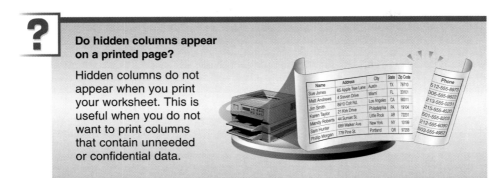

Do hidden columns appear on a printed page?

Hidden columns do not appear when you print your worksheet. This is useful when you do not want to print columns that contain unneeded or confidential data.

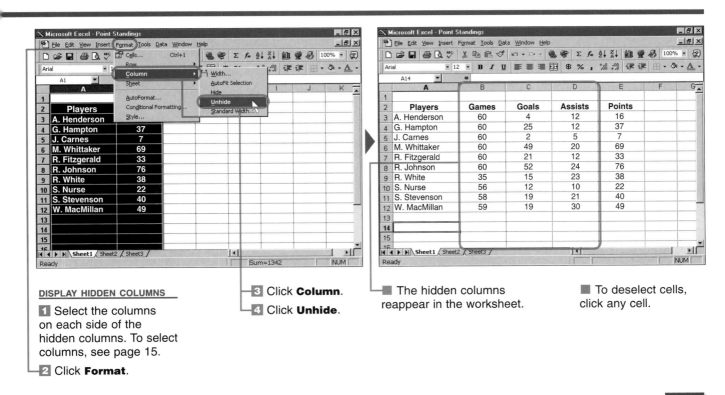

DISPLAY HIDDEN COLUMNS

1 Select the columns on each side of the hidden columns. To select columns, see page 15.

2 Click **Format**.

3 Click **Column**.

4 Click **Unhide**.

■ The hidden columns reappear in the worksheet.

■ To deselect cells, click any cell.

HIDE ROWS

You can hide rows in your worksheet to temporarily remove unnecessary or confidential data from your screen.

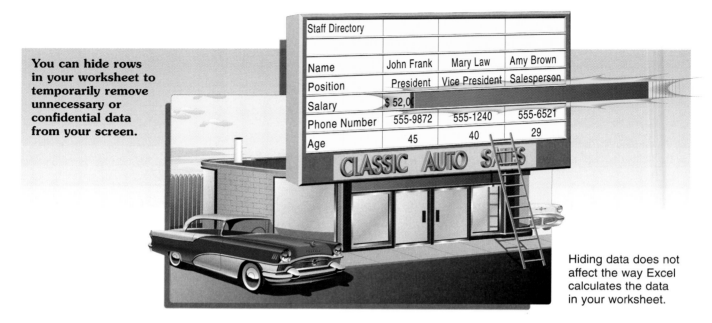

Staff Directory			
Name	John Frank	Mary Law	Amy Brown
Position	President	Vice President	Salesperson
Salary	$ 52,0		
Phone Number	555-9872	555-1240	555-6521
Age	45	40	29

Hiding data does not affect the way Excel calculates the data in your worksheet.

■ HIDE ROWS ■

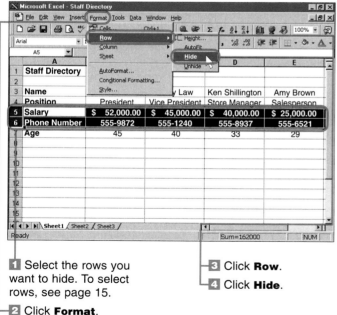

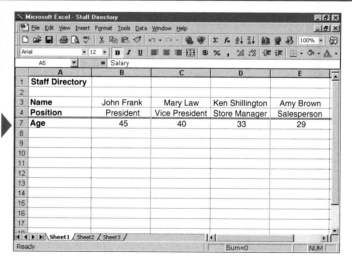

1 Select the rows you want to hide. To select rows, see page 15.

2 Click **Format**.

3 Click **Row**.

4 Click **Hide**.

■ Excel hides the rows you selected.

Is hiding rows an effective way to protect data in my worksheet?

Hiding rows is not a secure way to prevent others from viewing confidential data. Other people can redisplay the hidden rows at any time and view the data.

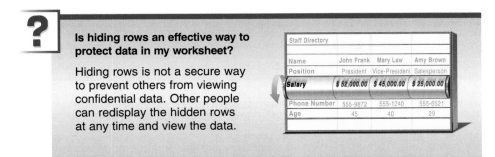

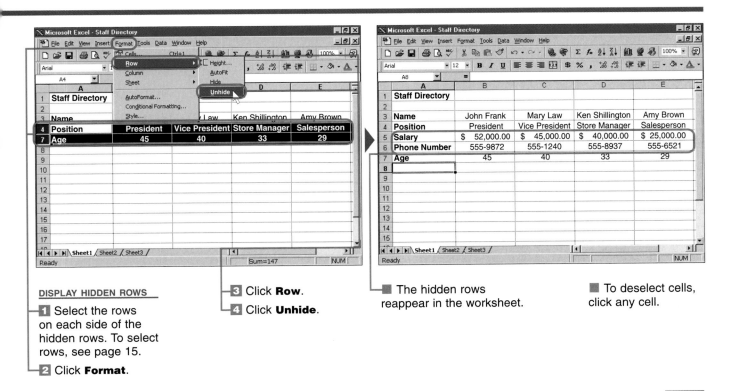

DISPLAY HIDDEN ROWS

1 Select the rows on each side of the hidden rows. To select rows, see page 15.

2 Click **Format**.

3 Click **Row**.

4 Click **Unhide**.

■ The hidden rows reappear in the worksheet.

■ To deselect cells, click any cell.

FREEZE ROWS AND COLUMNS

You can freeze rows
and columns in your
worksheet so they will
not move. This allows
you to keep headings
displayed on your
screen as you move
through a large
worksheet.

FREEZE ROWS AND COLUMNS

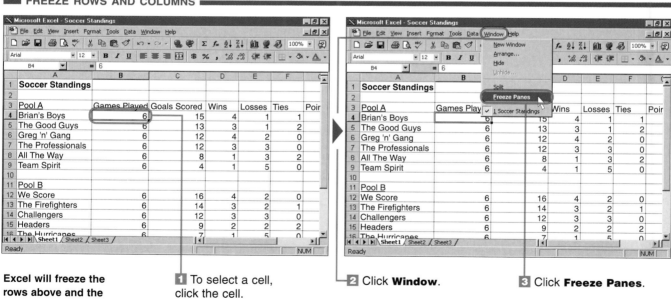

Excel will freeze the
rows above and the
columns to the left
of the cell you select.

1 To select a cell,
click the cell.

2 Click **Window**.

3 Click **Freeze Panes**.

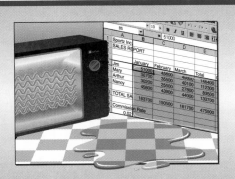

How do I unfreeze rows and columns in my worksheet?

When you no longer want to keep rows and columns frozen on your screen, perform steps **2** and **3** below, except select **Unfreeze Panes** in step **3**.

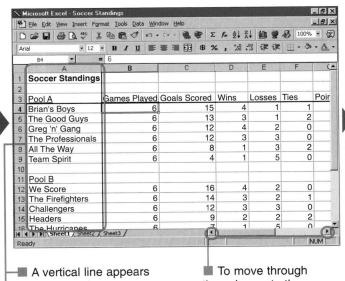

■ A vertical line appears in your worksheet.

■ The columns to the left of the vertical line are frozen. These columns remain on the screen as you move through the worksheet.

■ To move through the columns to the right of the vertical line, click ◀ or ▶.

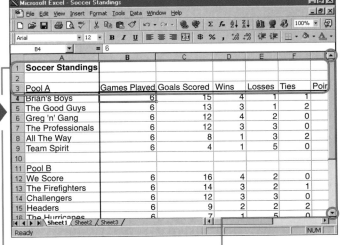

■ A horizontal line appears in your worksheet.

■ The rows above the horizontal line are frozen. These rows remain on the screen as you move through the worksheet.

■ To move through the rows below the horizontal line, click ▲ or ▼.

SPLIT A WORKSHEET

You can split your worksheet into separate sections. This lets you view different areas of a large worksheet at the same time.

SPLIT A WORKSHEET VERTICALLY

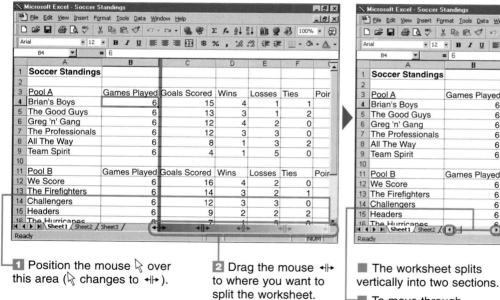

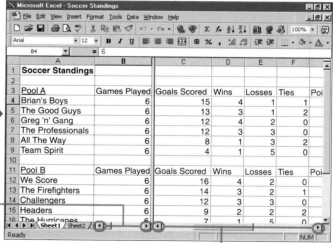

1 Position the mouse ⌖ over this area (⌖ changes to ◄║►).

2 Drag the mouse ◄║► to where you want to split the worksheet.

■ The worksheet splits vertically into two sections.

■ To move through the columns to the left of the dividing line, click ◄ or ►.

■ To move through the columns to the right of the dividing line, click ◄ or ►.

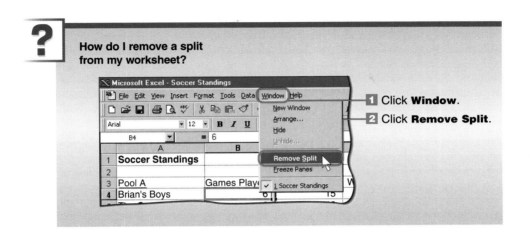

? How do I remove a split from my worksheet?

1 Click **Window**.

2 Click **Remove Split**.

SPLIT A WORKSHEET HORIZONTALLY

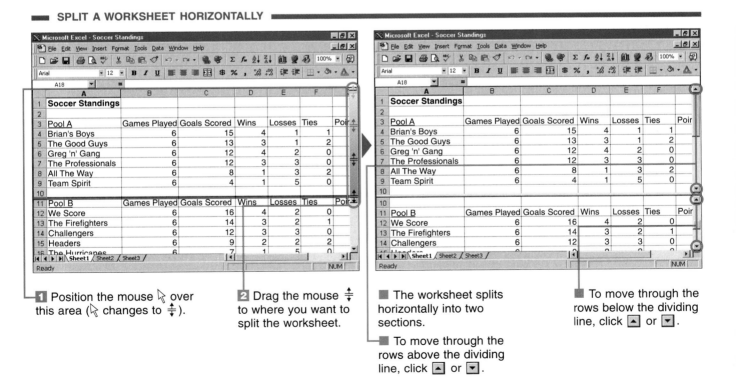

1 Position the mouse ⌖ over this area (⌖ changes to ⬍).

2 Drag the mouse ⬍ to where you want to split the worksheet.

■ The worksheet splits horizontally into two sections.

■ To move through the rows above the dividing line, click ▲ or ▼.

■ To move through the rows below the dividing line, click ▲ or ▼.

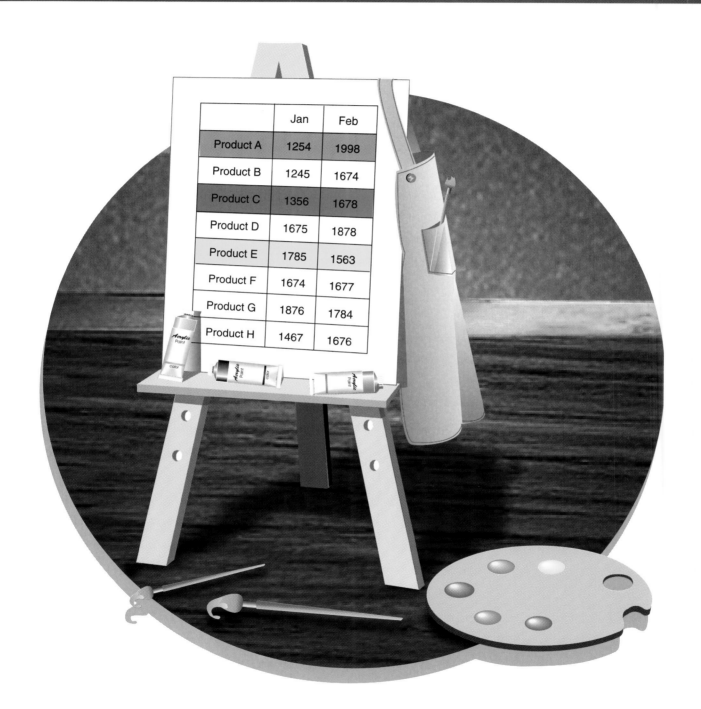

CHAPTER 6

Format Your Worksheets

Would you like to improve the appearance of your worksheet? This chapter shows you how to change the width of columns, add borders to cells, change the color of data and much more.

CHANGE COLUMN WIDTH

You can improve the
appearance of data
in your worksheet
by changing
the width
of columns.

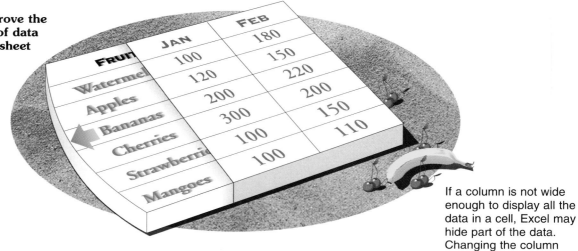

If a column is not wide
enough to display all the
data in a cell, Excel may
hide part of the data.
Changing the column
width allows you to
display the hidden data.

CHANGE COLUMN WIDTH

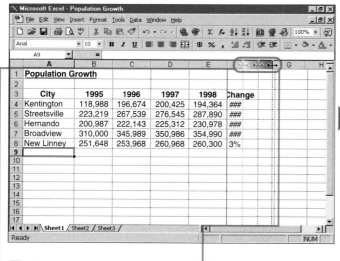

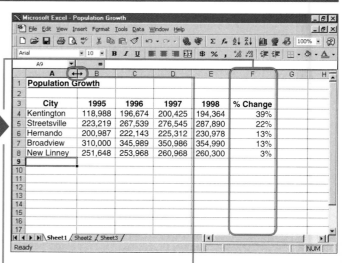

1 To change the width
of a column, position the
mouse ⇩ over the right
edge of the column heading
(⇩ changes to ↔).

2 Drag the column
edge until the dotted
line displays the column
width you want.

■ The column displays
the new width.

FIT LONGEST ITEM

You can have Excel
change a column
width to fit the longest
item in the column.

1 Double-click the
right edge of the
column heading.

CHANGE ROW HEIGHT

You can change the height of rows to increase the space between the rows of data in your worksheet. This can help make the data easier to read.

CHANGE ROW HEIGHT

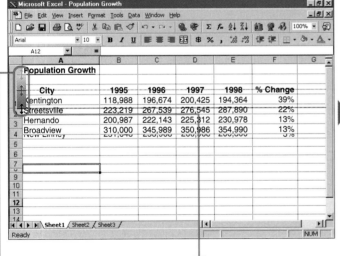

1 To change the height of a row, position the mouse ⇩ over the bottom edge of the row heading (⇩ changes to ↕).

2 Drag the row edge until the dotted line displays the row height you want.

■ The row displays the new height.

FIT TALLEST ITEM

You can have Excel change a row height to fit the tallest item in the row.

1 Double-click the bottom edge of the row heading.

BOLD, ITALIC AND UNDERLINE

You can use the bold, italic and underline styles to emphasize data in your worksheet.

BOLD, ITALIC AND UNDERLINE

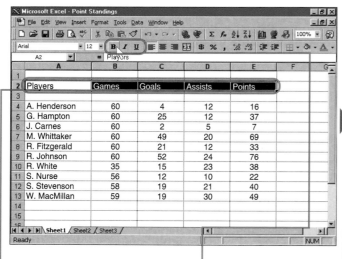

1 Select the cells containing the data you want to emphasize. To select cells, see page 14.

2 Click one of the following options.

B	Bold
I	Italic
U	Underline

■ The data displays the style you selected.

■ To deselect cells, click any cell.

■ To remove a bold, italic or underline style, repeat steps **1** and **2**.

CHANGE HORIZONTAL ALIGNMENT OF DATA

You can change
the position of data
between the left and
right edges of a cell
in your worksheet.

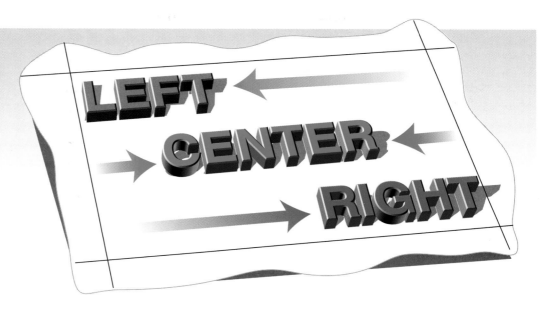

CHANGE HORIZONTAL ALIGNMENT OF DATA

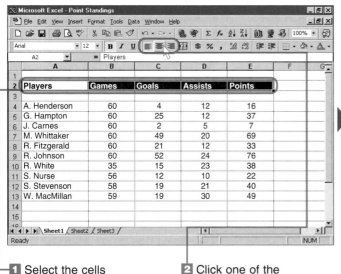

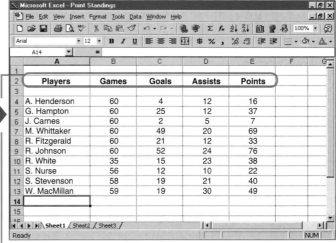

1 Select the cells
containing the data
you want to align
differently. To select
cells, see page 14.

2 Click one of the
following options.

▤ Left align

▤ Center

▤ Right align

■ Excel aligns the data.

■ To deselect cells,
click any cell.

CHANGE APPEARANCE OF DATA

You can enhance the appearance of data in your worksheet by changing the font and size of the data.

FRUIT	January	February
Apples	120	150
Bananas	200	220
Cherries	300	200
Grapes	100	90
Peaches	80	60

CHANGE FONT OF DATA

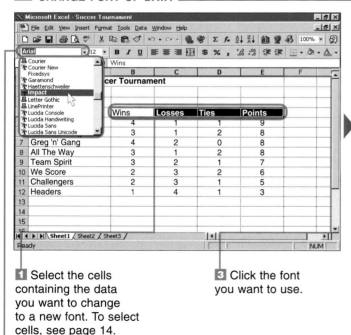

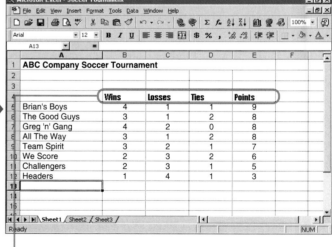

1 Select the cells containing the data you want to change to a new font. To select cells, see page 14.

2 Click ▾ in this area to display a list of the available fonts.

3 Click the font you want to use.

■ The data displays the font you selected.

■ To deselect cells, click any cell.

What determines which fonts are available in Excel?

The fonts available in Excel depend on the fonts installed on your computer and printer. Excel includes several fonts, but additional fonts may be available from the other programs on your computer. Your printer may also have built-in fonts you can use.

CHANGE SIZE OF DATA

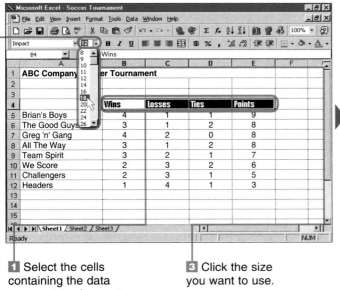

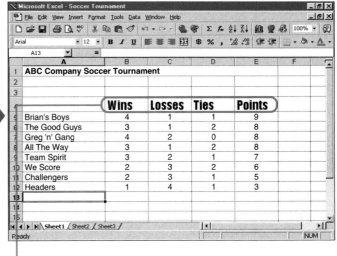

1 Select the cells containing the data you want to change to a new size. To select cells, see page 14.

2 Click ▾ in this area to display a list of the available sizes.

3 Click the size you want to use.

■ The data displays the size you selected.

■ To deselect cells, click any cell.

CHANGE APPEARANCE OF DATA

You can change the design, style and size of data in your worksheet at the same time.

	January	February	March
Jim	$51,000.00	$45,600.00	$49,800.00
Mary	$36,700.00	$35,500.00	$40,100.00
Arthur	$30,200.00	$25,500.00	$27,800.00

USING FORMAT CELLS DIALOG BOX

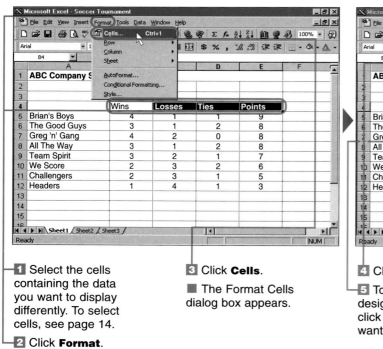

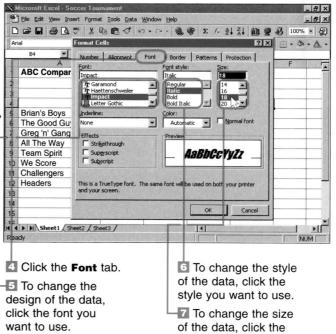

1 Select the cells containing the data you want to display differently. To select cells, see page 14.

2 Click **Format**.

3 Click **Cells**.

■ The Format Cells dialog box appears.

4 Click the **Font** tab.

5 To change the design of the data, click the font you want to use.

6 To change the style of the data, click the style you want to use.

7 To change the size of the data, click the size you want to use.

Can I add special effects to data in my worksheet?

Excel offers three special effects you can add to data—superscript, subscript and strikethrough.

The superscript and subscript effects are often used in mathematical formulas. The strikethrough effect is useful for showing data that has been revised.

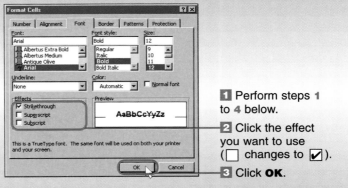

1 Perform steps **1** to **4** below.

2 Click the effect you want to use (☐ changes to ☑).

3 Click **OK**.

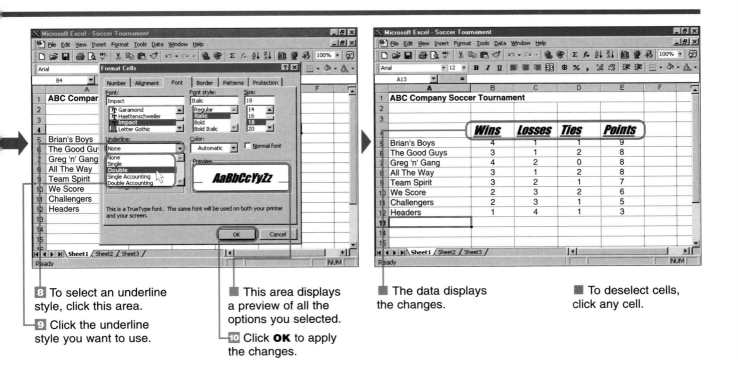

8 To select an underline style, click this area.

9 Click the underline style you want to use.

■ This area displays a preview of all the options you selected.

10 Click **OK** to apply the changes.

■ The data displays the changes.

■ To deselect cells, click any cell.

CHANGE NUMBER FORMAT

You can quickly change the way numbers in your worksheet look without retyping the numbers.

SALES		
Salesperson	Jan	Feb
Richard	1564	1687
Nancy	2008	2114
Steve	1789	1487
Jason	1002	1298
Susan	2354	1809

SALES		
Salesperson	Jan	Feb
Richard	$1,564.00	$1,687.00
Nancy	$2,008.00	$2,114.00
Steve	$1,789.00	$1,487.00
Jason	$1,002.00	$1,298.00
Susan	$2,354.00	$1,809.00

When you change the number format, the values of the numbers do not change.

CHANGE THE NUMBER STYLE

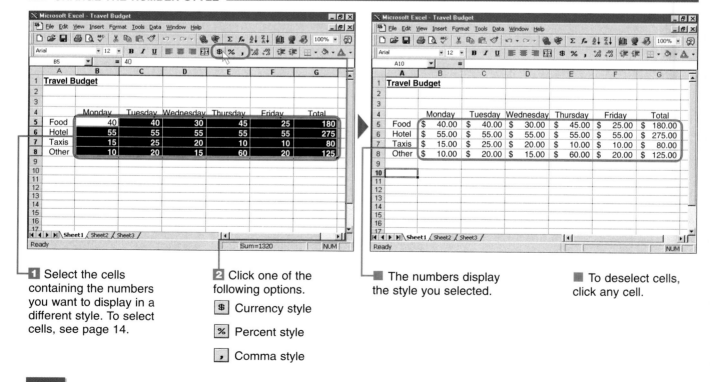

1 Select the cells containing the numbers you want to display in a different style. To select cells, see page 14.

2 Click one of the following options.

$ Currency style

% Percent style

, Comma style

■ The numbers display the style you selected.

■ To deselect cells, click any cell.

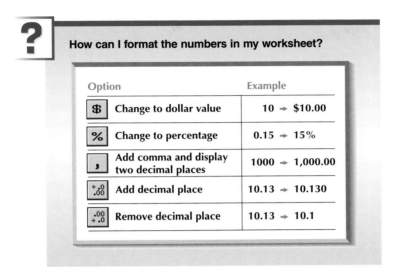

How can I format the numbers in my worksheet?

Option		Example
$	Change to dollar value	10 → $10.00
%	Change to percentage	0.15 → 15%
,	Add comma and display two decimal places	1000 → 1,000.00
.00	Add decimal place	10.13 → 10.130
.00	Remove decimal place	10.13 → 10.1

ADD OR REMOVE A DECIMAL PLACE

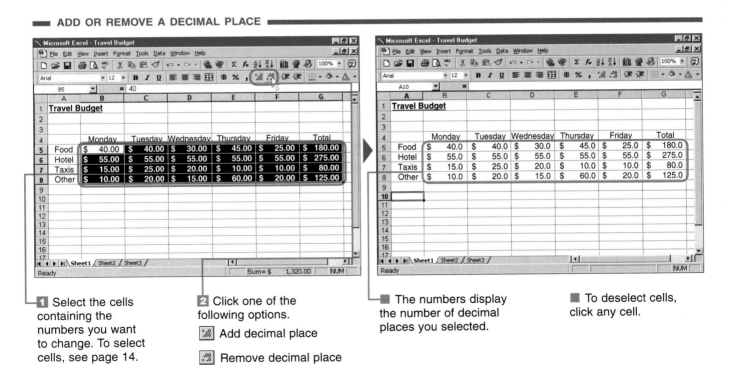

1 Select the cells containing the numbers you want to change. To select cells, see page 14.

2 Click one of the following options.

.00 Add decimal place

.00 Remove decimal place

■ The numbers display the number of decimal places you selected.

■ To deselect cells, click any cell.

CHANGE NUMBER FORMAT

Excel offers many different formats that you can use to make the numbers in your worksheet easier to read.

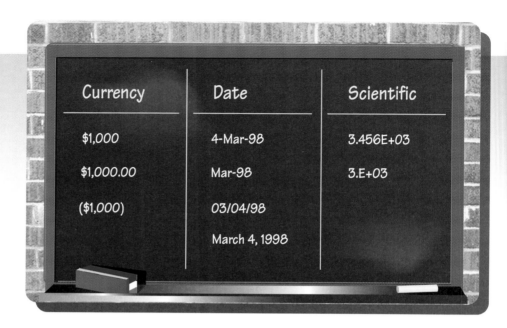

Currency	Date	Scientific
$1,000	4-Mar-98	3.456E+03
$1,000.00	Mar-98	3.E+03
($1,000)	03/04/98	
	March 4, 1998	

USING FORMAT CELLS DIALOG BOX

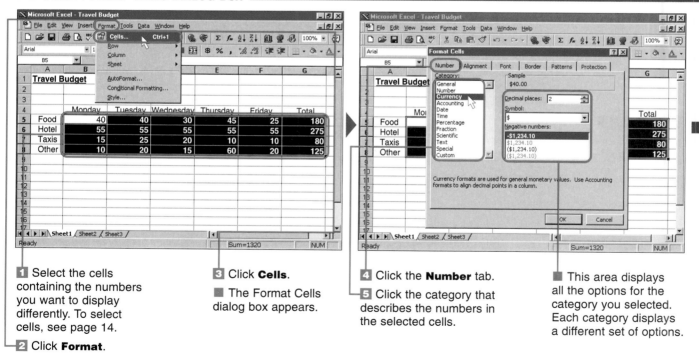

1 Select the cells containing the numbers you want to display differently. To select cells, see page 14.

2 Click **Format**.

3 Click **Cells**.

■ The Format Cells dialog box appears.

4 Click the **Number** tab.

5 Click the category that describes the numbers in the selected cells.

■ This area displays all the options for the category you selected. Each category displays a different set of options.

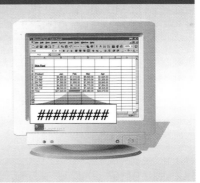

?

Why did number signs (#) appear in a cell after I changed the number format?

If number signs (#) appear in a cell, the column is not wide enough to display the entire number. To change the column width, see page 116.

#########

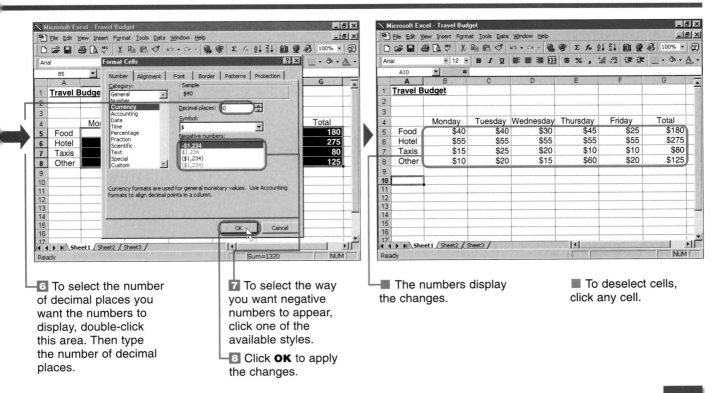

6 To select the number of decimal places you want the numbers to display, double-click this area. Then type the number of decimal places.

7 To select the way you want negative numbers to appear, click one of the available styles.

8 Click **OK** to apply the changes.

■ The numbers display the changes.

■ To deselect cells, click any cell.

INDENT DATA

You can indent data to move the data away from the left edge of a cell.

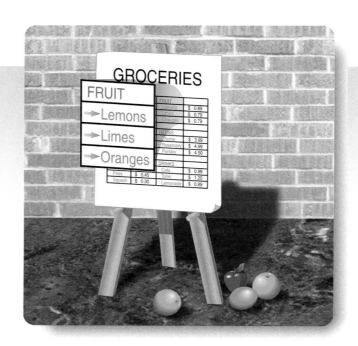

INDENT DATA

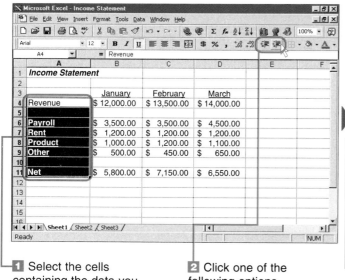

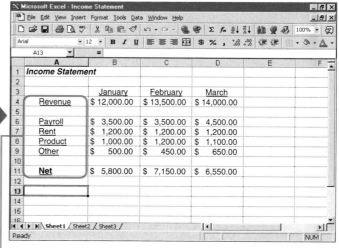

1 Select the cells containing the data you want to indent. To select cells, see page 14.

2 Click one of the following options.

 Move data to the left

 Move data to the right

■ Excel indents the data.

■ To deselect cells, click any cell.

You can center data across several columns in your worksheet. This is useful for centering titles over your data.

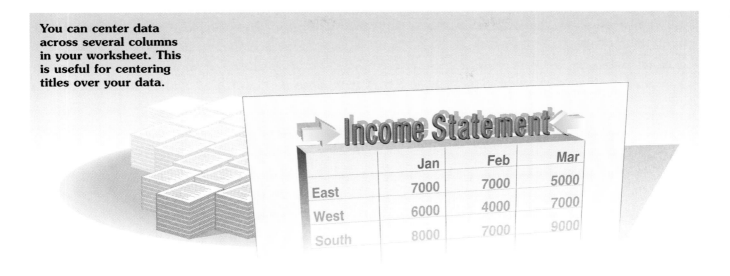

CENTER DATA ACROSS COLUMNS

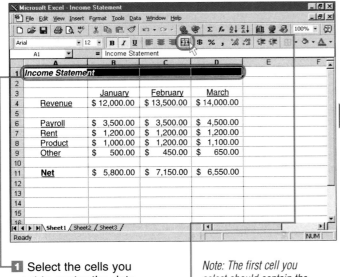

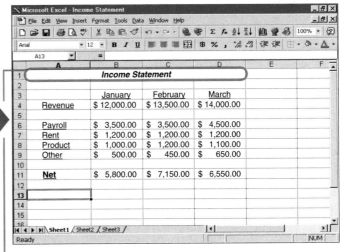

1 Select the cells you want to center the data across. To select cells, see page 14.

Note: The first cell you select should contain the data you want to center.

2 Click 🔳 .

■ Excel centers the data across the cells you selected.

■ To deselect cells, click any cell.

WRAP TEXT IN CELLS

You can display
long lines of text
within cells by
wrapping the text.

WRAP TEXT IN CELLS

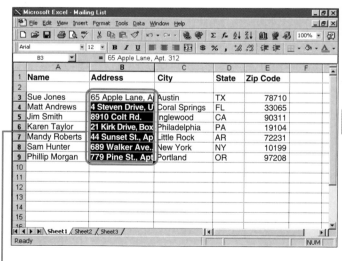

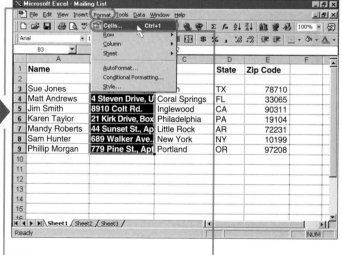

1 Select the cells
containing the text you
want to wrap. To select
cells, see page 14.

2 Click **Format**.

3 Click **Cells**.

■ The Format Cells
dialog box appears.

130

Can I display all the text in a cell without wrapping the text?

You can have Excel reduce the size of the text to fit within a cell. Perform steps **1** to **6** below, except select **Shrink to fit** in step **5** (☐ changes to ☑). If you later change the width of the column, Excel will automatically re-adjust the size of the text to fit the new width.

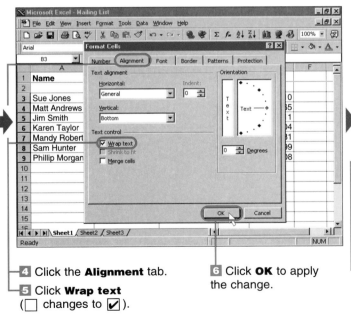

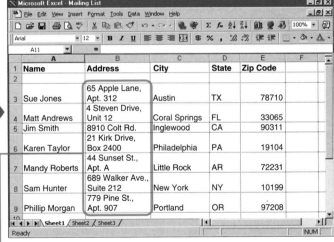

-4 Click the **Alignment** tab.

-5 Click **Wrap text** (☐ changes to ☑).

-6 Click **OK** to apply the change.

■ The text wraps within the cells you selected. The row heights change automatically to fit the wrapped text.

■ To deselect cells, click any cell.

CHANGE VERTICAL ALIGNMENT OF DATA

You can change the way Excel aligns data between the top and bottom edges of a cell.

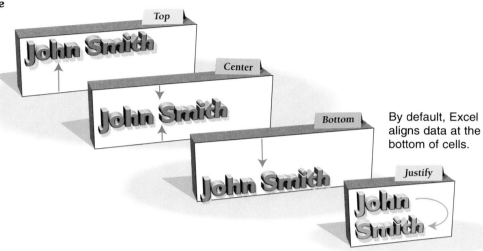

By default, Excel aligns data at the bottom of cells.

CHANGE VERTICAL ALIGNMENT OF DATA

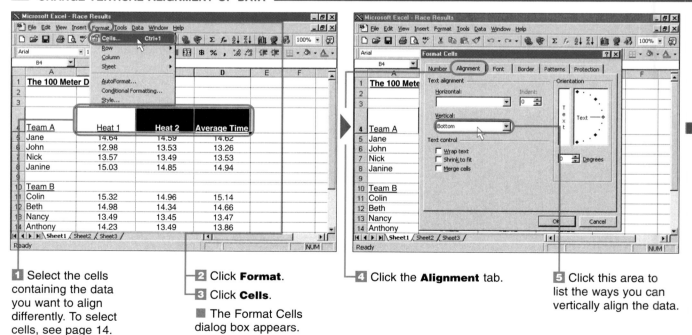

1 Select the cells containing the data you want to align differently. To select cells, see page 14.

2 Click **Format**.

3 Click **Cells**.

■ The Format Cells dialog box appears.

4 Click the **Alignment** tab.

5 Click this area to list the ways you can vertically align the data.

?

Why didn't I notice a change when I vertically aligned my data?

You may need to increase the height of the row to view the change to the vertical alignment. To change the height of rows, see page 117.

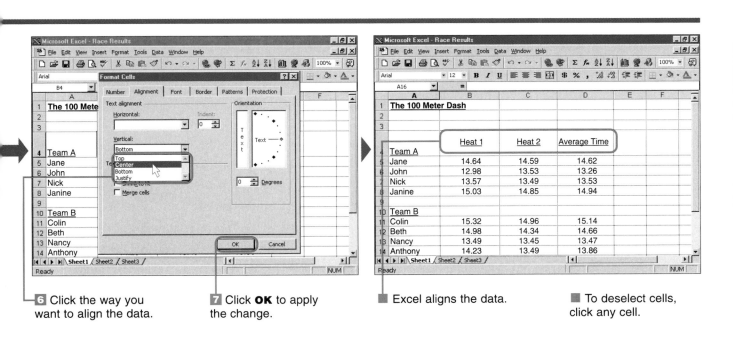

6 Click the way you want to align the data.

7 Click **OK** to apply the change.

■ Excel aligns the data.

■ To deselect cells, click any cell.

ROTATE DATA IN CELLS

You can rotate data within cells in your worksheet. This can help you emphasize row and column headings.

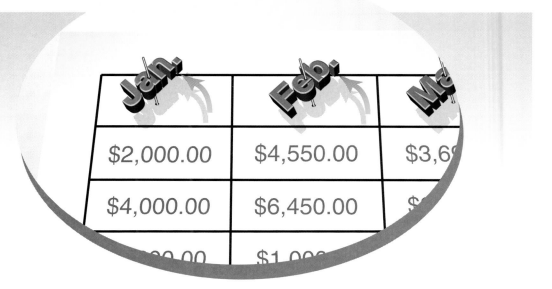

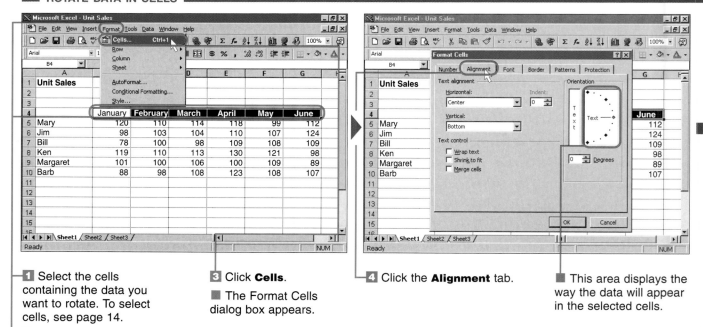

1 Select the cells containing the data you want to rotate. To select cells, see page 14.

2 Click **Format**.

3 Click **Cells**.

■ The Format Cells dialog box appears.

4 Click the **Alignment** tab.

■ This area displays the way the data will appear in the selected cells.

134

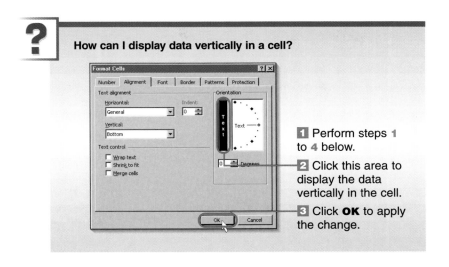

How can I display data vertically in a cell?

1 Perform steps **1** to **4** below.

2 Click this area to display the data vertically in the cell.

3 Click **OK** to apply the change.

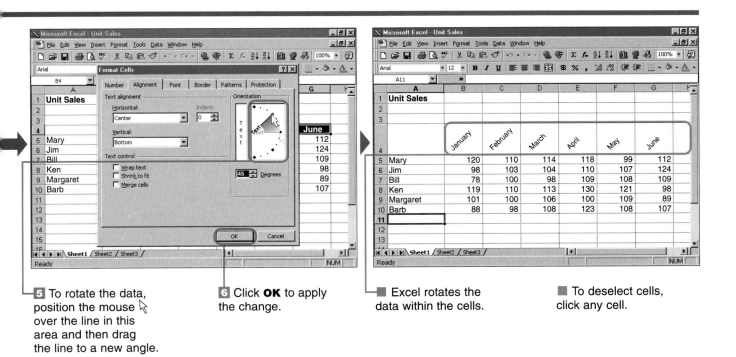

5 To rotate the data, position the mouse over the line in this area and then drag the line to a new angle.

6 Click **OK** to apply the change.

■ Excel rotates the data within the cells.

■ To deselect cells, click any cell.

ADD BORDERS

You can add borders to enhance the appearance of your worksheet or divide a worksheet into sections.

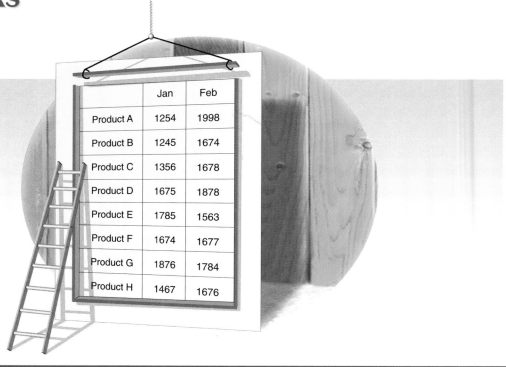

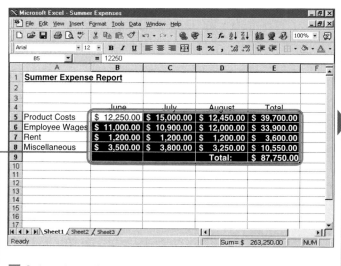

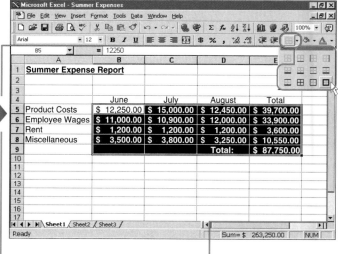

1 Select the cells you want to display borders. To select cells, see page 14.

2 Click ▾ in this area to display the types of borders you can add to the cells.

3 Click the type of border you want to add.

136

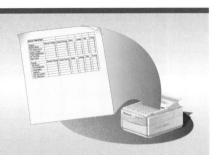

Can I print lines in my worksheet without adding borders?

Instead of adding borders to your worksheet, you can have Excel automatically print lines, called gridlines, around each cell. To print gridlines, see page 162.

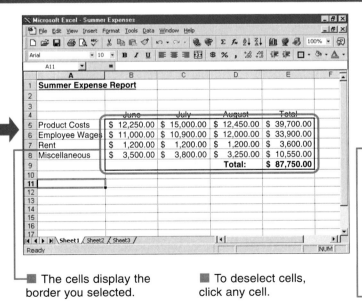

■ The cells display the border you selected.

■ To deselect cells, click any cell.

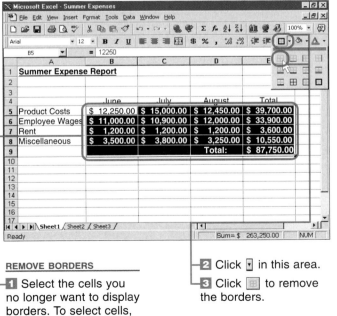

REMOVE BORDERS

1 Select the cells you no longer want to display borders. To select cells, see page 14.

2 Click ⚏ in this area.

3 Click ⊞ to remove the borders.

CHANGE COLOR

You can make your worksheet more attractive by adding color to cells or data.

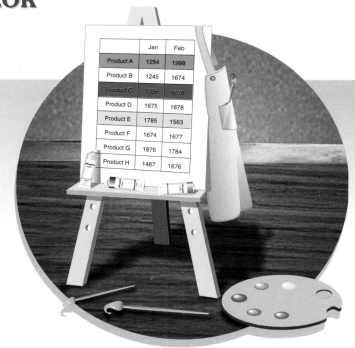

■ CHANGE CELL COLOR ■

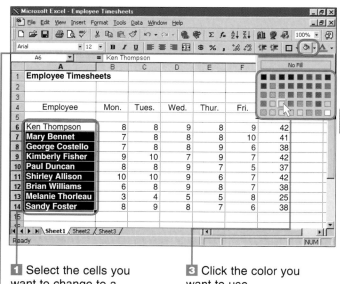

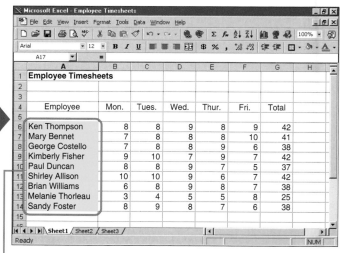

1 Select the cells you want to change to a different color. To select cells, see page 14.

2 Click ▼ in this area to display the available colors.

3 Click the color you want to use.

■ The cells change to the new color.

■ To deselect cells, click any cell.

■ If you no longer want the cells to display color, repeat steps **1** to **3**, except select **No Fill** in step **3**.

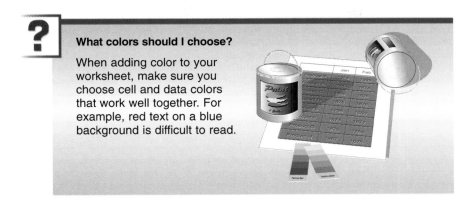

What colors should I choose?

When adding color to your worksheet, make sure you choose cell and data colors that work well together. For example, red text on a blue background is difficult to read.

CHANGE DATA COLOR

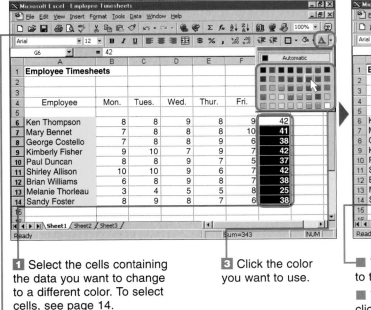

1 Select the cells containing the data you want to change to a different color. To select cells, see page 14.

2 Click ▾ in this area to display the available colors.

3 Click the color you want to use.

■ The data changes to the new color.

■ To deselect cells, click any cell.

■ If you no longer want the data to display color, repeat steps **1** to **3**, except select **Automatic** in step **3**.

COPY FORMATTING

If you like the
appearance of
a cell in your
worksheet, you
can make other
cells look exactly
the same.

COPY FORMATTING

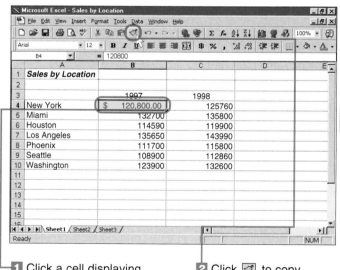

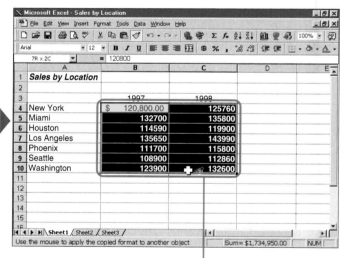

1 Click a cell displaying
the formatting you want
to copy to other cells.

2 Click 🖋 to copy
the formatting.

■ The mouse ⫠ changes
to ⊕🖋 when over the
worksheet.

3 Select the cells you
want to display the same
formatting. To select cells,
see page 14.

What types of formatting can I copy?

Number Formatting

Number formatting can include currency, percentage and date formats.

Data Formatting

Data formatting can include the font, size, color and alignment of data.

Cell Formatting

Cell formatting can include borders and colors.

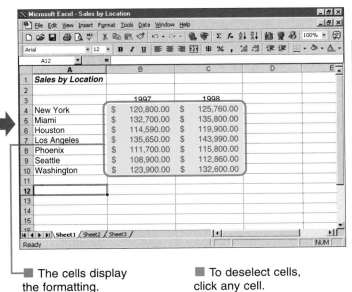

■ The cells display the formatting.

■ To deselect cells, click any cell.

You can copy formatting to several locations.

1 Click a cell displaying the formatting you want to copy to other cells.

2 Double-click 🖌 .

3 Select the cells you want to display the same formatting. Repeat this step until you have selected all the cells you want to display the formatting.

4 Click 🖌 .

CLEAR FORMATTING

You can easily remove all the formatting from cells in your worksheet.

CLEAR FORMATTING

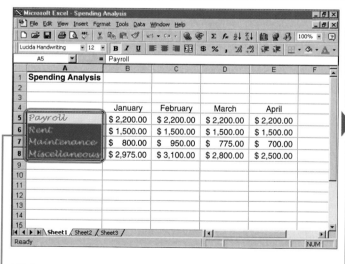

1 Select the cells containing the formatting you want to remove. To select cells, see page 14.

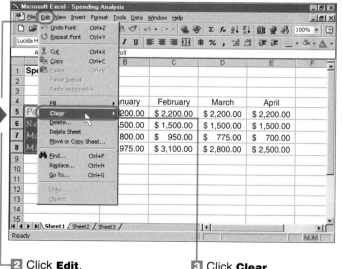

2 Click **Edit**.

3 Click **Clear**.

How can I keep the formatting but remove the data from cells?

To keep the formatting but remove the data from cells, select the cells containing the data you want to remove. Then press the Delete key.

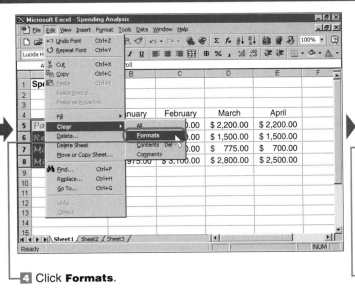

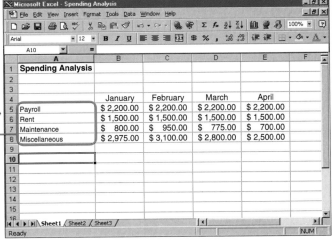

◢ Click **Formats**.

■ All the formatting disappears from the cells you selected.

■ To deselect cells, click any cell.

APPLY CONDITIONAL FORMATTING

You can have Excel apply formatting to data when the data meets a condition you specify. This can help you quickly locate important data on a large worksheet.

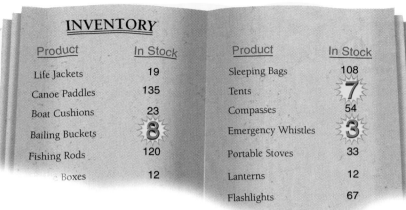

For example, when the number of units in stock falls below 10, you can have Excel display the number in red.

APPLY CONDITIONAL FORMATTING

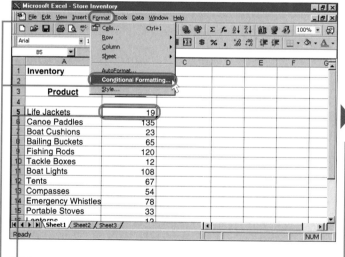

1 Click the cell containing the data you want Excel to format when the data meets a condition.

2 Click **Format**.

3 Click **Conditional Formatting**.

■ The Conditional Formatting dialog box appears.

*Note: The first time you display the Conditional Formatting dialog box, the Office Assistant may appear. Click **No** to hide the Office Assistant.*

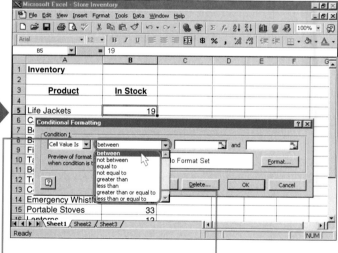

4 Click this area to list the operators you can use for the condition.

5 Click the operator you want to use.

Note: For information on operators, see the top of page 145.

? **What is an operator?**

An operator tells Excel how to compare the data in a cell to the value you specify. For example, you can use the **greater than** operator when you want Excel to determine whether the data in a cell has a value of more than 100.

greater than **100**

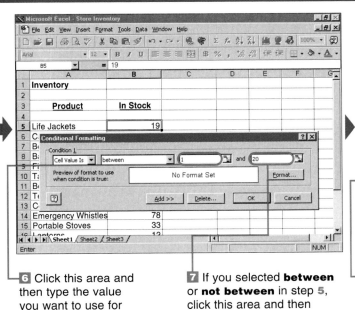

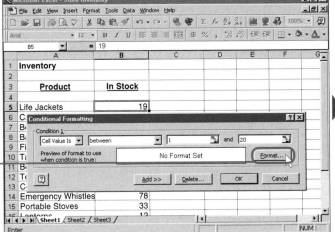

6 Click this area and then type the value you want to use for the condition.

7 If you selected **between** or **not between** in step **5**, click this area and then type the second value.

8 Click **Format** to specify how you want to format the data when the data meets the condition.

■ The Format Cells dialog box appears.

CONTINUED ▷

APPLY CONDITIONAL FORMATTING

You can specify the color, font style or underline style you want to use for data that meets a condition.

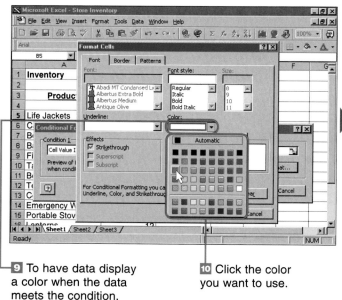

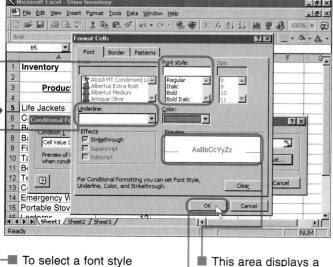

9 To have data display a color when the data meets the condition, click this area.

10 Click the color you want to use.

■ To select a font style or underline style for data that meets the condition, see page 122.

■ This area displays a preview of the options you selected.

11 Click **OK** to confirm the changes.

Can I copy conditional formatting?

Copying conditional formatting is useful when you want other cells in your worksheet to display the same formatting under the same conditions. You can copy conditional formatting as you would copy any formatting in a worksheet. To copy formatting, see page 140.

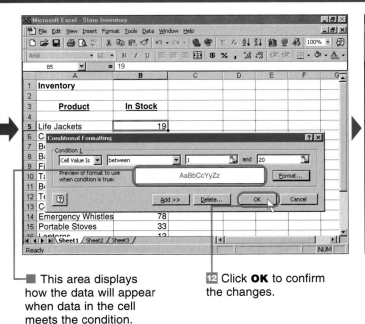

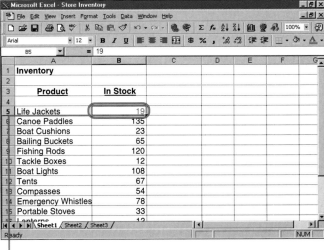

■ This area displays how the data will appear when data in the cell meets the condition.

🔢 Click **OK** to confirm the changes.

■ The data in the cell displays the formatting if the data meets the condition you specified.

■ To remove conditional formatting, clear the formatting from the cell. To clear formatting, see page 142.

QUICKLY APPLY A DESIGN

Excel offers many ready-to-use designs you can choose from to give your worksheet a new appearance.

A ready-to-use design provides the formatting so you can concentrate on the content of your worksheet.

QUICKLY APPLY A DESIGN

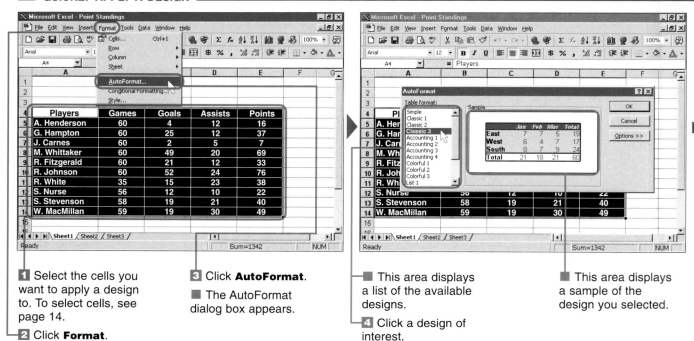

1 Select the cells you want to apply a design to. To select cells, see page 14.

2 Click **Format**.

3 Click **AutoFormat**.

■ The AutoFormat dialog box appears.

■ This area displays a list of the available designs.

4 Click a design of interest.

■ This area displays a sample of the design you selected.

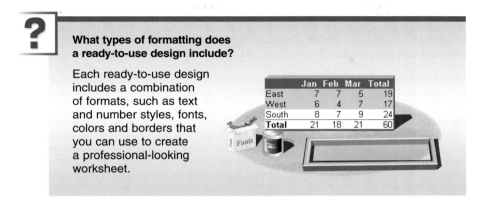

What types of formatting does a ready-to-use design include?

Each ready-to-use design includes a combination of formats, such as text and number styles, fonts, colors and borders that you can use to create a professional-looking worksheet.

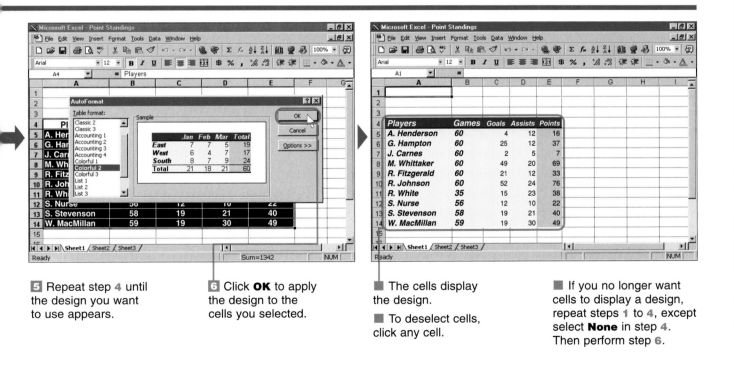

5 Repeat step **4** until the design you want to use appears.

6 Click **OK** to apply the design to the cells you selected.

■ The cells display the design.

■ To deselect cells, click any cell.

■ If you no longer want cells to display a design, repeat steps **1** to **4**, except select **None** in step **4**. Then perform step **6**.

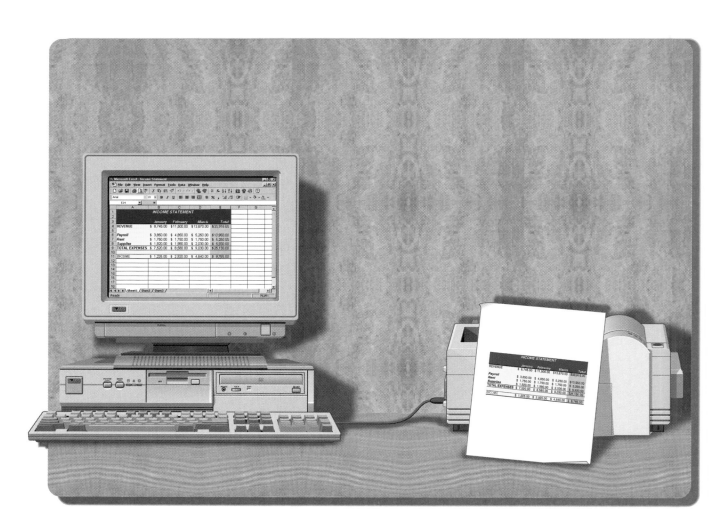

CHAPTER 7

Print Your Worksheets

*Are you ready to print your worksheet?
In this chapter you will learn how to
preview your worksheet and change
the way the worksheet appears on a
printed page.*

PREVIEW A WORKSHEET

You can see on your
screen how your
worksheet will look
when printed. This
lets you ensure the
worksheet will print
the way you want.

PREVIEW A WORKSHEET

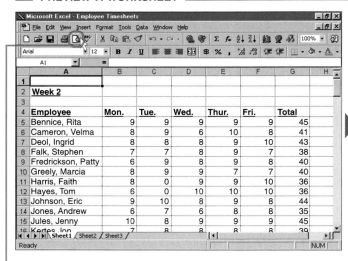

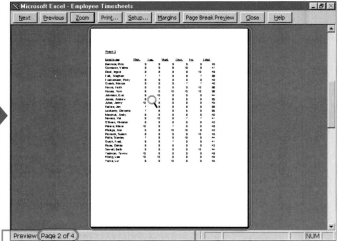

■1 Click 🔍 to preview
the worksheet.

■ The Print Preview
window appears.

■ This area indicates
which page is displayed
and the total number of
pages in the worksheet.

■2 To magnify an area
of the page, position the
mouse ⍀ over the area
(⍀ changes to 🔍).

■3 Click the area to
magnify the area.

?

Why does my worksheet appear in black and white in the Print Preview window?

If you use a black-and-white printer, your worksheet appears in black and white in the Print Preview window. If you use a color printer, the worksheet appears in color.

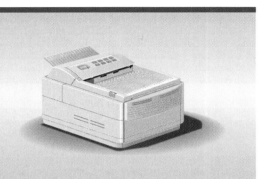

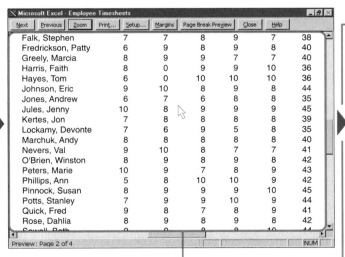

■ A magnified view of the area appears.

4 To once again display the entire page, click the page.

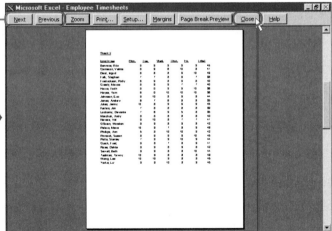

■ If the worksheet contains more than one page, click **Next** or **Previous** to view the next or previous page.

Note: You can also use the scroll bar to view other pages.

5 Click **Close** to close the Print Preview window.

PRINT A WORKSHEET

You can produce a paper copy of the worksheet displayed on your screen.

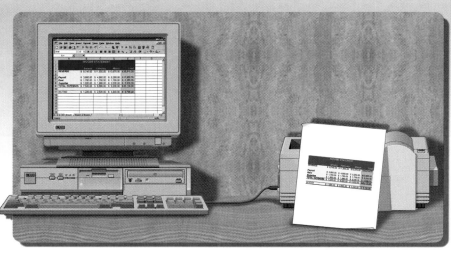

Before printing, make sure your printer is turned on and contains paper.

PRINT A WORKSHEET

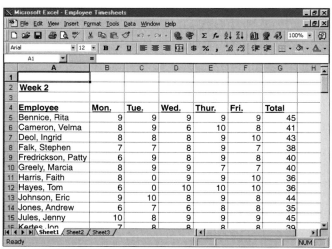

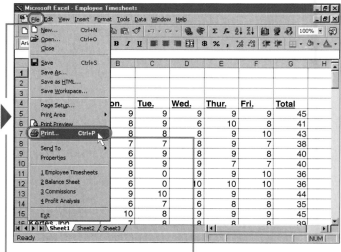

1 To print a worksheet, click any cell in the worksheet.

■ To print only part of the worksheet, select the cells you want to print. To select cells, see page 14.

2 Click **File**.

3 Click **Print**.

■ The Print dialog box appears.

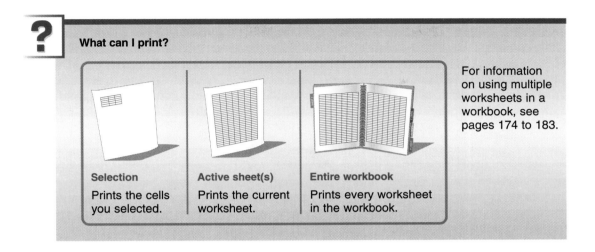

What can I print?

Selection

Prints the cells you selected.

Active sheet(s)

Prints the current worksheet.

Entire workbook

Prints every worksheet in the workbook.

For information on using multiple worksheets in a workbook, see pages 174 to 183.

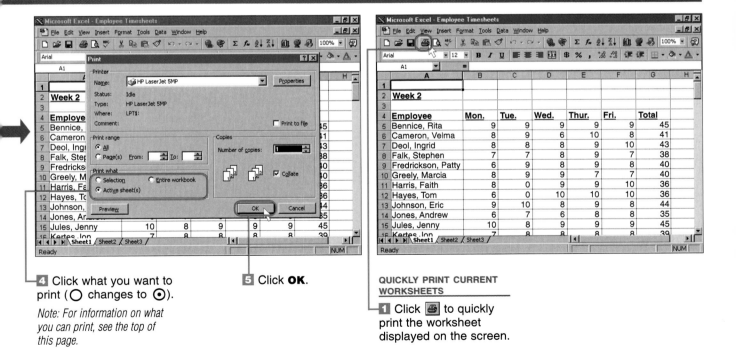

4 Click what you want to print (○ changes to ⊙).

Note: For information on what you can print, see the top of this page.

5 Click **OK**.

QUICKLY PRINT CURRENT WORKSHEETS

1 Click 🖨 to quickly print the worksheet displayed on the screen.

SET A PRINT AREA

If you always print the same area of your worksheet, you can set a print area to quickly print the data. Excel will print only the data in the print area.

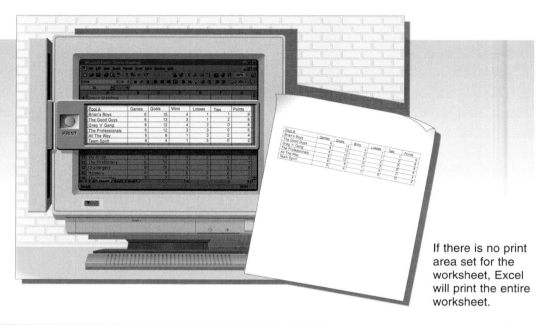

If there is no print area set for the worksheet, Excel will print the entire worksheet.

SET A PRINT AREA

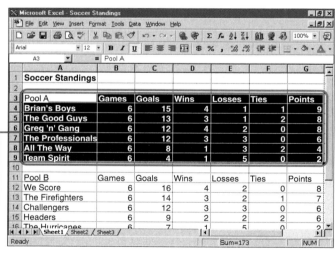

1 Select the cells containing the data you want to include in the print area. To select cells, see page 14.

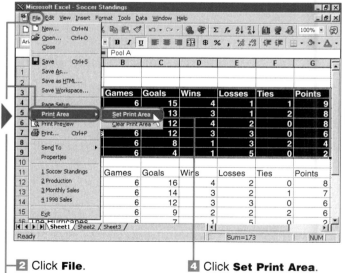

2 Click **File**.

3 Click **Print Area**.

4 Click **Set Print Area**.

? I set a print area, but now I want to print other data in my worksheet. What can I do?

You can temporarily override a print area you have set and print other data in the worksheet. Select the cells containing the data you want to print and then perform steps **2** to **5** starting on page 154, choosing **Selection** in step **4** (○ changes to ⊙).

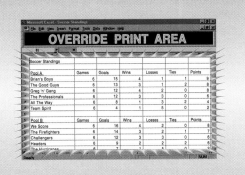

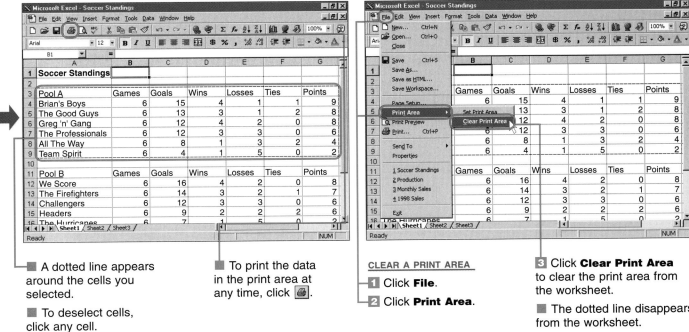

■ A dotted line appears around the cells you selected.

■ To deselect cells, click any cell.

■ To print the data in the print area at any time, click 🖨.

CLEAR A PRINT AREA

1 Click **File**.

2 Click **Print Area**.

3 Click **Clear Print Area** to clear the print area from the worksheet.

■ The dotted line disappears from the worksheet.

CHANGE MARGINS

A margin is the amount of space between data and an edge of your paper. You can change the margins for your worksheet.

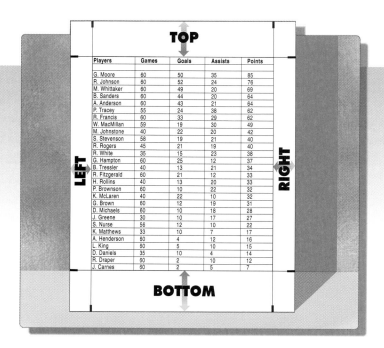

CHANGE MARGINS

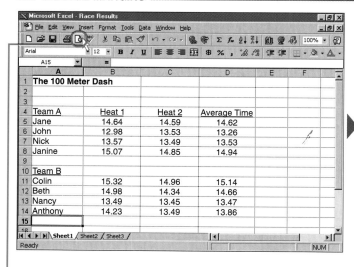

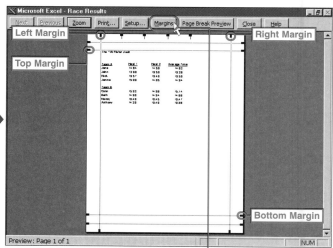

1 Click 🔍 to display the worksheet in the Print Preview window.

■ The worksheet appears in the Print Preview window. For information on previewing a worksheet, see page 152.

2 If the margins are not displayed, click **Margins**.

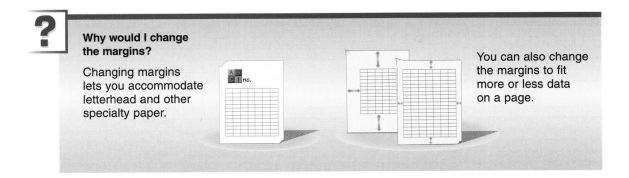

Why would I change the margins?

Changing margins lets you accommodate letterhead and other specialty paper.

You can also change the margins to fit more or less data on a page.

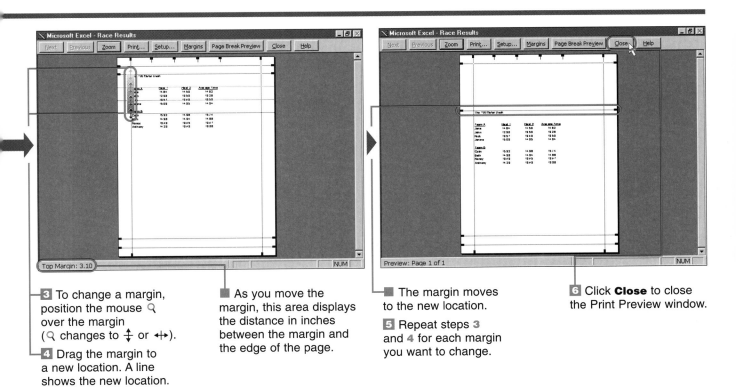

Top Margin: 3.10

3 To change a margin, position the mouse ⊖ over the margin (⊖ changes to ↕ or ↔).

4 Drag the margin to a new location. A line shows the new location.

■ As you move the margin, this area displays the distance in inches between the margin and the edge of the page.

■ The margin moves to the new location.

5 Repeat steps **3** and **4** for each margin you want to change.

6 Click **Close** to close the Print Preview window.

CENTER DATA ON A PAGE

You can center data horizontally and vertically between the margins on a page.

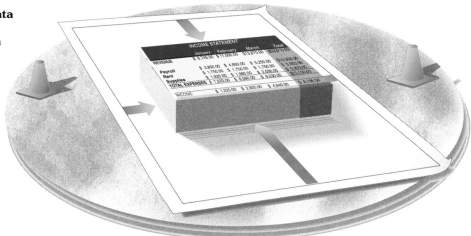

CENTER DATA ON A PAGE

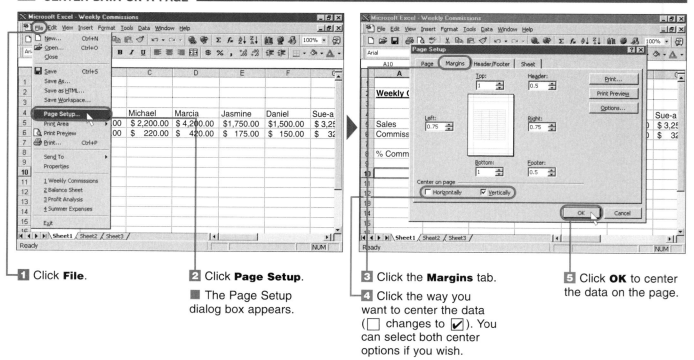

1 Click **File**.

2 Click **Page Setup**.

■ The Page Setup dialog box appears.

3 Click the **Margins** tab.

4 Click the way you want to center the data (☐ changes to ☑). You can select both center options if you wish.

5 Click **OK** to center the data on the page.

CHANGE PAGE ORIENTATION

You can change the orientation of your printed worksheet.

Portrait

Landscape

By default, Excel prints worksheets in the portrait orientation. The landscape orientation is useful when you want a wide worksheet to fit on one page.

CHANGE PAGE ORIENTATION

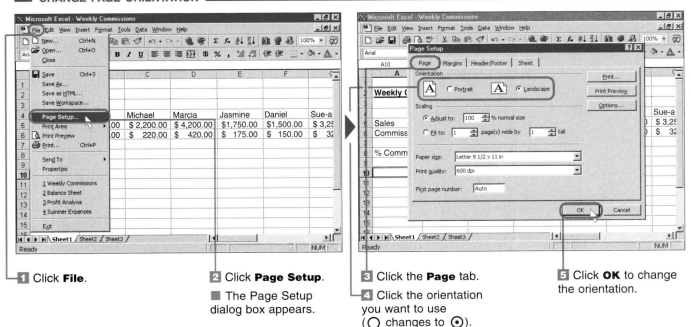

1 Click **File**.

2 Click **Page Setup**.

■ The Page Setup dialog box appears.

3 Click the **Page** tab.

4 Click the orientation you want to use
(○ changes to ⊙).

5 Click **OK** to change the orientation.

CHANGE PRINT OPTIONS

Excel offers several print options that let you change the way your worksheet appears on a printed page.

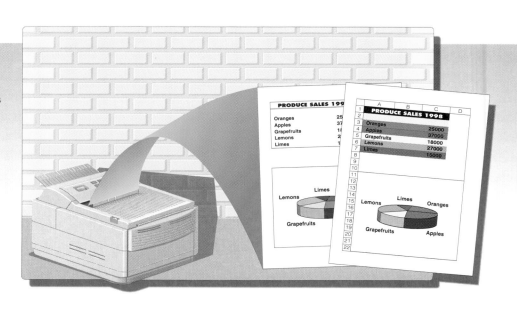

CHANGE PRINT OPTIONS

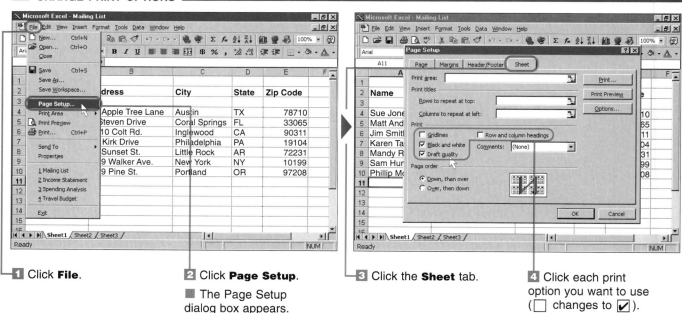

1 Click **File**.

2 Click **Page Setup**.

■ The Page Setup dialog box appears.

3 Click the **Sheet** tab.

4 Click each print option you want to use (☐ changes to ☑).

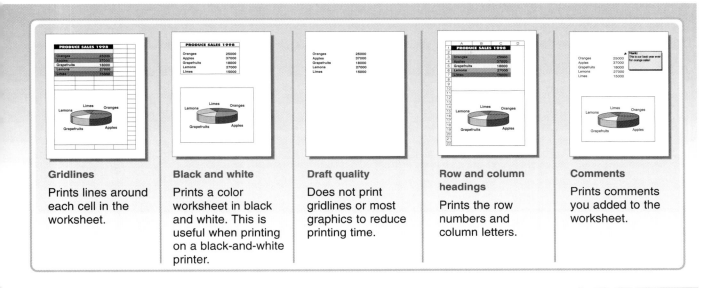

Gridlines

Prints lines around each cell in the worksheet.

Black and white

Prints a color worksheet in black and white. This is useful when printing on a black-and-white printer.

Draft quality

Does not print gridlines or most graphics to reduce printing time.

Row and column headings

Prints the row numbers and column letters.

Comments

Prints comments you added to the worksheet.

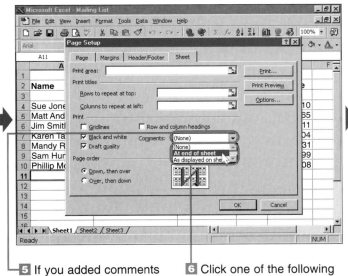

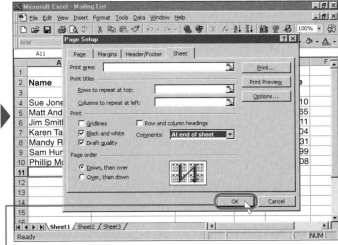

■5 If you added comments to the worksheet, click this area to print the comments.

Note: For information on comments, see page 72.

■6 Click one of the following options to specify where you want to print the comments.

At end of sheet - Prints comments on separate page

As displayed on sheet - Prints comments on worksheet

■7 Click **OK** to confirm the changes.

■ The print options you selected only change the way the worksheet appears on a printed page. They do not affect the way the worksheet appears on the screen.

INSERT A PAGE BREAK

You can insert a page break when you want to start a new page at a specific place in your worksheet. A page break defines where one page ends and another begins.

When you fill a page with data, Excel automatically starts a new page by inserting a page break for you.

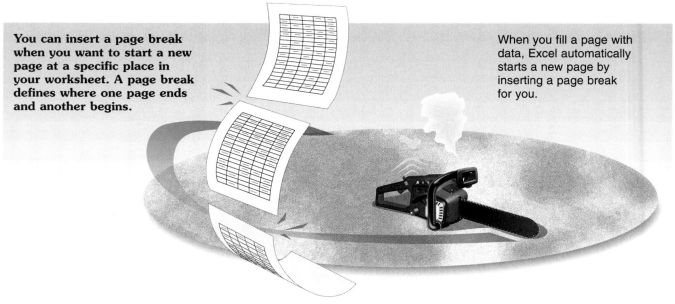

■ INSERT A PAGE BREAK

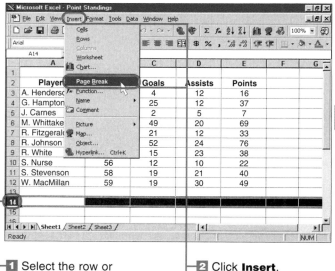

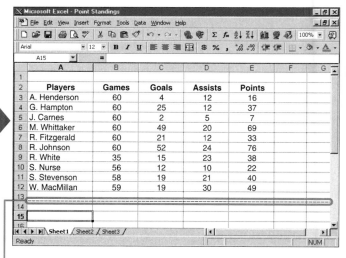

1 Select the row or column you want to appear at the beginning of the new page. To select a row or column, see page 15.

2 Click **Insert**.

3 Click **Page Break**.

■ A dotted line appears on the screen. The line will not appear when you print the worksheet.

■ To deselect cells, click any cell.

■ To remove a page break, click a cell directly below or directly to the right of the page break line. Then repeat steps **2** and **3**, except select **Remove Page Break** in step **3**.

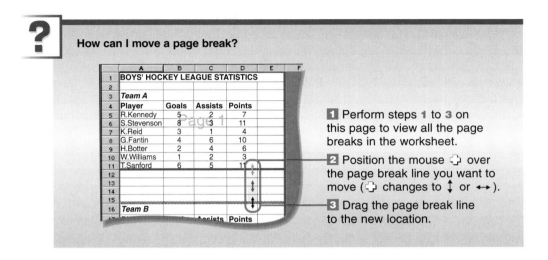

How can I move a page break?

1 Perform steps **1** to **3** on this page to view all the page breaks in the worksheet.

2 Position the mouse ⬦ over the page break line you want to move (⬦ changes to ↕ or ↔).

3 Drag the page break line to the new location.

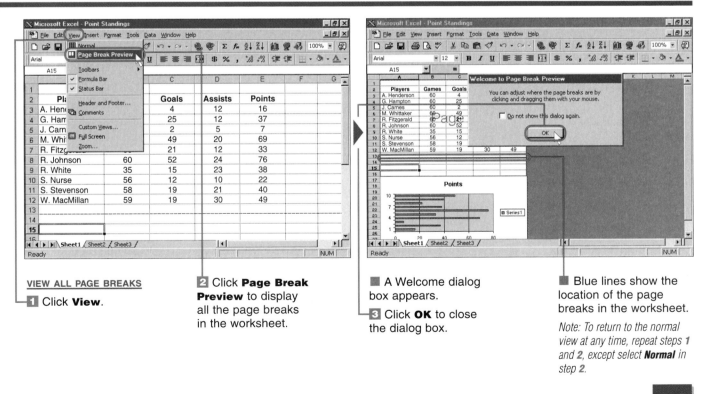

VIEW ALL PAGE BREAKS

1 Click **View**.

2 Click **Page Break Preview** to display all the page breaks in the worksheet.

■ A Welcome dialog box appears.

3 Click **OK** to close the dialog box.

■ Blue lines show the location of the page breaks in the worksheet.

*Note: To return to the normal view at any time, repeat steps 1 and 2, except select **Normal** in step 2.*

ADD A HEADER OR FOOTER

You can add a header or footer to display information such as the workbook title and the page number on each page of your worksheet.

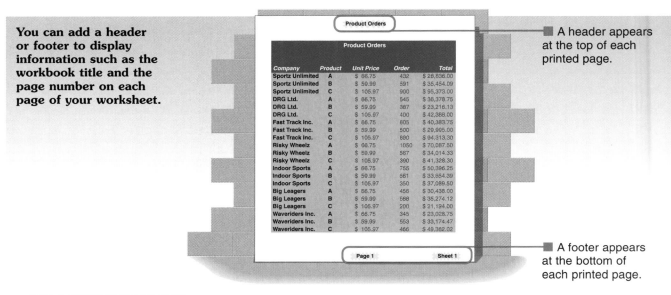

■ A header appears at the top of each printed page.

■ A footer appears at the bottom of each printed page.

ADD A HEADER OR FOOTER

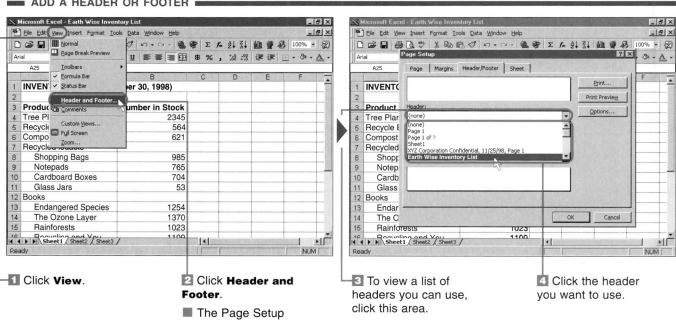

1 Click **View**.

2 Click **Header and Footer**.

■ The Page Setup dialog box appears.

3 To view a list of headers you can use, click this area.

4 Click the header you want to use.

How can I see what a header or footer will look like before I print my worksheet?

You can use the Print Preview feature to view a header or footer on your worksheet before you print the worksheet. To use the Print Preview feature, see page 152.

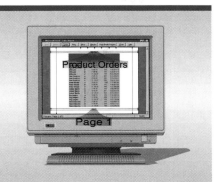

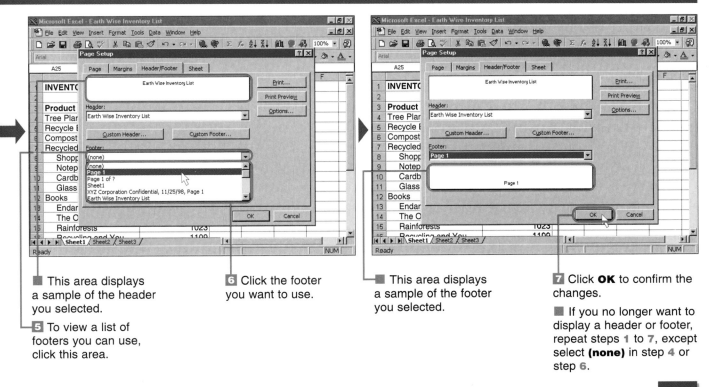

■ This area displays a sample of the header you selected.

5 To view a list of footers you can use, click this area.

6 Click the footer you want to use.

■ This area displays a sample of the footer you selected.

7 Click **OK** to confirm the changes.

■ If you no longer want to display a header or footer, repeat steps **1** to **7**, except select **(none)** in step **4** or step **6**.

CHANGE SIZE OF PRINTED DATA

You can reduce
the size of printed
data to print your
worksheet on a
specific number
of pages.

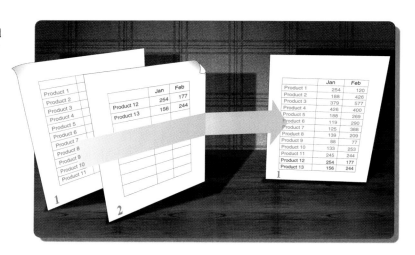

This feature is useful
when the last page of
your worksheet contains
a small amount of data
that you want to fit on
the second-last page.

CHANGE SIZE OF PRINTED DATA

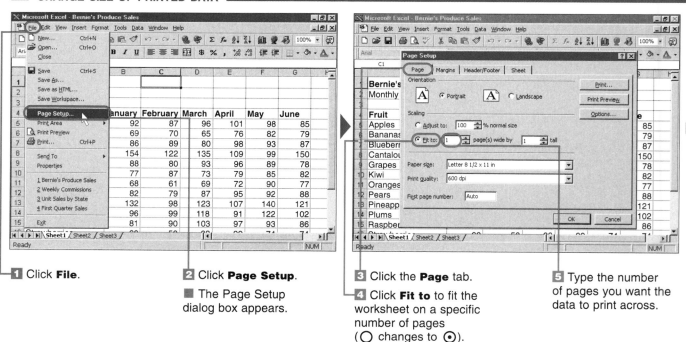

1 Click **File**.

2 Click **Page Setup**.

■ The Page Setup
dialog box appears.

3 Click the **Page** tab.

4 Click **Fit to** to fit the
worksheet on a specific
number of pages
(○ changes to ⊙).

5 Type the number
of pages you want the
data to print across.

168

What information does Excel require to change the size of my printed data?

When you change the size of your printed data, you need to tell Excel how many pages you want the data to print across and down.

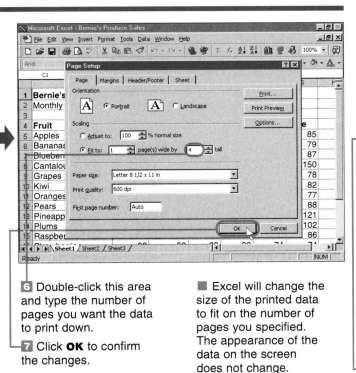

MANUALLY CHANGE SIZE OF PRINTED DATA

6 Double-click this area and type the number of pages you want the data to print down.

7 Click **OK** to confirm the changes.

■ Excel will change the size of the printed data to fit on the number of pages you specified. The appearance of the data on the screen does not change.

You can manually reduce or enlarge the size of printed data.

1 Perform steps **1** to **3** on page 168.

2 Click **Adjust to** (○ changes to ⊙).

3 Type the percentage you want to use and then press the Enter key.

Note: A percentage over 100 increases the size of the printed data. A percentage under 100 decreases the size of the printed data.

REPEAT TITLES ON PRINTED PAGES

You can display the
same row or column
titles on every printed
page. This helps you
review worksheets
that print on more
than one page.

REPEAT TITLES ON PRINTED PAGES

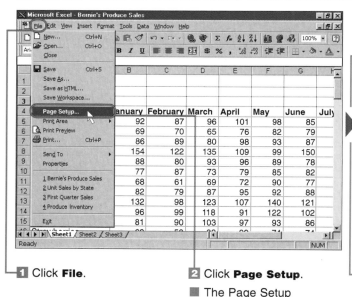

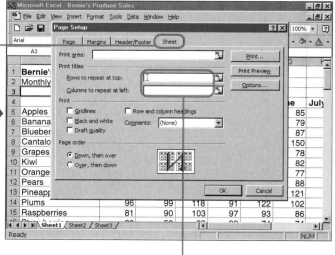

1 Click **File**.

2 Click **Page Setup**.

■ The Page Setup
dialog box appears.

3 Click the **Sheet** tab.

4 Click one of the following
options.

Rows to repeat at top -
Repeats titles across top
of each page

Columns to repeat at left -
Repeats titles down left side
of each page

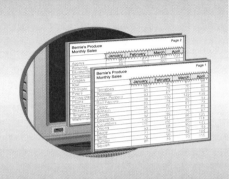

How can I see the repeated titles on my screen?

When you repeat titles on printed pages, the changes only affect the printed data. The data on your screen does not change. You can use the Print Preview feature to view the repeated titles before you print the worksheet. To use the Print Preview feature, see page 152.

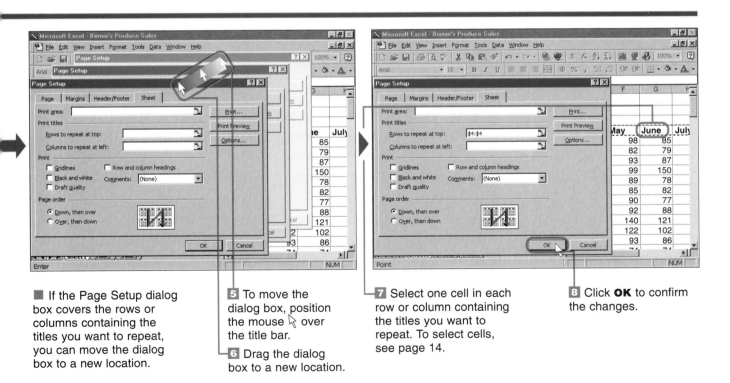

■ If the Page Setup dialog box covers the rows or columns containing the titles you want to repeat, you can move the dialog box to a new location.

5 To move the dialog box, position the mouse ⌖ over the title bar.

6 Drag the dialog box to a new location.

7 Select one cell in each row or column containing the titles you want to repeat. To select cells, see page 14.

8 Click **OK** to confirm the changes.

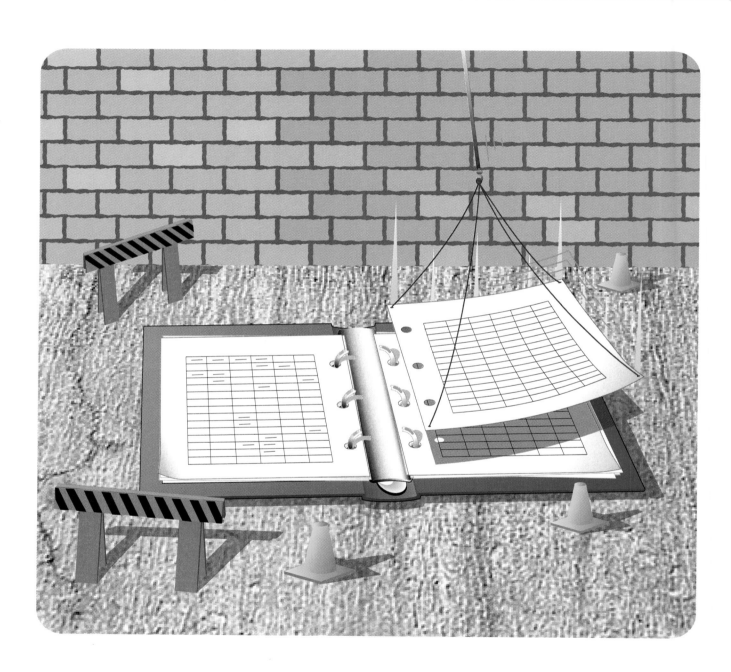

CHAPTER 8

Work With Multiple Worksheets

Are you interested in working with more than one worksheet at a time? This chapter teaches you how to switch between worksheets, move or copy data between worksheets and more.

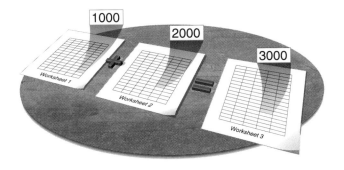

SWITCH BETWEEN WORKSHEETS

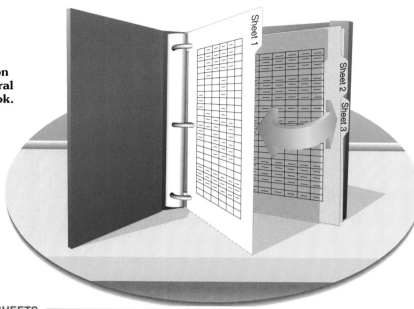

The worksheet displayed on your screen is one of several worksheets in the workbook. You can easily switch between the worksheets.

SWITCH BETWEEN WORKSHEETS

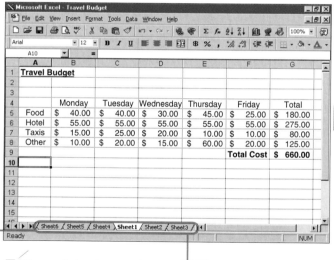

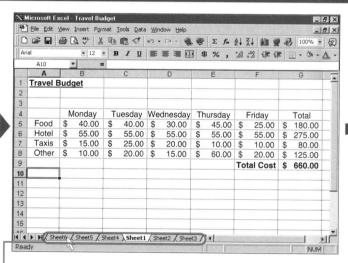

■ The worksheet currently displayed on the screen has a white tab.

■ The other worksheets in the workbook have gray tabs. The contents of these worksheets are hidden.

1 To display the contents of a different worksheet, click the tab of the worksheet.

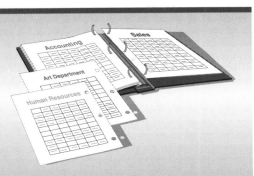

?

Why would I need more than one worksheet?

Worksheets allow you to keep related data in a single file, called a workbook. For example, you can store data for each division of a company on a separate worksheet in one workbook.

BROWSE THROUGH TABS

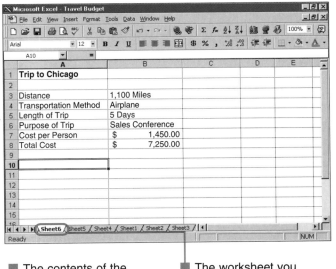

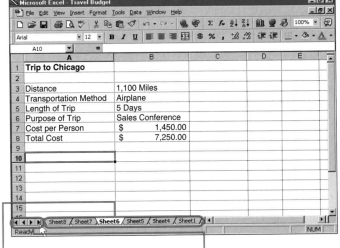

■ The contents of the worksheet appear.

■ The worksheet you selected now displays a white tab.

■ This area displays the worksheet tabs. If the workbook has many worksheets, you may not be able to see all the tabs.

Note: To insert additional worksheets, see page 176.

1 To browse through the tabs, click one of the following options.

|◄| Display first tab

|◄| Display tab to the left

|►| Display tab to the right

|►| Display last tab

INSERT A WORKSHEET

You can insert a new worksheet to add related information to your workbook.

INSERT A WORKSHEET

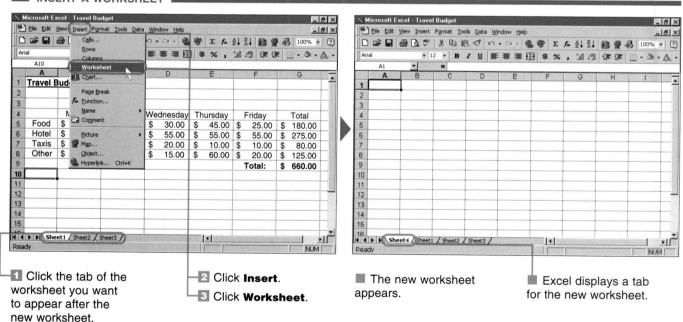

1 Click the tab of the worksheet you want to appear after the new worksheet.

2 Click **Insert**.

3 Click **Worksheet**.

■ The new worksheet appears.

■ Excel displays a tab for the new worksheet.

DELETE A WORKSHEET

You can permanently
remove a worksheet
you no longer need.

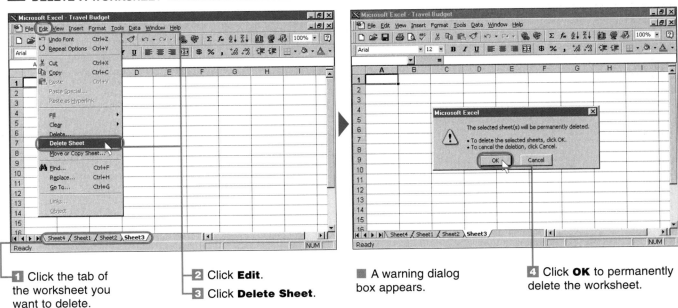

DELETE A WORKSHEET

1 Click the tab of
the worksheet you
want to delete.

2 Click **Edit**.

3 Click **Delete Sheet**.

■ A warning dialog
box appears.

4 Click **OK** to permanently
delete the worksheet.

RENAME A WORKSHEET

You can give each worksheet in your workbook a descriptive name. Descriptive names can help you locate information of interest.

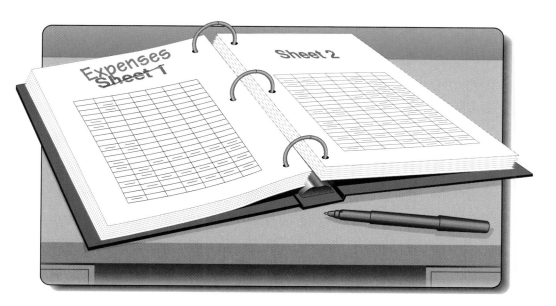

RENAME A WORKSHEET

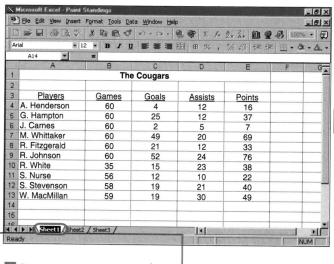

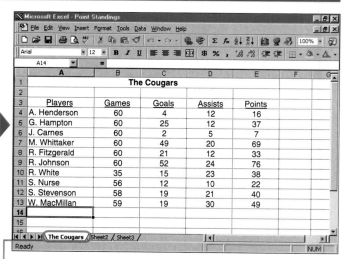

1 Double-click the tab of the worksheet you want to rename.

■ The current name is highlighted.

2 Type a new name and then press the Enter key.

Note: A worksheet name can contain up to 31 characters, including spaces.

You can reorganize data by moving a worksheet to a new location in your workbook.

MOVE A WORKSHEET

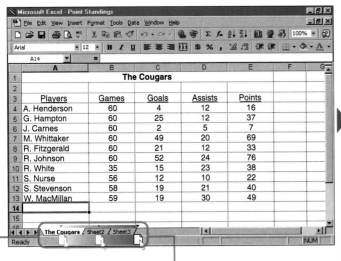

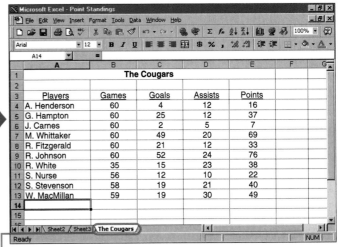

1 Position the mouse ⟍ over the tab of the worksheet you want to move.

2 Drag the worksheet to a new location.

■ An arrow (▼) shows where the worksheet will appear.

■ The worksheet appears in the new location.

■ To copy a worksheet, perform steps **1** and **2**, except press and hold down the `Ctrl` key as you perform step **2**.

MOVE OR COPY DATA BETWEEN WORKSHEETS

You can move or copy data from one worksheet to another. This saves you time when you want to use data from another worksheet.

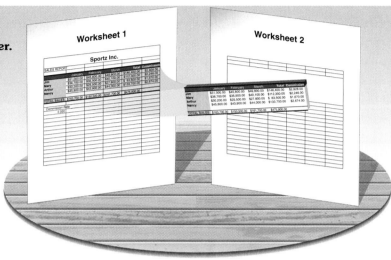

Worksheet 1

Worksheet 2

When you move data, the data disappears from its original location in the workbook. When you copy data, the data appears in both the original and new locations.

MOVE OR COPY DATA BETWEEN WORKSHEETS

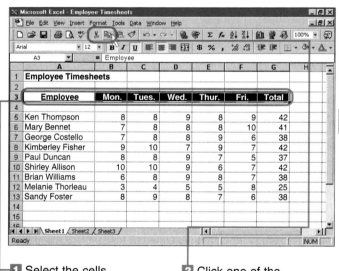

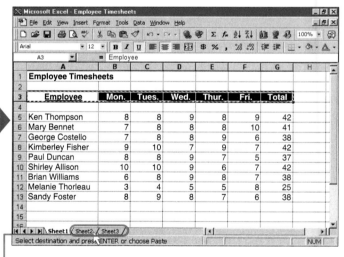

1 Select the cells containing the data you want to place in another worksheet. To select cells, see page 14.

2 Click one of the following options.

✂ Move data

📋 Copy data

3 Click the tab of the worksheet where you want to place the data.

Note: To place the data in another workbook, open the workbook before performing step 3. To open a workbook, see page 36.

? **Why did the cell references in my formula change when I copied the formula from one worksheet to another?**

When you copy a formula containing relative cell references, Excel automatically changes the cell references in the formula for the new location.

	A	B	C
1	4	3	A1+B1=7
2			
3			
4			
5			
6			

	A	B	C
1			
2			
3			
4	2	3	A4+B4=5
5			
6			

If you do not want Excel to automatically change the cell references in the formula, you can use absolute cell references.

For information on relative and absolute cell references, see pages 94 to 97.

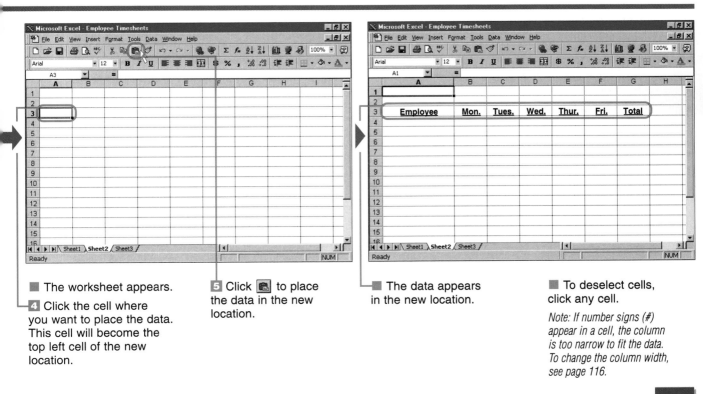

■ The worksheet appears.

4 Click the cell where you want to place the data. This cell will become the top left cell of the new location.

5 Click 🔳 to place the data in the new location.

■ The data appears in the new location.

■ To deselect cells, click any cell.

Note: If number signs (#) appear in a cell, the column is too narrow to fit the data. To change the column width, see page 116.

ENTER A FORMULA ACROSS WORKSHEETS

You can enter a formula in one worksheet that uses data from other worksheets.

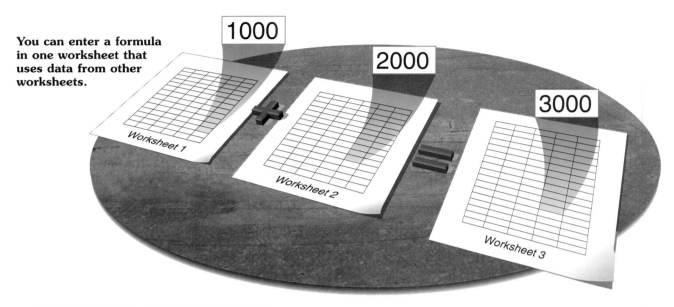

■■■ ENTER A FORMULA ACROSS WORKSHEETS ■■■

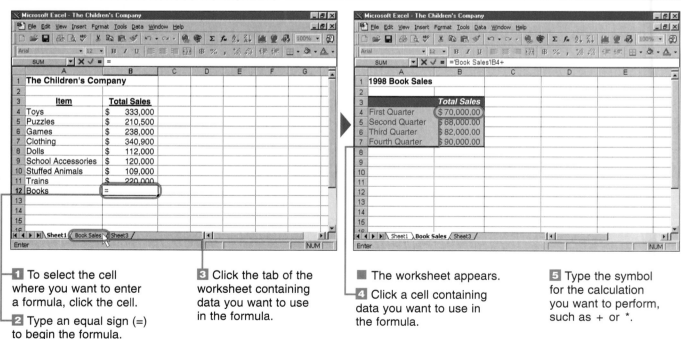

1 To select the cell where you want to enter a formula, click the cell.

2 Type an equal sign (=) to begin the formula.

3 Click the tab of the worksheet containing data you want to use in the formula.

■ The worksheet appears.

4 Click a cell containing data you want to use in the formula.

5 Type the symbol for the calculation you want to perform, such as + or *.

What happens if I change a number used in a formula?

If you change a number used in a formula, Excel will automatically calculate a new result. This ensures that your calculations are always up-to-date.

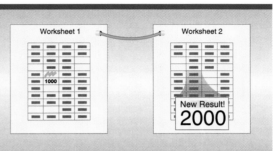

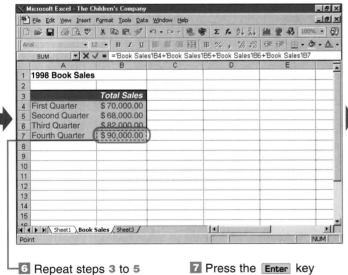

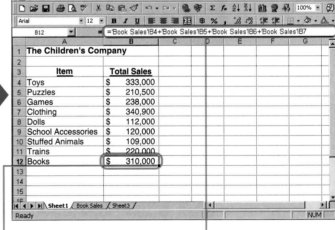

6 Repeat steps **3** to **5** until you have selected all the cells containing data you want to use in the formula.

*Note: In this example, cells **B4** to **B7** are added together.*

7 Press the Enter key to complete the formula.

■ The result of the calculation appears in the cell you selected in step **1**.

8 To view the formula you entered, click the cell containing the formula.

■ The formula bar displays the worksheet name and cell reference for each cell used in the formula.

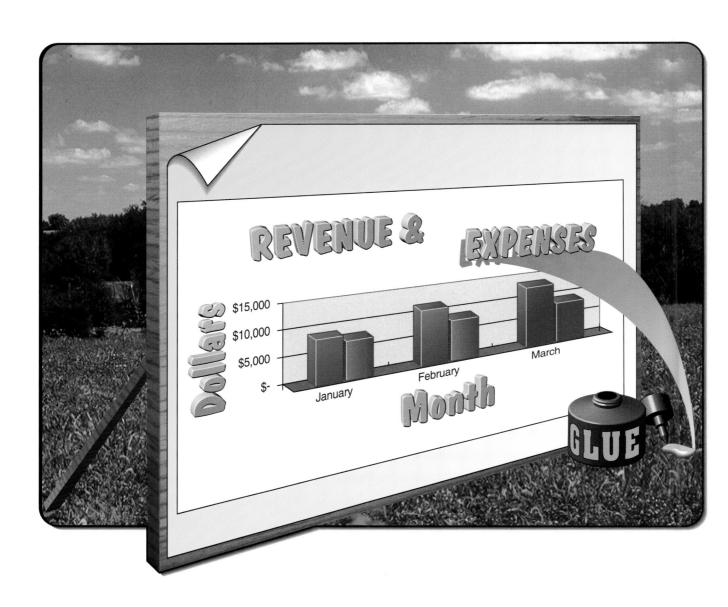

CHAPTER 9

Work With Charts

Would you like to display your worksheet data in a chart? In this chapter you will learn how to create, change and print charts.

INTRODUCTION TO CHARTS

A chart allows you to visually display your worksheet data. Excel offers many different chart types.

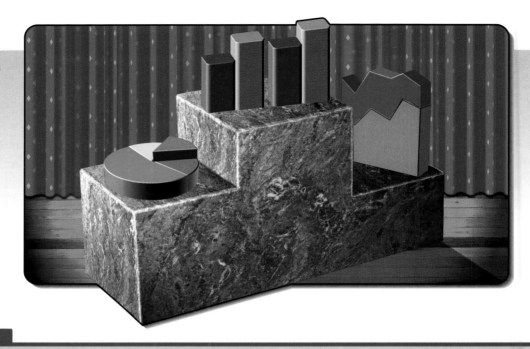

PARTS OF A CHART

Data Series

A group of related data representing one row or column from your worksheet. Each data series is represented by a specific color, pattern or symbol.

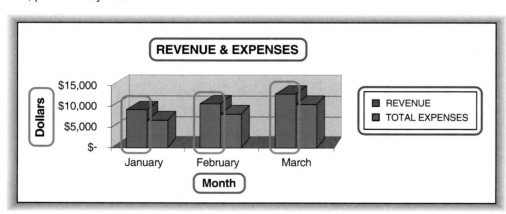

Chart Title

Identifies the subject of your chart.

Legend

Identifies the color, pattern or symbol that represents each data series in your chart.

Y-axis Title

Indicates the unit of measure used in your chart.

X-axis Title

Indicates the categories used in your chart.

COMMON CHART TYPES

Area

An area chart is useful for showing the amount of change in data over time. Each line represents a data series.

Line

A line chart is useful for showing changes to data at regular intervals. Each line represents a data series.

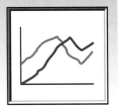

Column

A column chart is useful for showing changes to data over time or comparing individual items. Each column represents an item in a data series.

Bar

A bar chart is useful for comparing individual items. Each bar represents an item in a data series.

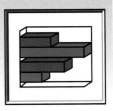

Pie

A pie chart is useful for showing the relationship of parts to a whole. Each piece of a pie represents an item in a data series. A pie chart can show only one data series at a time.

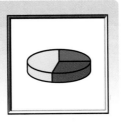

Doughnut

A doughnut chart is useful for showing the relationship of parts to a whole. Unlike a pie chart, a doughnut chart can display more than one data series. Each ring represents a data series.

Radar

A radar chart is useful for comparing the items in several data series. Each data series is shown as a line around a central point.

XY (Scatter)

An xy (scatter) chart is useful for showing the relationship between two or more data series measured at uneven intervals.

CREATE A CHART

You can use the Chart Wizard to create a chart that graphically displays your worksheet data. The wizard asks you a series of questions and then creates a chart based on your answers.

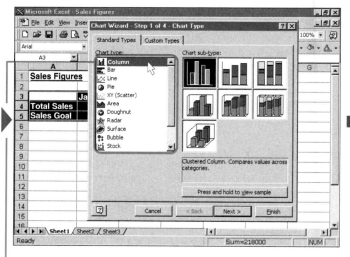

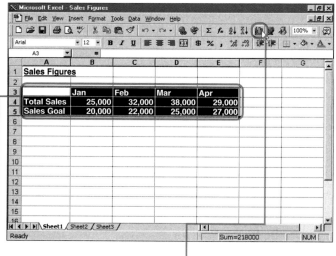

1 Select the cells containing the data you want to display in a chart, including the row and column labels. To select cells, see page 14.

2 Click 📊.

■ The Chart Wizard appears.

*Note: The first time you create a chart, the Office Assistant may appear. Click **No** to hide the Office Assistant.*

3 Click the type of chart you want to create.

Note: After you create a chart, you can easily change the chart type. For information, see page 192.

Do I have to create a new chart each time I change the data in my worksheet?

No. When you edit the data you used to create the chart, Excel will automatically update the chart to display the changes.

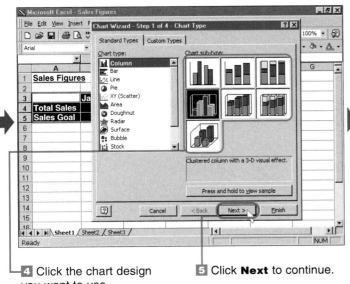

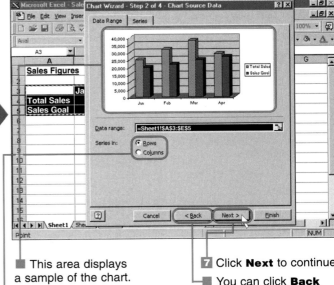

■4■ Click the chart design you want to use.

Note: The available designs depend on the type of chart you selected in step 3.

■5■ Click **Next** to continue.

■ This area displays a sample of the chart.

■6■ Click an option to select the way you want Excel to plot the data from the worksheet (○ changes to ◉).

■7■ Click **Next** to continue.

■ You can click **Back** at any time to return to a previous step and change your selections.

CONTINUED

CREATE A CHART

You can add titles to your chart to make the chart easier to understand.

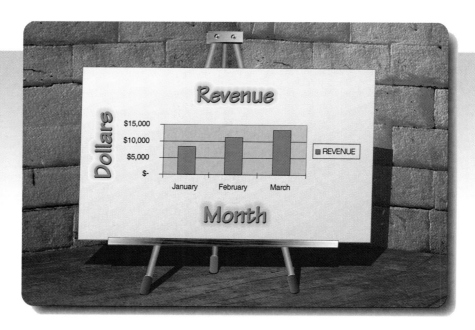

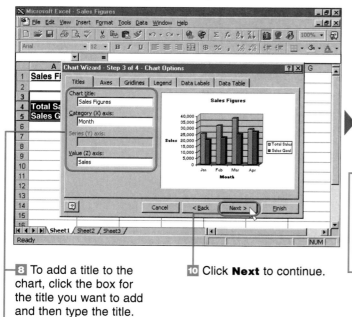

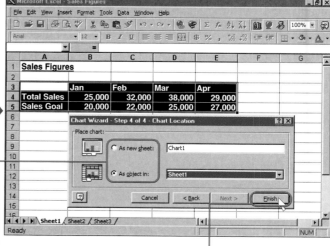

8 To add a title to the chart, click the box for the title you want to add and then type the title.

9 Repeat step **8** for each title you want to add.

10 Click **Next** to continue.

11 Click an option to specify where you want to display the chart (○ changes to ◉).

Note: For information on where you can display the chart, see the top of page 191.

12 Click **Finish** to complete the chart.

?

Where can I display my chart?

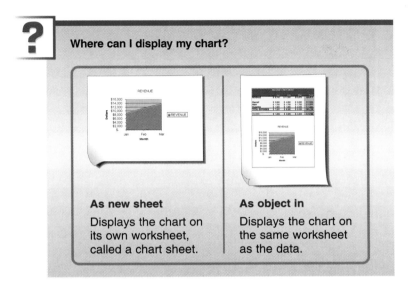

As new sheet
Displays the chart on
its own worksheet,
called a chart sheet.

As object in
Displays the chart on
the same worksheet
as the data.

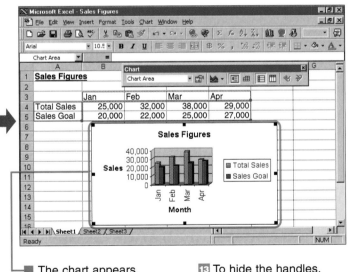

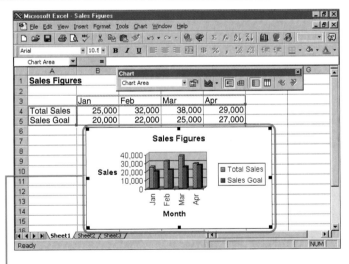

■ The chart appears.
Handles (■) around the
chart let you change
the size of the chart.

13 To hide the handles,
click outside the chart.

*Note: To move or size a chart,
see page 194.*

DELETE A CHART

1 Click a blank area in
the chart. Handles (■)
appear around the chart.

2 Press the Delete key.

*Note: You can delete a chart
displayed on a chart sheet as
you would delete a worksheet.
To delete a worksheet, see
page 177.*

CHANGE CHART TYPE

After you create a chart, you can select a different type of chart that will better suit your data.

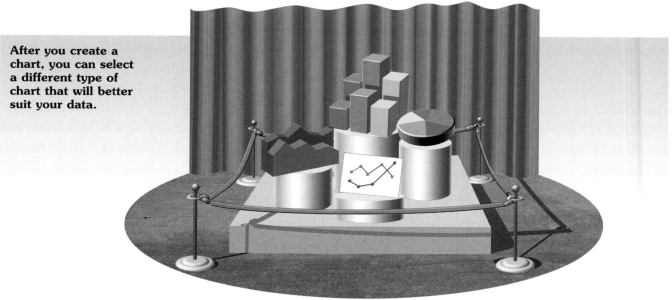

CHANGE CHART TYPE

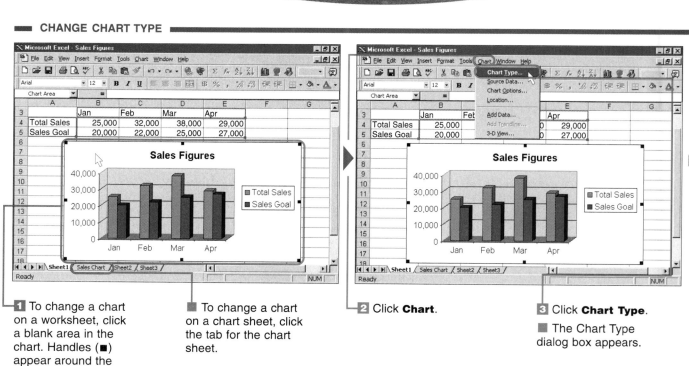

1 To change a chart on a worksheet, click a blank area in the chart. Handles (■) appear around the chart.

■ To change a chart on a chart sheet, click the tab for the chart sheet.

2 Click **Chart**.

3 Click **Chart Type**.

■ The Chart Type dialog box appears.

? What type of chart should I choose?

The type of chart you should choose depends on your data. For example, area, column and line charts are ideal for showing changes to values over time, whereas pie charts are ideal for showing percentages.

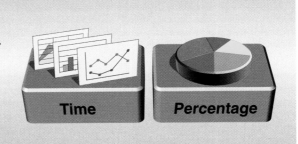

Time   Percentage

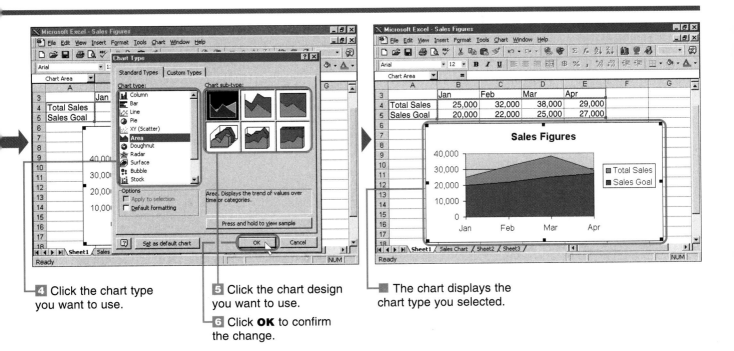

4 Click the chart type you want to use.

5 Click the chart design you want to use.

6 Click **OK** to confirm the change.

■ The chart displays the chart type you selected.

MOVE OR SIZE A CHART

After you create
a chart, you can
change the location
or size of the chart.

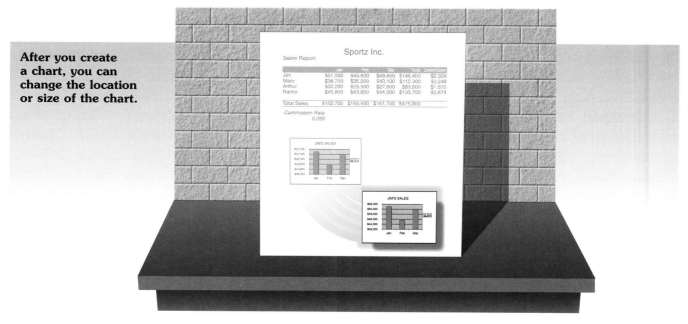

MOVE A CHART

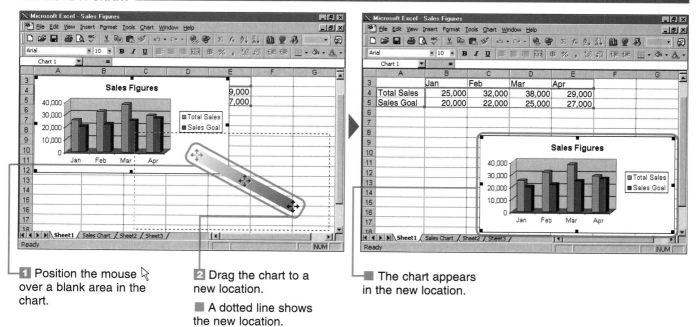

1 Position the mouse ℞ over a blank area in the chart.

2 Drag the chart to a new location.

■ A dotted line shows the new location.

■ The chart appears in the new location.

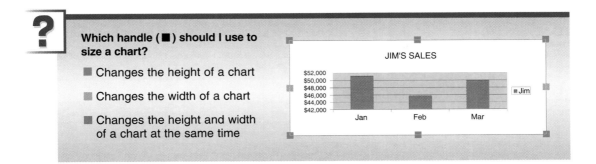

Which handle (■) should I use to size a chart?

■ Changes the height of a chart

■ Changes the width of a chart

■ Changes the height and width of a chart at the same time

JIM'S SALES

■ SIZE A CHART ■

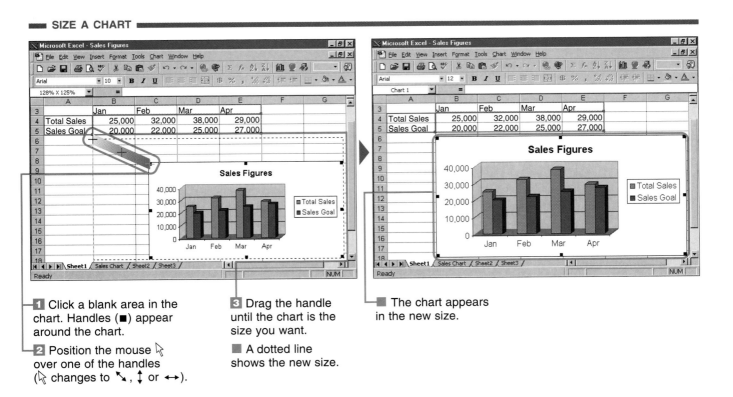

1 Click a blank area in the chart. Handles (■) appear around the chart.

2 Position the mouse ⌀ over one of the handles (⌀ changes to ⬉, ↕ or ↔).

3 Drag the handle until the chart is the size you want.

■ A dotted line shows the new size.

■ The chart appears in the new size.

PRINT A CHART

You can print
your chart with
the worksheet
data or on its
own page.

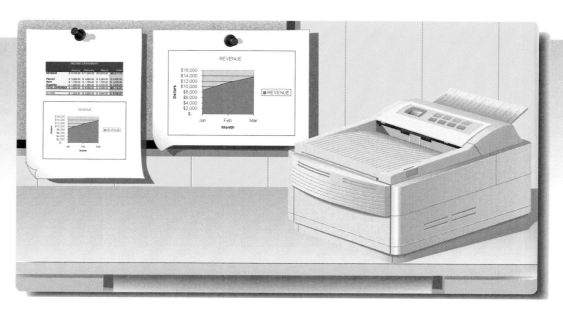

PRINT A CHART WITH WORKSHEET DATA

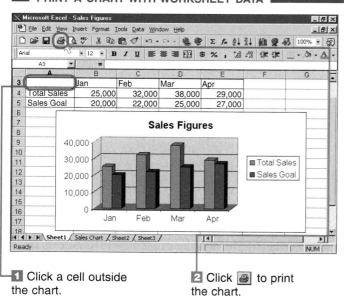

1 Click a cell outside
the chart.

2 Click 🖨 to print
the chart.

*Note: For more information
on printing, see pages 152
to 171.*

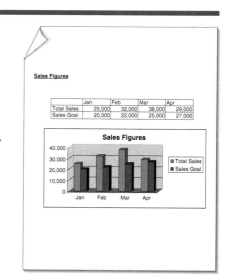

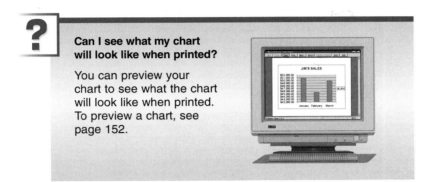

Can I see what my chart will look like when printed?

You can preview your chart to see what the chart will look like when printed. To preview a chart, see page 152.

PRINT A CHART ON ITS OWN PAGE

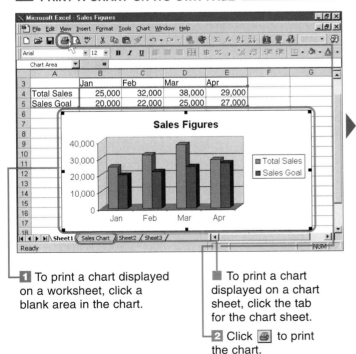

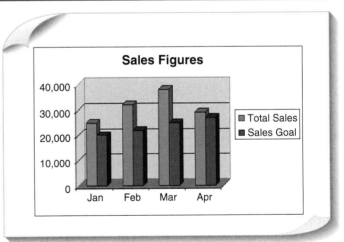

■1 To print a chart displayed on a worksheet, click a blank area in the chart.

■ To print a chart displayed on a chart sheet, click the tab for the chart sheet.

■2 Click 🖨 to print the chart.

Note: When you print a chart on its own page, the chart will expand to fill the page. The printed chart may look different from the chart on the worksheet.

ADD DATA TO A CHART

After you create a chart, you can easily add new data to the chart.

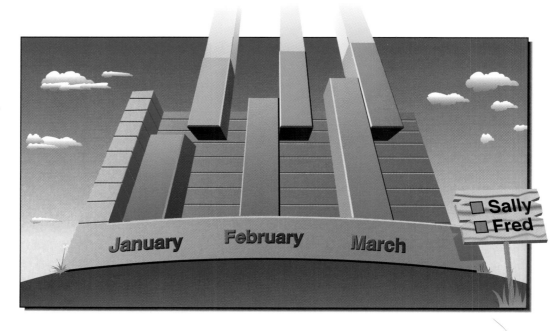

ADD DATA TO A CHART

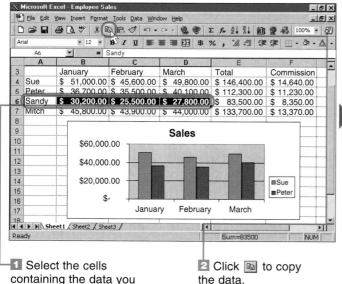

1 Select the cells containing the data you want to add to the chart, including the row or column labels. To select cells, see page 14.

2 Click 🖹 to copy the data.

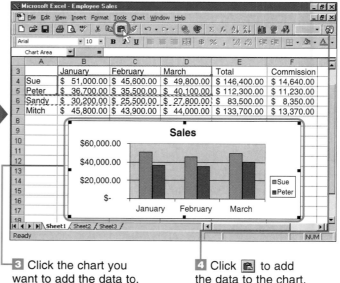

3 Click the chart you want to add the data to.

4 Click 🖹 to add the data to the chart.

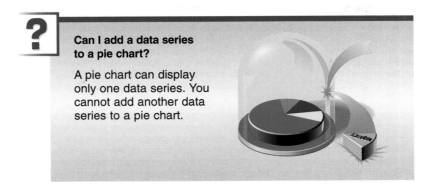

**Can I add a data series
to a pie chart?**

A pie chart can display
only one data series. You
cannot add another data
series to a pie chart.

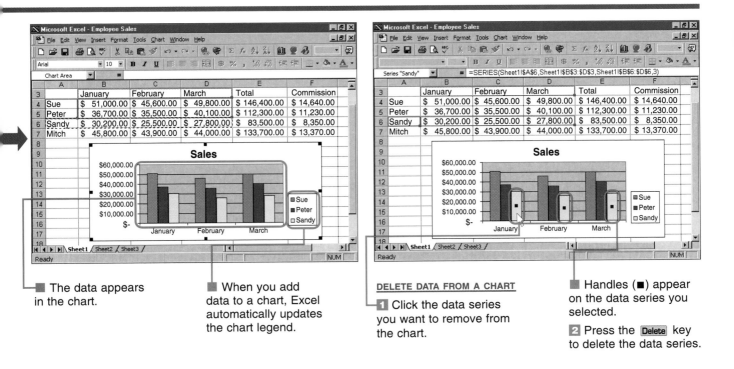

■ The data appears
in the chart.

■ When you add
data to a chart, Excel
automatically updates
the chart legend.

DELETE DATA FROM A CHART

■1 Click the data series
you want to remove from
the chart.

■ Handles (■) appear
on the data series you
selected.

■2 Press the Delete key
to delete the data series.

CHANGE APPEARANCE OF DATA SERIES

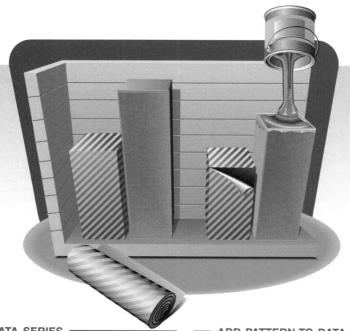

You can change
the color of a data
series in a chart.
You can also add
a pattern to a data
series.

If you are printing your
chart on a black-and-white
printer, adding a pattern to
a data series may make it
easier to identify the data
series in the chart.

CHANGE COLOR OF DATA SERIES

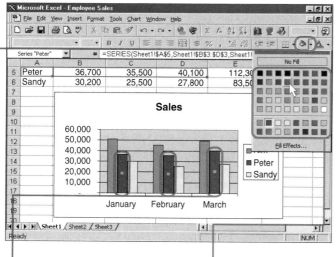

ADD PATTERN TO DATA SERIES

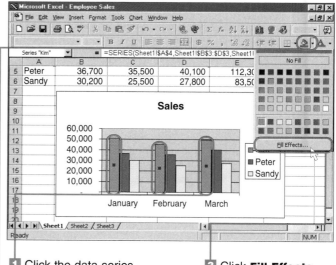

■1 Click the data series
you want to change
to a different color.
Handles (■) appear
on the data series.

■2 Click ⬝ in this area
to display the available
colors.

■3 Click the color
you want to use.

■ The data series
changes to the new
color.

■1 Click the data series
you want to add a pattern
to. Handles (■) appear
on the data series.

■2 Click ⬝ in this area.

■3 Click **Fill Effects**.

■ The Fill Effects
dialog box appears.

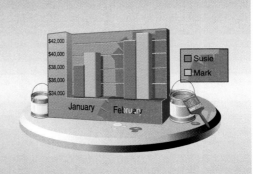

Can I change the color of other parts of a chart?

You can change the color of other parts of a chart, such as the background of the chart or the chart legend. Click the part of the chart you want to change and then perform steps 2 and 3 on page 200 to select the color you want to use.

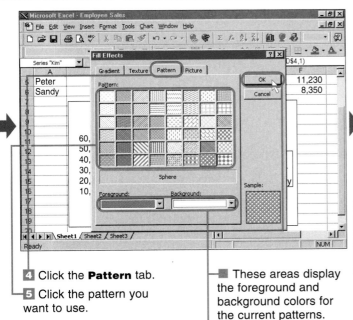

4 Click the **Pattern** tab.

5 Click the pattern you want to use.

■ These areas display the foreground and background colors for the current patterns. You can click an area to select a different color.

6 Click **OK** to confirm the change.

■ The data series displays the pattern you selected.

■ To deselect the data series, click outside the chart.

CHANGE CHART TITLES

You can change the
titles in your chart
to make the titles
more meaningful.

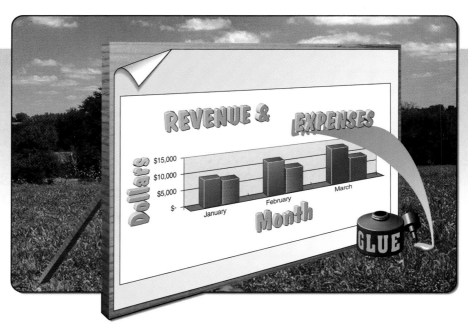

CHANGE CHART TITLES

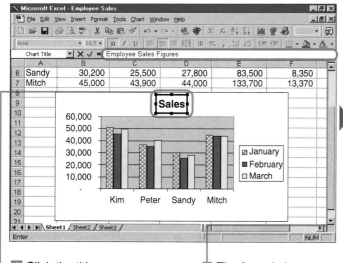

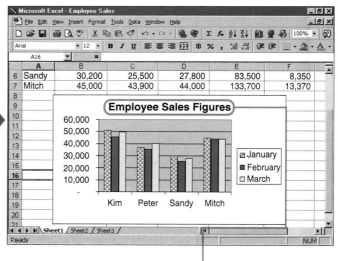

1 Click the title you
want to change. A border
appears around the title.

2 Type the new title.

■ The formula bar
displays the title as
you type.

3 Press the **Enter** key
to add the title to the
chart.

■ The chart displays
the new title.

■ To deselect the title,
click outside the chart.

ROTATE CHART TEXT

You can rotate text on a
chart axis to improve the
appearance of the chart.

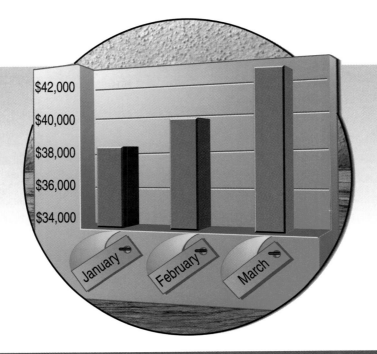

ROTATE CHART TEXT

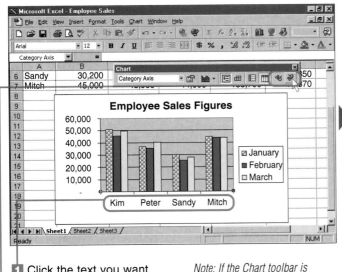

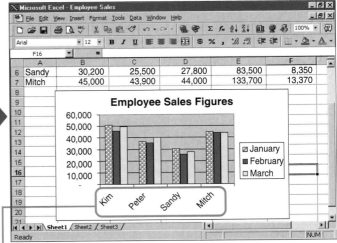

1 Click the text you want
to rotate.

2 Click one of the
following options.

[icon] Rotate text downward

[icon] Rotate text upward

*Note: If the Chart toolbar is
not displayed, see page 104
to display the toolbar.*

■ Excel rotates the
text in the chart.

■ To deselect the text,
click outside the chart.

■ To return the text
to its original position,
repeat steps **1** and **2**.

FORMAT CHART TEXT

You can change the
appearance of the
text and numbers
in a chart.

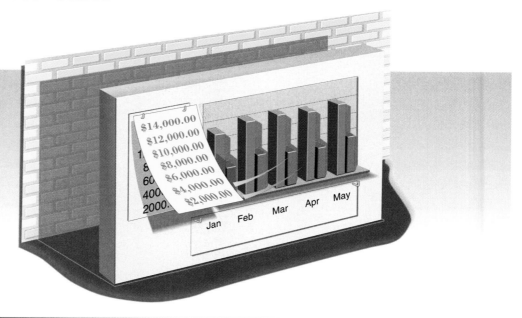

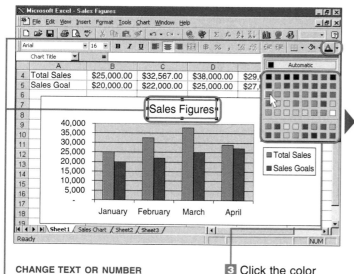

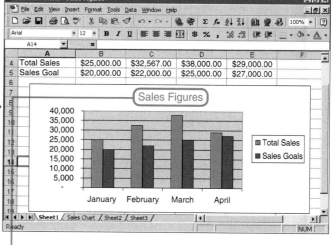

CHANGE TEXT OR NUMBER COLOR

1 Click the text or numbers you want to change to a different color.

2 Click ▾ in this area to display the available colors.

3 Click the color you want to use.

■ The text or numbers change to the new color.

■ To deselect the text or numbers, click outside the chart.

? **How else can I change the appearance of the text and numbers in a chart?**

Change the Font

Click the text or numbers you want to change and then perform steps **2** and **3** on page 120.

Change the Font Size

Click the text or numbers you want to change and then perform steps **2** and **3** on page 121.

Add or Remove Decimal Places from Numbers

Click the numbers you want to change and then perform step **2** on page 125.

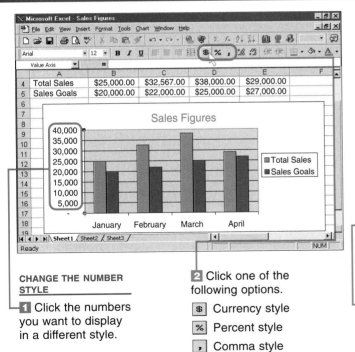

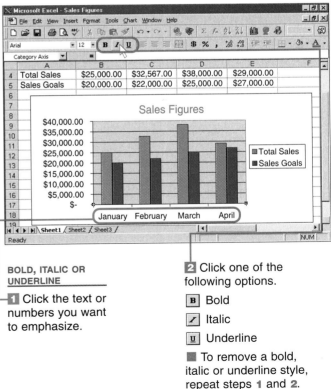

CHANGE THE NUMBER STYLE

1 Click the numbers you want to display in a different style.

2 Click one of the following options.

$ Currency style

% Percent style

, Comma style

BOLD, ITALIC OR UNDERLINE

1 Click the text or numbers you want to emphasize.

2 Click one of the following options.

B Bold

I Italic

U Underline

■ To remove a bold, italic or underline style, repeat steps **1** and **2**.

CHANGE THE WAY DATA IS PLOTTED

You can change the way Excel plots the data in your chart. This allows you to emphasize different information in the chart.

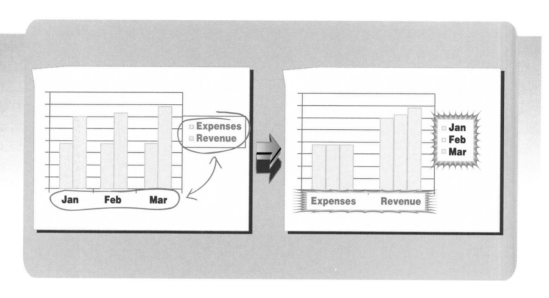

CHANGE THE WAY DATA IS PLOTTED

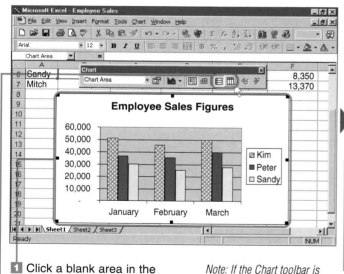

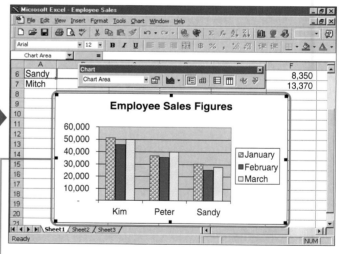

1 Click a blank area in the chart you want to change.

2 Click one of the following options.

▤ Plot data by row

▥ Plot data by column

Note: If the Chart toolbar is not displayed, see page 104 to display the toolbar.

■ The chart displays the change.

ADD A DATA TABLE TO A CHART

You can add a table to
your chart to display
the data used to create
the chart.

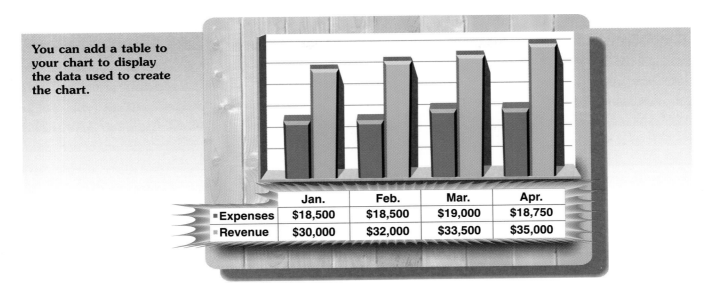

	Jan.	Feb.	Mar.	Apr.
▪Expenses	$18,500	$18,500	$19,000	$18,750
▪Revenue	$30,000	$32,000	$33,500	$35,000

ADD A DATA TABLE TO A CHART

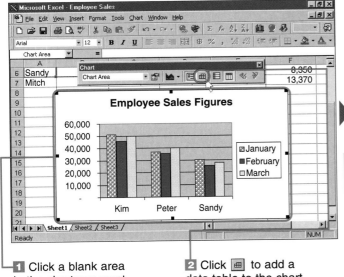

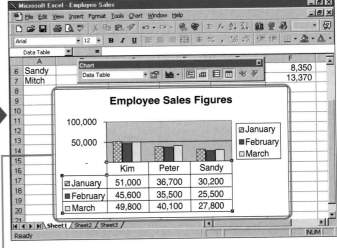

1 Click a blank area
in the chart you want
to change.

*Note: You cannot add a
data table to some types
of charts.*

2 Click ⊞ to add a
data table to the chart.

*Note: If the Chart toolbar is
not displayed, see page 104
to display the toolbar.*

▪ The chart displays
the data table.

▪ To remove the data
table from the chart,
repeat steps **1** and **2**.

CHANGE VIEW OF A 3-D CHART

You can change the elevation, rotation and perspective of a 3-D chart. This can help you emphasize the important parts of your chart.

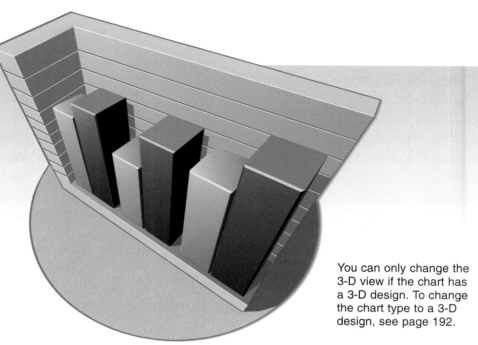

You can only change the 3-D view if the chart has a 3-D design. To change the chart type to a 3-D design, see page 192.

CHANGE VIEW OF A 3-D CHART

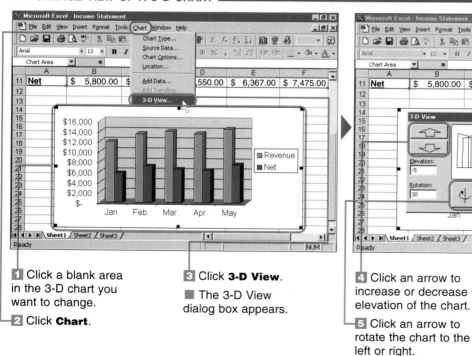

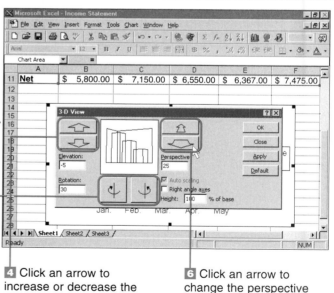

1 Click a blank area in the 3-D chart you want to change.

2 Click **Chart**.

3 Click **3-D View**.

■ The 3-D View dialog box appears.

4 Click an arrow to increase or decrease the elevation of the chart.

5 Click an arrow to rotate the chart to the left or right.

6 Click an arrow to change the perspective of the chart.

Note: The perspective options are not available for some chart types.

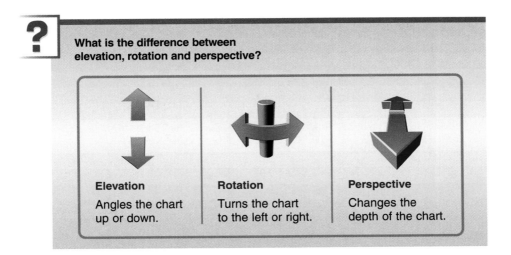

What is the difference between elevation, rotation and perspective?

Elevation
Angles the chart up or down.

Rotation
Turns the chart to the left or right.

Perspective
Changes the depth of the chart.

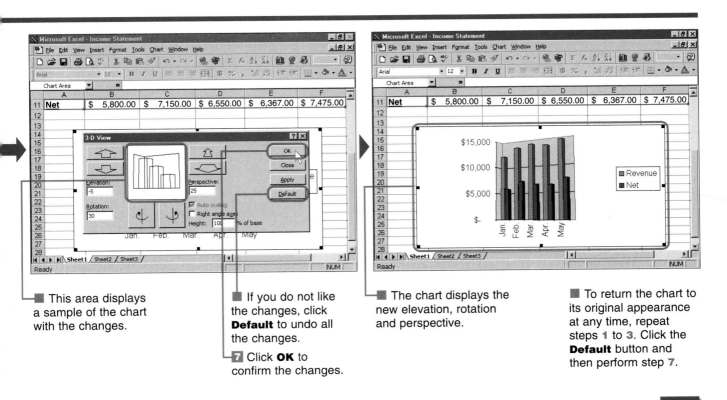

■ This area displays a sample of the chart with the changes.

■ If you do not like the changes, click **Default** to undo all the changes.

7 Click **OK** to confirm the changes.

■ The chart displays the new elevation, rotation and perspective.

■ To return the chart to its original appearance at any time, repeat steps **1** to **3**. Click the **Default** button and then perform step **7**.

DISPLAY DATA IN A MAP

You can create a map
to display data that
relates to specific
geographic areas.

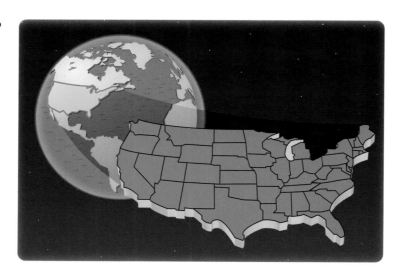

Before you can create
a map, you need to
install the Microsoft
Map component from
the CD-ROM disc you
used to install Excel.

CREATE A MAP

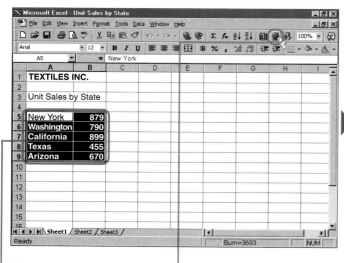

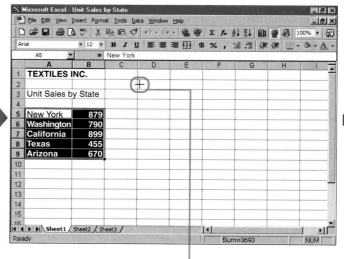

■1 Select the cells
containing the data
you want to display in
a map. To select cells,
see page 14.

*Note: One column must
contain geographic data, such
as country or state names.*

■2 Click 🗺.

■ The mouse ⌖
changes to **+** when
over the worksheet.

■3 Click the location
where you want the
top left corner of the
map to appear.

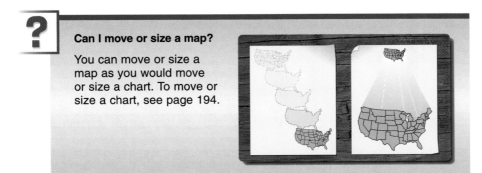

Can I move or size a map?

You can move or size a map as you would move or size a chart. To move or size a chart, see page 194.

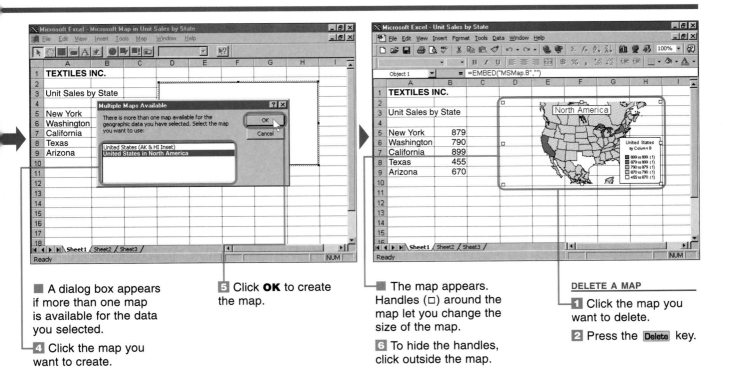

■ A dialog box appears if more than one map is available for the data you selected.

◀ Click the map you want to create.

⑤ Click **OK** to create the map.

■ The map appears. Handles (□) around the map let you change the size of the map.

⑥ To hide the handles, click outside the map.

DELETE A MAP

❶ Click the map you want to delete.

❷ Press the Delete key.

DISPLAY DATA IN A MAP

If you change data
used in your map,
you can update the
map to reflect the
changes.

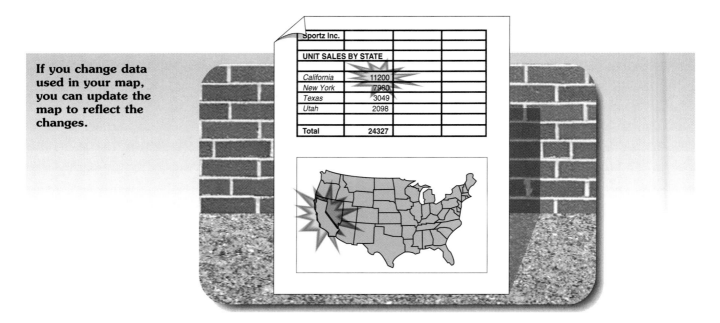

UPDATE A MAP

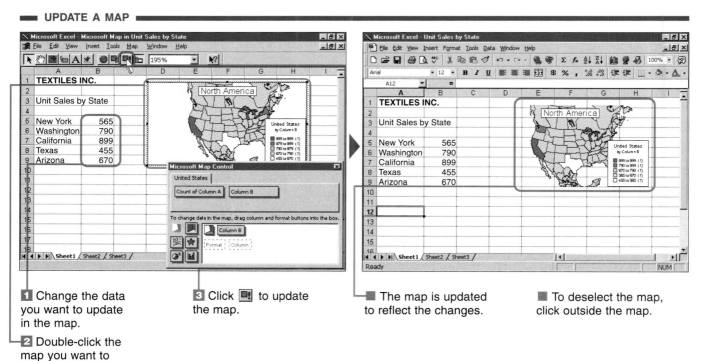

1 Change the data
you want to update
in the map.

2 Double-click the
map you want to
update.

3 Click 📵 to update
the map.

■ The map is updated
to reflect the changes.

■ To deselect the map,
click outside the map.

You can add text
to your map to
label areas or
insert notes.

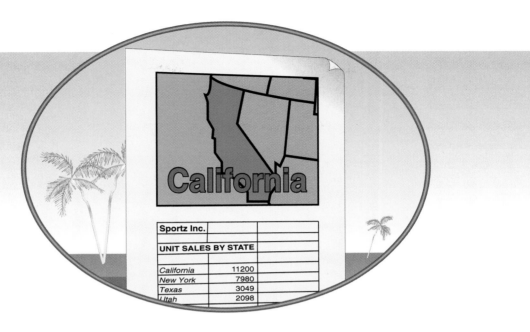

ADD TEXT TO A MAP

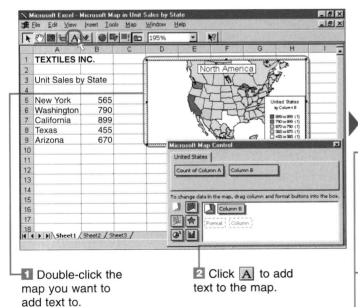

1 Double-click the
map you want to
add text to.

2 Click **A** to add
text to the map.

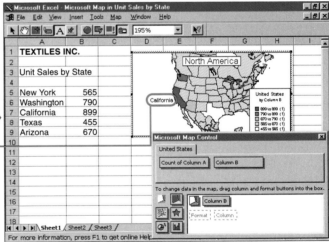

3 Click the location
where you want the
text to appear.

4 Type the text and then
press the **Enter** key.

■ To deselect the map,
click outside the map.

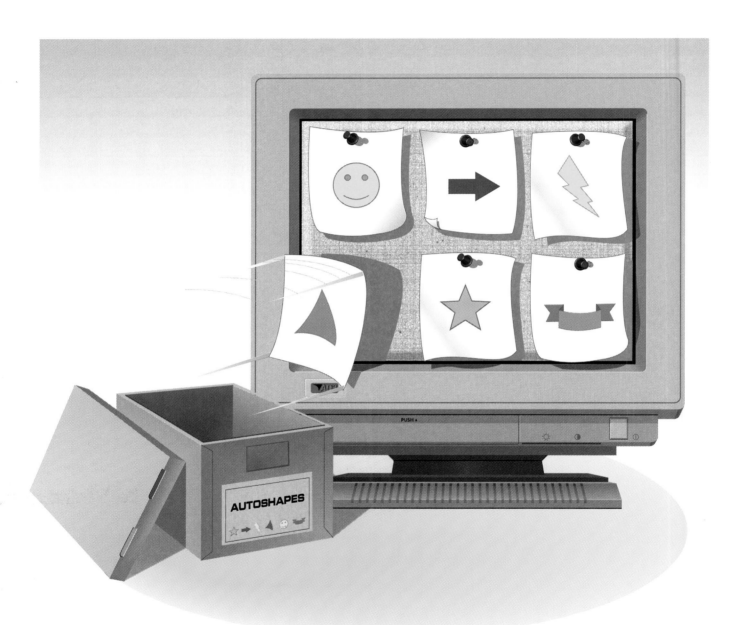

CHAPTER 10

Work With Graphics

Are you interested in using graphics to enhance the appearance of your worksheet? This chapter shows you how.

ADD AN AUTOSHAPE

Excel provides many ready-made shapes, called AutoShapes, that you can add to your worksheet.

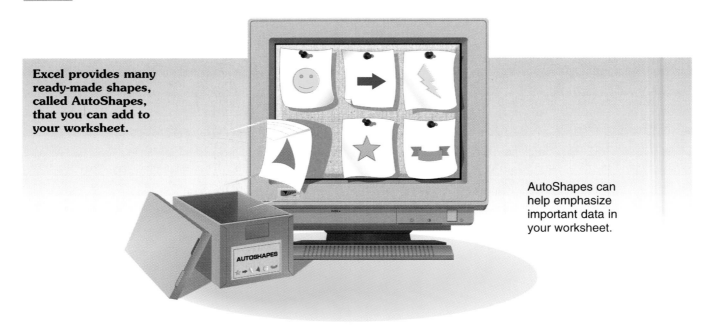

AutoShapes can help emphasize important data in your worksheet.

ADD AN AUTOSHAPE

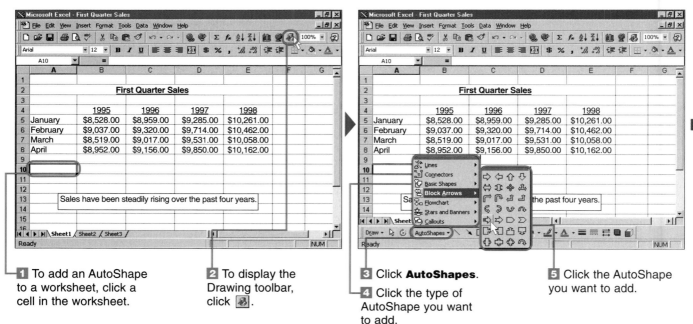

1 To add an AutoShape to a worksheet, click a cell in the worksheet.

2 To display the Drawing toolbar, click 🖺.

3 Click **AutoShapes**.

4 Click the type of AutoShape you want to add.

5 Click the AutoShape you want to add.

Can I add text to an AutoShape?

You can add text to most AutoShapes. This is particularly useful for AutoShapes such as banners. To add text to an AutoShape, click the AutoShape and then type the text you want the AutoShape to display.

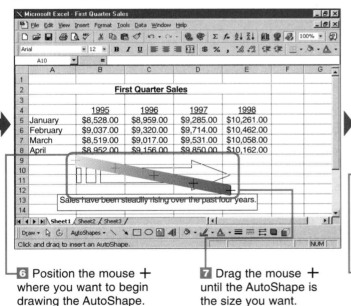

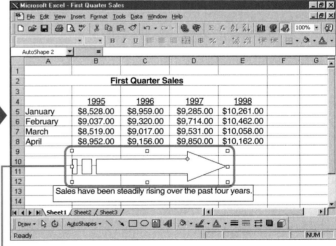

6 Position the mouse + where you want to begin drawing the AutoShape.

7 Drag the mouse + until the AutoShape is the size you want.

■ The AutoShape appears in the worksheet. The handles (□) around the AutoShape let you change the size of the shape.

8 To hide the handles, click outside the AutoShape.

Note: To move, size or delete an AutoShape, see pages 226 to 228.

ADD A TEXT BOX

You can add a text box to your worksheet to display additional information.

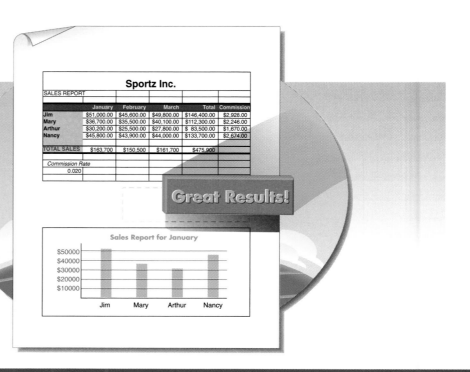

ADD A TEXT BOX

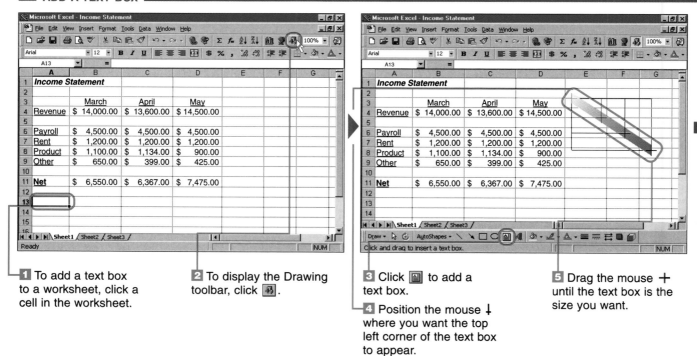

1 To add a text box to a worksheet, click a cell in the worksheet.

2 To display the Drawing toolbar, click 🐻.

3 Click 📧 to add a text box.

4 Position the mouse ↓ where you want the top left corner of the text box to appear.

5 Drag the mouse ✛ until the text box is the size you want.

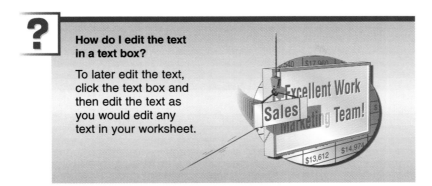

How do I edit the text in a text box?

To later edit the text, click the text box and then edit the text as you would edit any text in your worksheet.

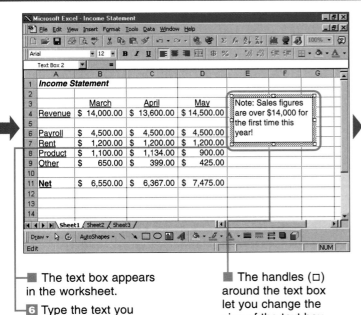

■ The text box appears in the worksheet.

6 Type the text you want to appear in the text box.

■ The handles (□) around the text box let you change the size of the text box.

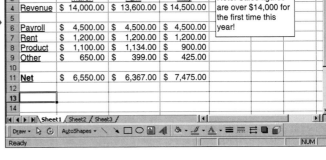

7 To hide the handles, click outside the text box.

Note: To move, size or delete a text box, see pages 226 to 228.

ADD A TEXT EFFECT

You can use the WordArt feature to add a text effect to your worksheet.

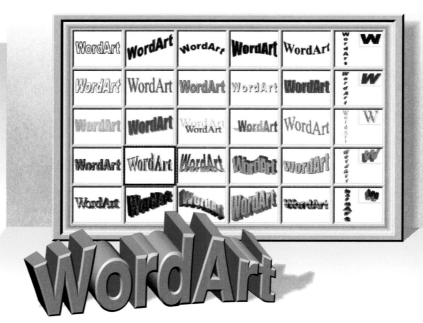

Text effects can enhance the appearance of a title or draw attention to important data.

ADD A TEXT EFFECT

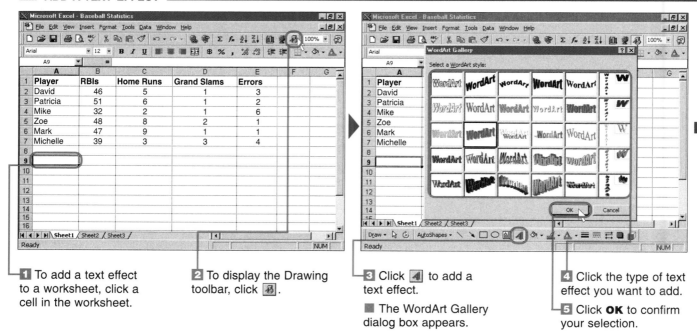

1 To add a text effect to a worksheet, click a cell in the worksheet.

2 To display the Drawing toolbar, click ⚄.

3 Click ◪ to add a text effect.

■ The WordArt Gallery dialog box appears.

4 Click the type of text effect you want to add.

5 Click **OK** to confirm your selection.

How do I edit a text effect?

Double-click the text effect to display the Edit WordArt Text dialog box. Then edit the text in the dialog box. When you are finished editing the text effect, click **OK**.

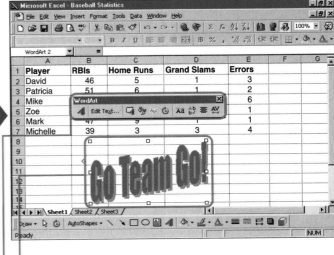

■ The Edit WordArt Text dialog box appears.

█ Type the text for the text effect.

█ Click **OK**.

■ The text effect appears in the worksheet. The handles (□) around the text effect let you change the size of the effect.

■ The WordArt toolbar also appears, providing tools to help you work with the text effect.

█ To hide the handles and the WordArt toolbar, click outside the text effect.

Note: To move, size or delete a text effect, see pages 226 to 228.

ADD CLIP ART

You can add a clip art image to your worksheet to illustrate a concept or make the worksheet more interesting.

Excel provides thousands of clip art images that you can choose from.

ADD CLIP ART

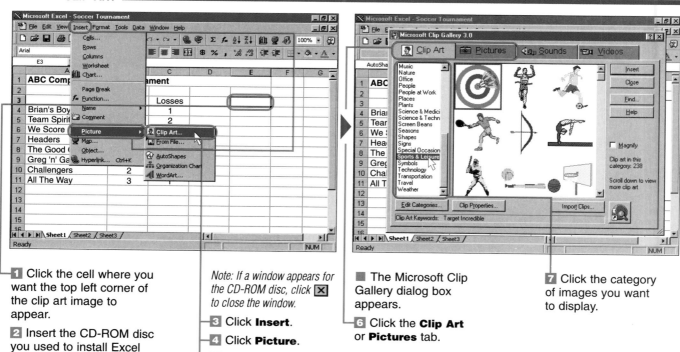

1 Click the cell where you want the top left corner of the clip art image to appear.

2 Insert the CD-ROM disc you used to install Excel into your CD-ROM drive.

Note: If a window appears for the CD-ROM disc, click ☒ to close the window.

3 Click **Insert**.

4 Click **Picture**.

5 Click **Clip Art**.

■ The Microsoft Clip Gallery dialog box appears.

6 Click the **Clip Art** or **Pictures** tab.

7 Click the category of images you want to display.

?

Where can I find more clip art images?

If you are connected to the Internet, you can visit Microsoft's Clip Gallery Live Web site to find additional clip art images that you can download to your computer.

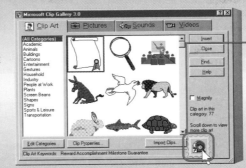

■ In the Microsoft Clip Gallery dialog box, click 🖼 to display the Clip Gallery Live Web site. Then follow the instructions on your screen.

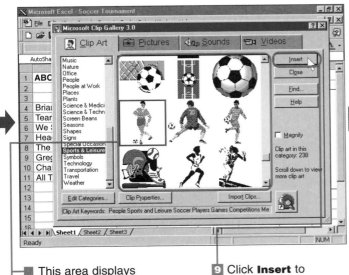

■ This area displays the images in the category you selected.

8 Click the image you want to add to the worksheet.

9 Click **Insert** to add the image to the worksheet.

■ The image appears in the worksheet. The handles (□) around the image let you change the size of the image.

■ The Picture toolbar also appears, providing tools to help you work with the image.

10 To hide the handles and the Picture toolbar, click outside the image.

Note: To move, size or delete an image, see pages 226 to 228.

ADD A PICTURE

You can add a
picture stored on
your computer to
your worksheet.

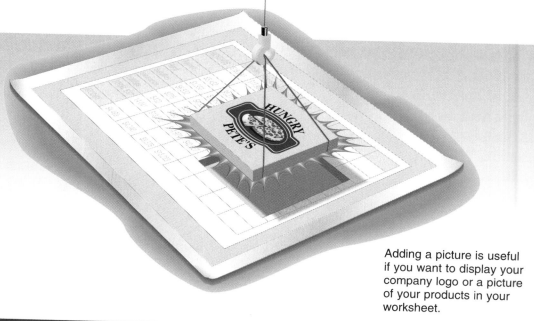

Adding a picture is useful
if you want to display your
company logo or a picture
of your products in your
worksheet.

ADD A PICTURE

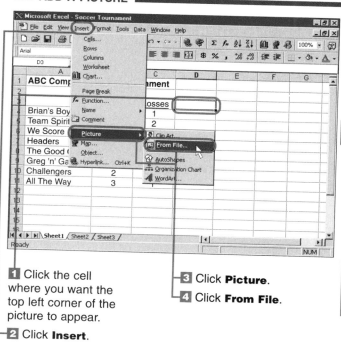

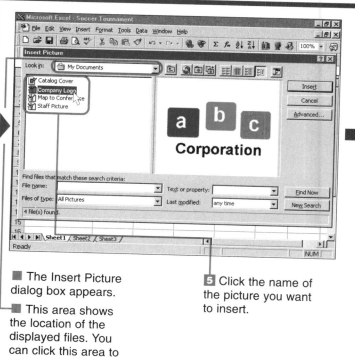

1 Click the cell
where you want the
top left corner of the
picture to appear.

2 Click **Insert**.

3 Click **Picture**.

4 Click **From File**.

■ The Insert Picture
dialog box appears.

■ This area shows
the location of the
displayed files. You
can click this area to
change the location.

5 Click the name of
the picture you want
to insert.

Where can I get pictures to use in my worksheets?

You can use a drawing program to create your own pictures or use a scanner to scan pictures into your computer. You can also find collections of pictures at most computer stores and on the World Wide Web.

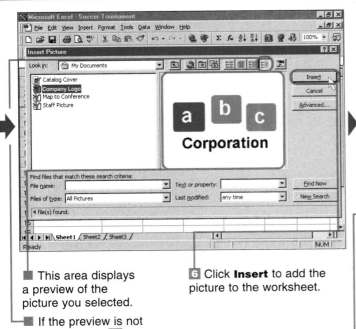

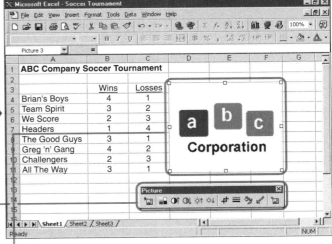

■ This area displays a preview of the picture you selected.

■ If the preview is not displayed, click 🔳.

6 Click **Insert** to add the picture to the worksheet.

■ The picture appears in the worksheet. The handles (□) around the picture let you change the size of the picture.

■ The Picture toolbar also appears, providing tools to help you work with the picture.

7 To hide the handles and the Picture toolbar, click outside the picture.

Note: To move, size or delete a picture, see pages 226 to 228.

MOVE OR SIZE A GRAPHIC

You can easily change the location or size of a graphic in your worksheet.

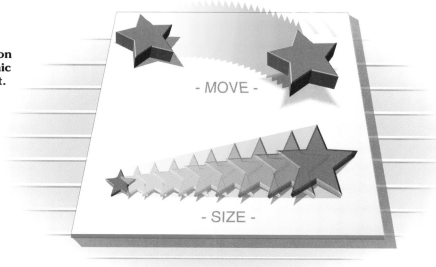

Popular types of graphics include AutoShapes, text boxes, text effects, clip art images and pictures.

MOVE A GRAPHIC

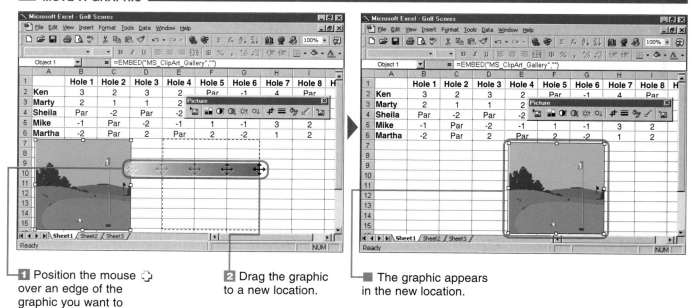

1 Position the mouse ⇲ over an edge of the graphic you want to move (⇲ changes to ✛).

2 Drag the graphic to a new location.

■ The graphic appears in the new location.

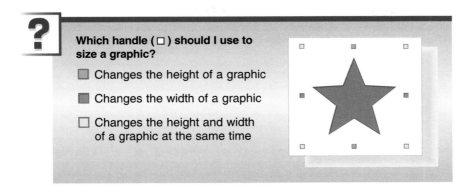

? Which handle (□) should I use to size a graphic?

■ Changes the height of a graphic

■ Changes the width of a graphic

□ Changes the height and width of a graphic at the same time

■ SIZE A GRAPHIC ■

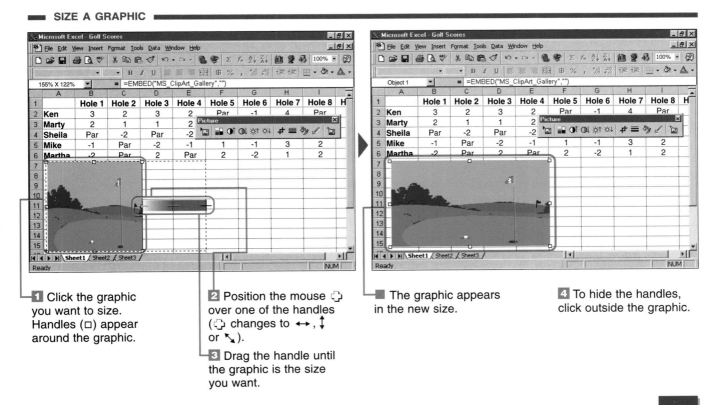

1 Click the graphic you want to size. Handles (□) appear around the graphic.

2 Position the mouse ⊕ over one of the handles (⊕ changes to ↔, ↕ or ↘).

3 Drag the handle until the graphic is the size you want.

■ The graphic appears in the new size.

4 To hide the handles, click outside the graphic.

DELETE A GRAPHIC

You can delete a graphic you no longer want to appear in your worksheet.

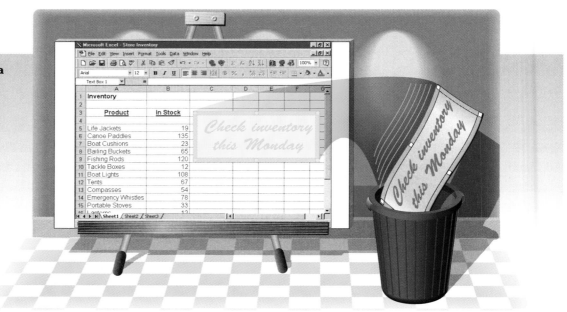

DELETE A GRAPHIC

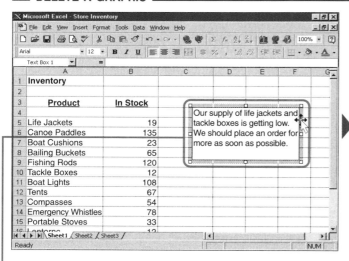

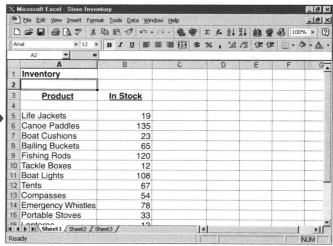

1 Click the graphic you want to delete.

2 If the graphic is a text box, click an edge of the text box to select the text box.

Note: For information on text boxes, see page 218.

3 Press the Delete key.

■ The graphic disappears.

You can make a graphic
in your worksheet appear
three-dimensional.

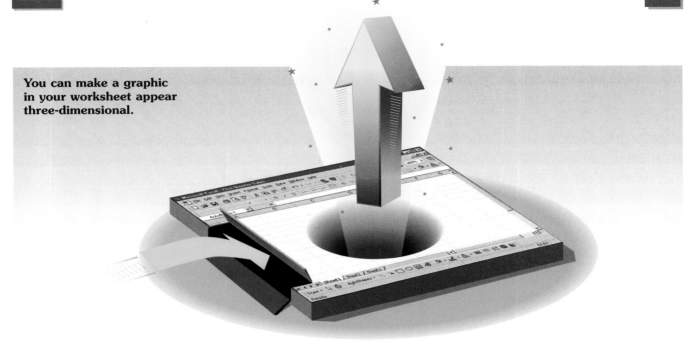

■ MAKE A GRAPHIC 3-D ■

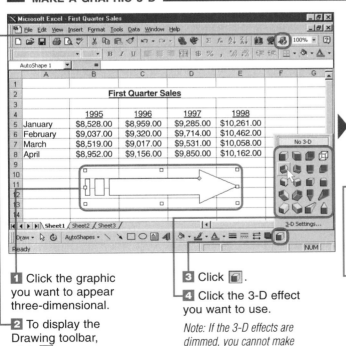

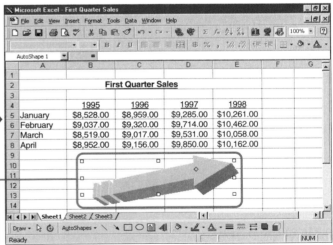

1 Click the graphic
you want to appear
three-dimensional.

2 To display the
Drawing toolbar,
click 🖼.

3 Click 🔲.

4 Click the 3-D effect
you want to use.

*Note: If the 3-D effects are
dimmed, you cannot make
the graphic you selected
three-dimensional.*

■ The graphic displays
the 3-D effect.

*Note: To remove a 3-D
effect from a graphic,
repeat steps 1 to 4, except
select No 3-D in step 4.*

CHANGE GRAPHIC COLOR

You can change the
color of a graphic
in your worksheet.

CHANGE GRAPHIC COLOR

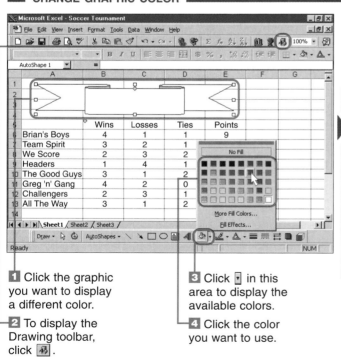

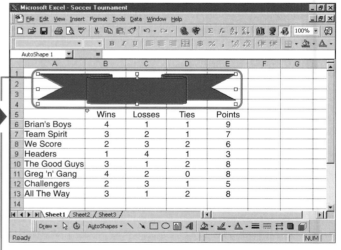

1 Click the graphic
you want to display
a different color.

2 To display the
Drawing toolbar,
click 🖉 .

3 Click 🔽 in this
area to display the
available colors.

4 Click the color
you want to use.

■ The graphic
displays the new color.

■ To remove the color
from a graphic, repeat
steps **1** to **4**, except
select **No Fill** in step **4**.

You can change
the color of the
line surrounding
a graphic.

CHANGE LINE COLOR

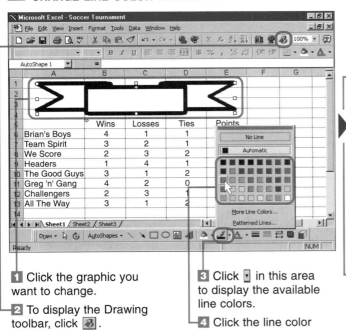

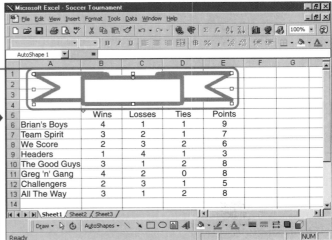

1 Click the graphic you
want to change.

2 To display the Drawing
toolbar, click ▣.

3 Click ▼ in this area
to display the available
line colors.

4 Click the line color
you want to use.

■ The line surrounding
the graphic displays the
new color.

■ To remove the line
surrounding a graphic,
repeat steps **1** to **4**,
except select **No Line**
in step **4**.

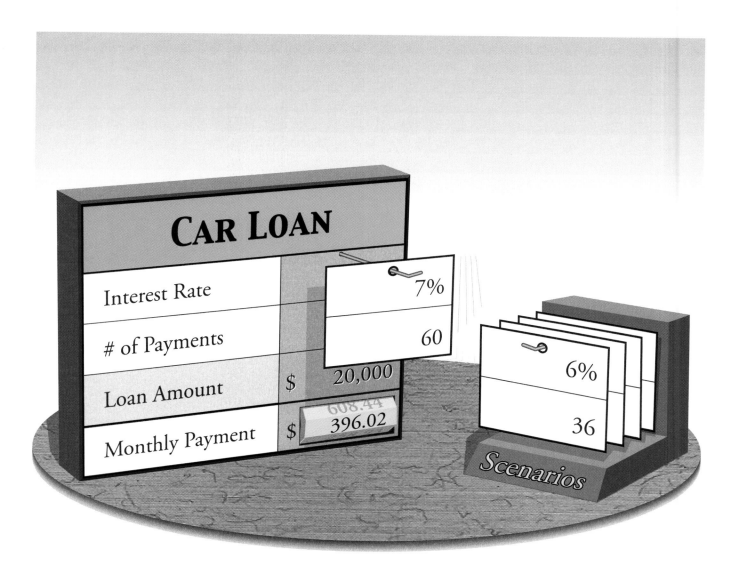

CHAPTER 11

Create Powerful Worksheets

Are you ready to learn some advanced Excel features? In this chapter you will learn how to use scenarios and macros to create powerful worksheets.

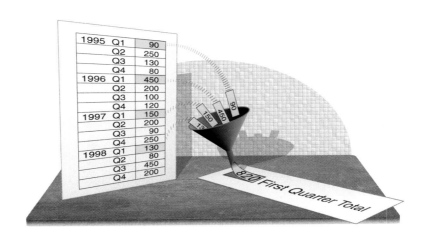

CREATE SCENARIOS

A scenario is a set of alternate values for data in your worksheet. You can create multiple scenarios to see how different values affect your worksheet data.

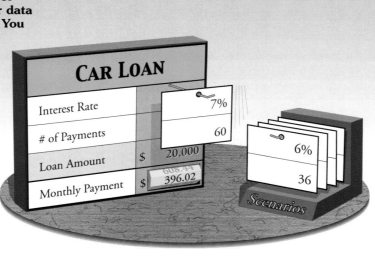

Creating scenarios allows you to consider various outcomes. For example, you can create scenarios to see how changing interest rates will affect your car payments.

CREATE SCENARIOS

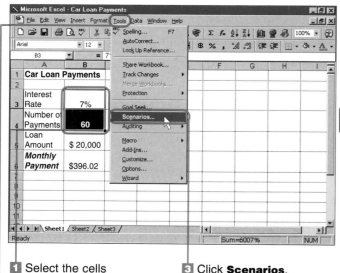

1 Select the cells containing the data you want to change in the scenarios. To select cells, see page 14.

2 Click **Tools**.

3 Click **Scenarios**.

■ The Scenario Manager dialog box appears.

4 Click **Add** to create a new scenario.

■ The Add Scenario dialog box appears.

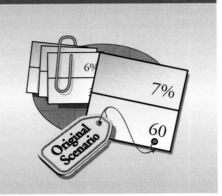

Why should I save the current values as a scenario?

Excel will only keep the current values if you save the values as a scenario. After you create a scenario for the current values, you can use the scenario to redisplay the original worksheet data at any time.

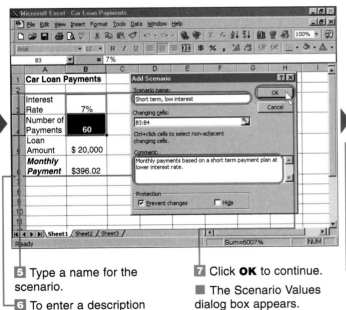

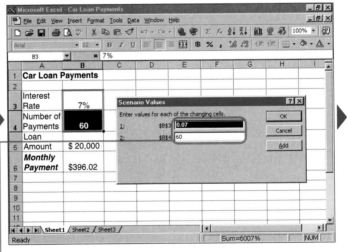

5 Type a name for the scenario.

6 To enter a description for the scenario, drag the mouse I over the text in this area to highlight the text. Then type a description.

7 Click **OK** to continue.

■ The Scenario Values dialog box appears.

■ These areas display the current values of the cells you selected.

■ To save the current values as your first scenario, skip to step **9** on page 236.

CONTINUED

CREATE SCENARIOS

Excel saves your scenarios with your worksheet. You can display a different scenario at any time.

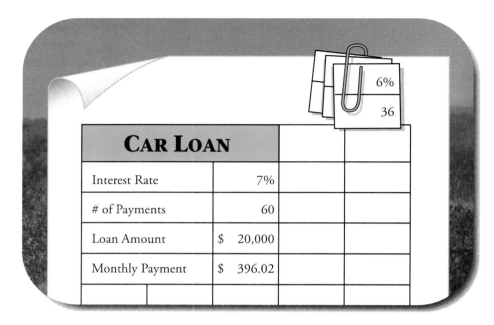

CAR LOAN		
Interest Rate	7%	
# of Payments	60	
Loan Amount	$ 20,000	
Monthly Payment	$ 396.02	

CREATE SCENARIOS (CONTINUED)

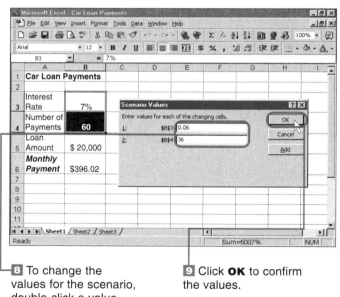

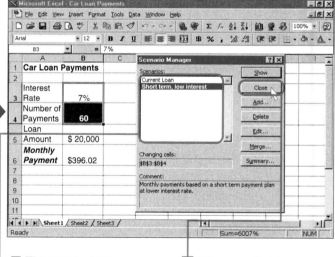

8 To change the values for the scenario, double-click a value and then type a new value. Repeat this step for all the values you want to change.

9 Click **OK** to confirm the values.

■ The Scenario Manager dialog box reappears.

■ The name of the scenario appears in this area.

10 To create another scenario, repeat steps **4** to **9**.

11 When you finish creating scenarios, click **Close** to close the dialog box.

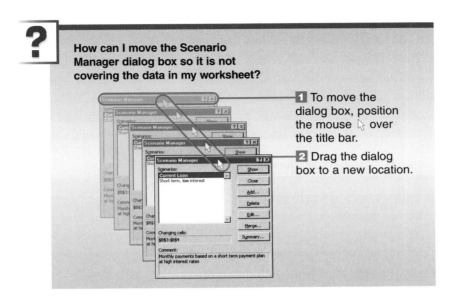

How can I move the Scenario Manager dialog box so it is not covering the data in my worksheet?

■1 To move the dialog box, position the mouse ⌖ over the title bar.

■2 Drag the dialog box to a new location.

DISPLAY SCENARIOS

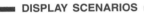

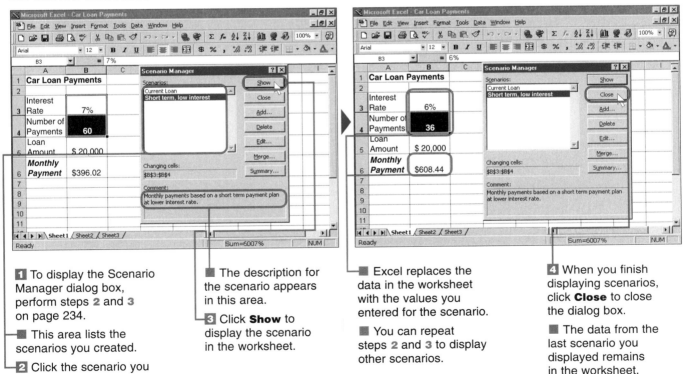

■1 To display the Scenario Manager dialog box, perform steps **2** and **3** on page 234.

■ This area lists the scenarios you created.

■2 Click the scenario you want to display.

■ The description for the scenario appears in this area.

■3 Click **Show** to display the scenario in the worksheet.

■ Excel replaces the data in the worksheet with the values you entered for the scenario.

■ You can repeat steps **2** and **3** to display other scenarios.

■4 When you finish displaying scenarios, click **Close** to close the dialog box.

■ The data from the last scenario you displayed remains in the worksheet.

CREATE A SCENARIO SUMMARY REPORT

You can create a summary report to display the values for each scenario and the effects of the scenarios on the calculations in your worksheet.

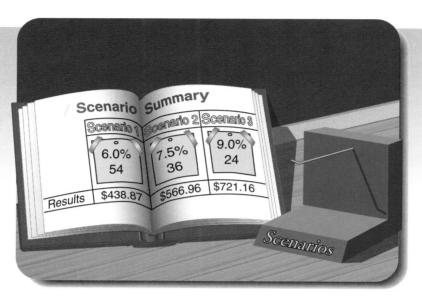

Summary reports are useful when you want to quickly review or print the results of all the scenarios you created.

CREATE A SCENARIO SUMMARY REPORT

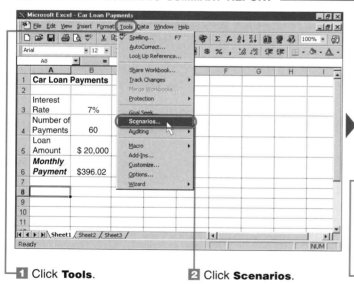

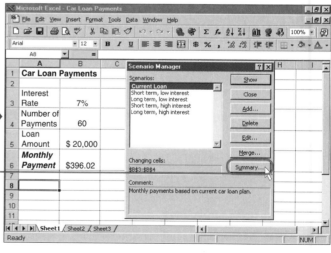

1 Click **Tools**.

2 Click **Scenarios**.

■ The Scenario Manager dialog box appears.

3 Click **Summary** to create a summary report.

■ The Scenario Summary dialog box appears.

? **Why does the Scenario Summary worksheet display plus (⊞) and minus (⊟) sign buttons?**

Excel groups data together in the Scenario Summary worksheet to make the data easier to work with. You can use the plus and minus sign buttons to hide or display details in each group of data.

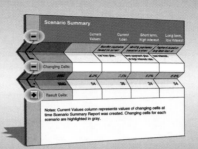

■ Click a plus sign (⊞) to display hidden data.

■ Click a minus sign (⊟) to hide data.

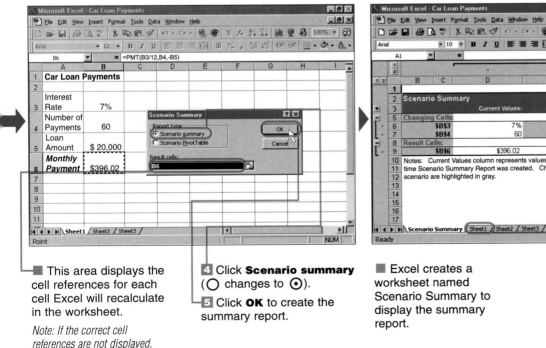

■ This area displays the cell references for each cell Excel will recalculate in the worksheet.

Note: If the correct cell references are not displayed, type each cell reference, separated by a comma (,).

4 Click **Scenario summary** (○ changes to ⊙).

5 Click **OK** to create the summary report.

■ Excel creates a worksheet named Scenario Summary to display the summary report.

■ To redisplay the contents of the original worksheet, click the tab of the original worksheet.

Note: For information on working with multiple worksheets, see pages 174 to 183.

RECORD A MACRO

A macro saves you time by combining a series of commands into a single command. Macros are ideal for tasks you perform repeatedly.

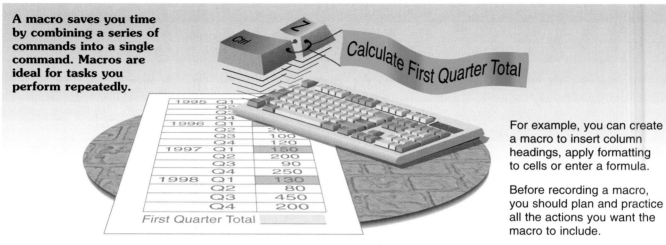

For example, you can create a macro to insert column headings, apply formatting to cells or enter a formula.

Before recording a macro, you should plan and practice all the actions you want the macro to include.

RECORD A MACRO

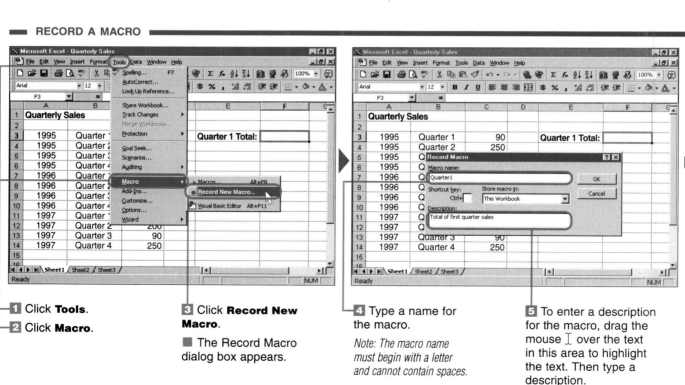

-1 Click **Tools**.

-2 Click **Macro**.

-3 Click **Record New Macro**.

■ The Record Macro dialog box appears.

-4 Type a name for the macro.

Note: The macro name must begin with a letter and cannot contain spaces.

-5 To enter a description for the macro, drag the mouse ⊥ over the text in this area to highlight the text. Then type a description.

? Where can I store a macro?

Personal Macro Workbook

If you want to use a macro with all your workbooks, you can store the macro in the Personal Macro Workbook.

New Workbook

You can have Excel create a new workbook to store the macro. You will only be able to use the macro when the new workbook is open.

This Workbook

You can store the macro in the current workbook. You will only be able to use the macro when this workbook is open.

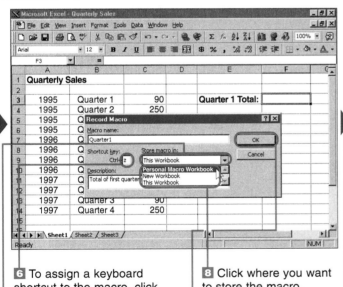

6 To assign a keyboard shortcut to the macro, click this area. Then type the letter you want to use with the Ctrl key as the shortcut.

7 This area shows the location where Excel will store the macro. Click this area to change the location.

8 Click where you want to store the macro.

9 Click **OK** to continue.

■ The Stop Recording toolbar appears.

10 If you want to be able to run the macro in any cell in a worksheet, click 圖.

11 Perform the actions you want the macro to include.

12 When you have completed all the actions you want the macro to include, click ■.

Note: To run a macro, see page 242.

RUN A MACRO

When you run a macro, Excel automatically performs the series of commands you recorded.

You should save your workbook before running a macro. After the macro runs, you will not be able to use the Undo feature to reverse the results of the macro or any changes you made before running the macro.

RUN A MACRO

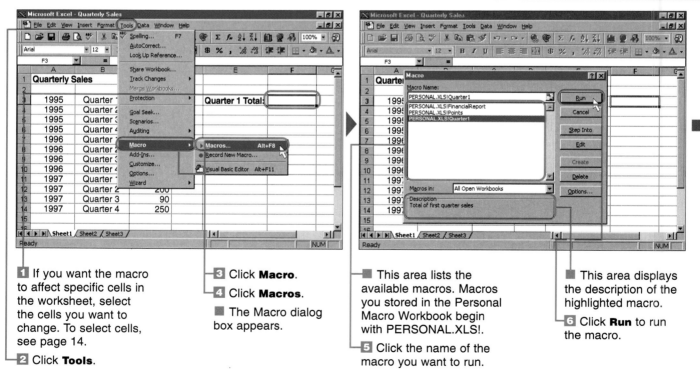

1 If you want the macro to affect specific cells in the worksheet, select the cells you want to change. To select cells, see page 14.

2 Click **Tools**.

3 Click **Macro**.

4 Click **Macros**.

■ The Macro dialog box appears.

■ This area lists the available macros. Macros you stored in the Personal Macro Workbook begin with PERSONAL.XLS!.

5 Click the name of the macro you want to run.

■ This area displays the description of the highlighted macro.

6 Click **Run** to run the macro.

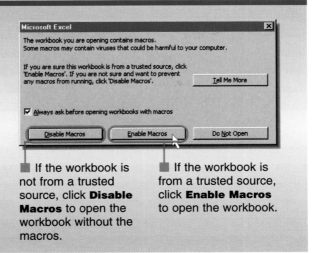

Why does a warning dialog box appear when I open a workbook containing a macro?

Some macros may contain viruses that could damage your computer.

■ If the workbook is not from a trusted source, click **Disable Macros** to open the workbook without the macros.

■ If the workbook is from a trusted source, click **Enable Macros** to open the workbook.

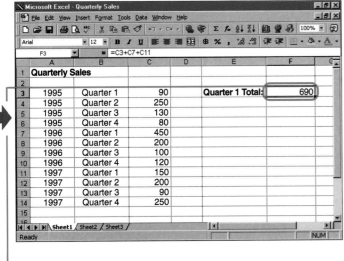

■ The macro performs the tasks you recorded.

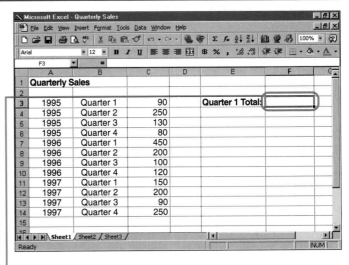

RUN A MACRO USING THE KEYBOARD

1 If you want the macro to affect specific cells in the worksheet, select the cells you want to change.

2 Press and hold down the **Ctrl** key and then press the key for the letter you used to create the keyboard shortcut.

■ The macro performs the tasks you recorded.

CHAPTER 12

Manage Data in a List

Would you like Excel to help you organize and analyze a large collection of data? In this chapter you will learn how to sort data, add subtotals to a list and more.

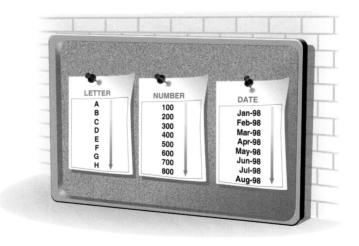

CREATE A LIST

You can create
a list to organize
a large collection
of data.

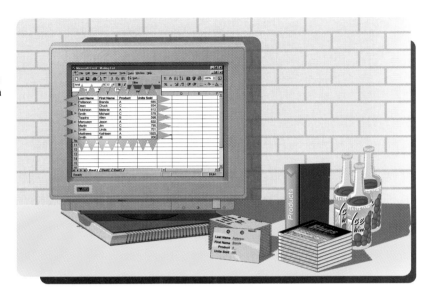

Common lists include
mailing lists, phone
directories, product lists,
library book catalogs,
music collections and
wine lists.

CREATE A LIST

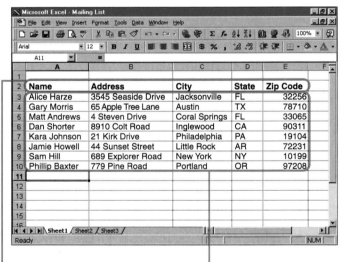

1 Type the column labels
that describe the data you
want to enter into each
column.

*Note: You should bold the column
labels to ensure that Excel will
recognize the text as column labels.
To bold text, see page 118.*

2 Enter the data for
each record. Do not
leave any blank rows
in the list.

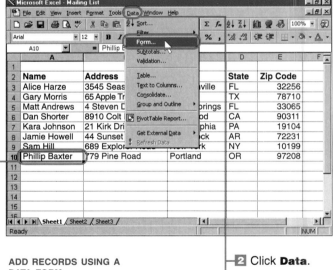

**ADD RECORDS USING A
DATA FORM**

1 Click a cell in the list.

2 Click **Data**.

3 Click **Form**.

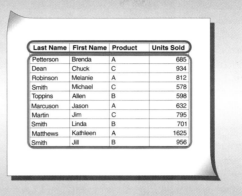

? What are column labels and records?

Column Labels

A column label describes the data in a column. The first row in a list contains the column labels for the list.

Records

A record is a group of related data. Each row in a list contains one record.

Last Name	First Name	Product	Units Sold
Petterson	Brenda	A	685
Dean	Chuck	C	934
Robinson	Melanie	A	812
Smith	Michael	C	578
Toppins	Allen	B	598
Marcuson	Jason	A	632
Martin	Jim	C	795
Smith	Linda	B	701
Matthews	Kathleen	A	1625
Smith	Jill	B	956

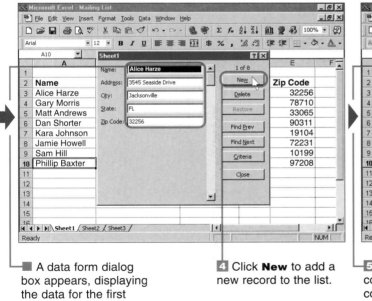

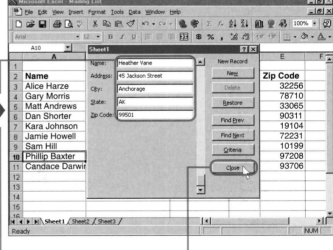

■ A data form dialog box appears, displaying the data for the first record in the list.

4 Click **New** to add a new record to the list.

5 Type the data that corresponds to the first column label and then press the `Tab` key. Repeat this step until you have entered all the data for the record.

6 Repeat steps **4** and **5** for each record you want to add.

7 Click **Close** when you have finished entering records.

EDIT RECORDS IN A LIST

You can edit records in
a list to update the data
or correct a mistake. You
can also delete a record
to remove data you no
longer need from the list.

EDIT RECORDS IN A LIST

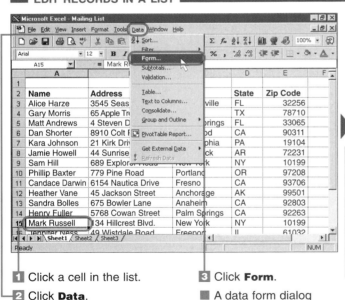

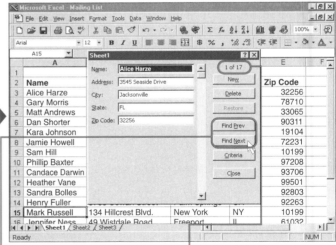

1 Click a cell in the list.

2 Click **Data**.

3 Click **Form**.

■ A data form dialog
box appears, displaying
the data for the first
record in the list.

4 Click one of the
following options to
browse through the
records.

Find Prev - Displays
previous record

Find Next - Displays
next record

■ This area shows the
number of the displayed
record and the total number
of records in the list.

*Note: You can also use the scroll
bar to browse through the records.*

248

Can I make changes to my list directly in the worksheet?

You can edit records directly in the worksheet to update or correct the data in your list. To edit data in a worksheet, see page 44.

You can also delete a row to remove a record you no longer need from your list. To delete a row, see page 64.

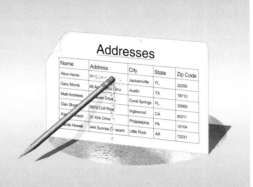

DELETE A RECORD

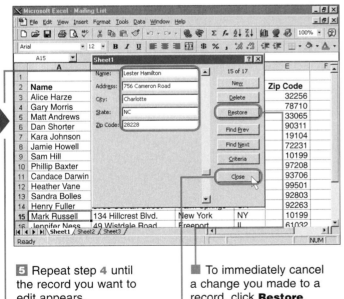

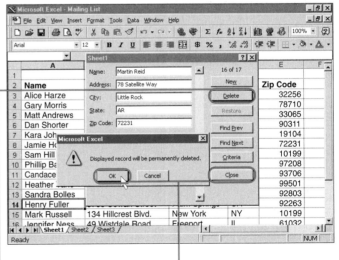

■ **5** Repeat step **4** until the record you want to edit appears.

■ **6** Double-click the data you want to change and then type the new data.

■ To immediately cancel a change you made to a record, click **Restore**.

■ **7** When you finish editing the data, click **Close** to close the data form dialog box.

■ **1** Perform steps **1** to **4** on page 248 to display the record you want to delete in the data form dialog box.

■ **2** Click **Delete**.

■ A dialog box appears, confirming the deletion.

■ **3** Click **OK** to permanently delete the record.

■ **4** Click **Close** to close the data form dialog box.

FIND RECORDS IN A LIST

You can search for records in your list that contain specific data.

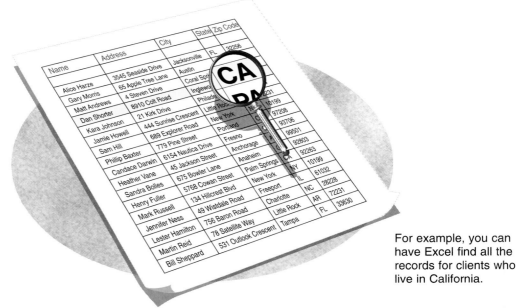

For example, you can have Excel find all the records for clients who live in California.

FIND RECORDS IN A LIST

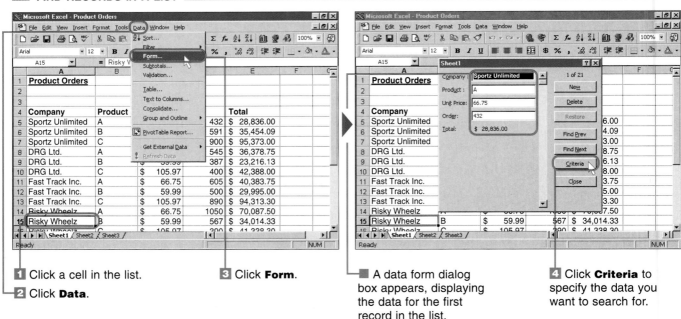

1 Click a cell in the list.

2 Click **Data**.

3 Click **Form**.

■ A data form dialog box appears, displaying the data for the first record in the list.

4 Click **Criteria** to specify the data you want to search for.

Can I use operators to search for specific data in the records?

There are several operators you can use to find specific data.

Operator	Example	Result
=	=100	Finds data equal to 100
>	>100	Finds data greater than 100
<	<100	Finds data less than 100
>=	>=100	Finds data greater than or equal to 100
<=	<=100	Finds data less than or equal to 100
<>	<>100	Finds data not equal to 100

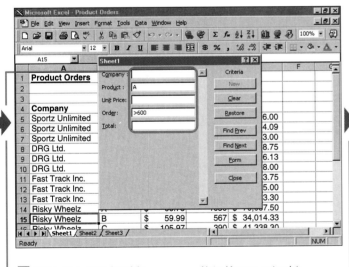

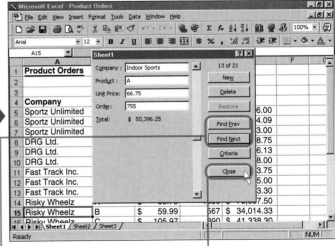

5 Click the area beside the label for the column containing the data you want to search for. Then type the data.

Note: You can enter data into more than one area. For example, you can find all the companies that bought more than 600 units of product A.

6 Click one of the following options.

Find Prev - Displays previous matching record

Find Next - Displays next matching record

7 Repeat step **6** until you have finished viewing all the matching records.

Note: Your computer beeps when you reach the first or last matching record.

8 Click **Close** to close the data form dialog box.

SORT RECORDS IN A LIST

You can organize your list by changing the order of the records.

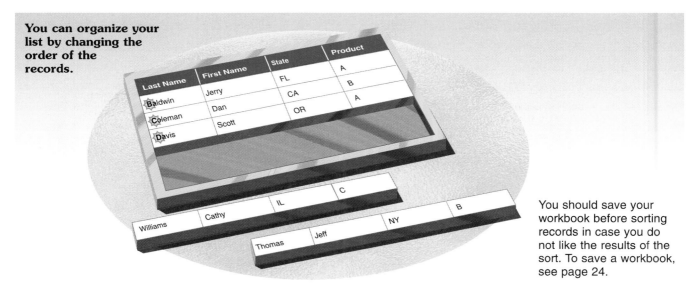

You should save your workbook before sorting records in case you do not like the results of the sort. To save a workbook, see page 24.

SORT BY ONE COLUMN

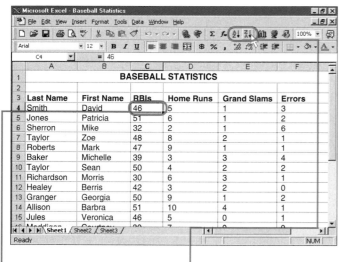

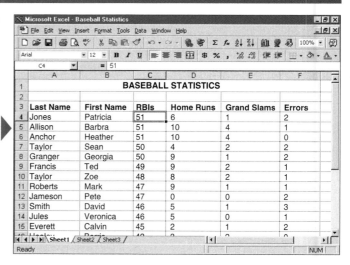

1 Click a cell in the column you want to sort by.

2 Click the way you want to sort the records.

[↓] Sort 0 to 9, A to Z

[↓] Sort 9 to 0, Z to A

■ The records in the list appear in the new order.

■ In this example, the records are sorted by RBIs.

Why would I sort my records by more than one column?

Sorting by more than one column allows you to further organize the records in your list. For example, if a last name appears more than once in your list, you can sort by a second column, such as First Name.

	A	B
1	**Last Name**	**First Name**
2	Carter	Michael
3	Jones	Beatrice
4	Jones	Allan
5	Jones	Cathy
6	Thompson	Mary

	A	B
1	**Last Name**	**First Name**
2	Carter	Michael
3	Jones	Allan
4	Jones	Beatrice
5	Jones	Cathy
6	Thompson	Mary

■ SORT BY TWO COLUMNS ■

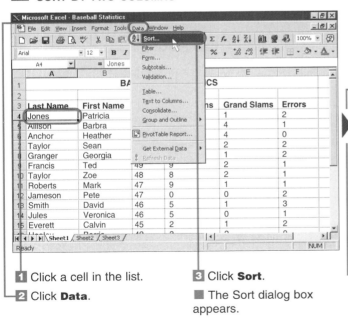

1 Click a cell in the list.

2 Click **Data**.

3 Click **Sort**.

■ The Sort dialog box appears.

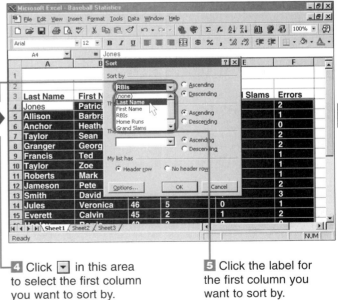

4 Click ▼ in this area to select the first column you want to sort by.

5 Click the label for the first column you want to sort by.

CONTINUED ▶

SORT RECORDS IN A LIST

You can sort the
records in your
list by letter,
number or date.

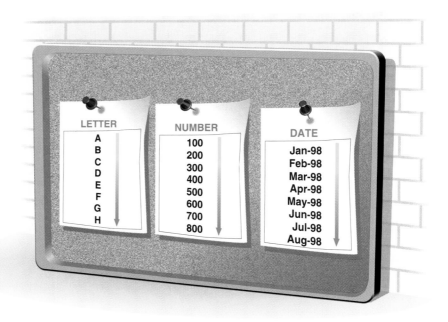

SORT BY TWO COLUMNS (CONTINUED)

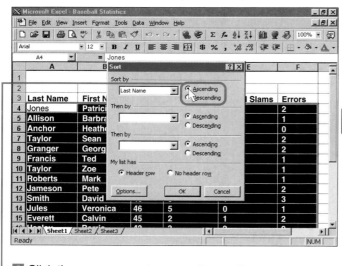

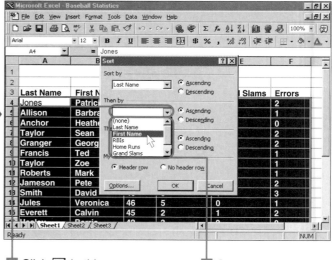

6 Click the way you want
to sort the first column
(○ changes to ⊙).

Ascending -
Sorts 0 to 9, A to Z

Descending -
Sorts 9 to 0, Z to A

7 Click ▼ in this area
to select the second
column you want to
sort by.

8 Click the label for
the second column
you want to sort by.

How often can I sort records in my list?

You can sort records in your list as often as you like. This is useful if you frequently add new records to the list.

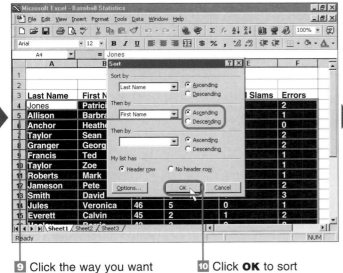

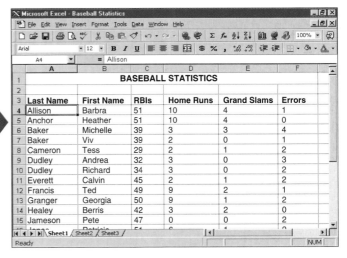

9 Click the way you want to sort the second column (○ changes to ⊙).

10 Click **OK** to sort the records.

■ The records in the list appear in the new order.

■ In this example, the records are sorted by last name. All records with the same last name are then sorted by first name.

FILTER RECORDS IN A LIST

You can filter your
list to display
only the records
containing the data
you want to view.

Using the AutoFilter
feature allows you to
analyze your data by
placing related records
together and hiding
the records you do
not want to view.

FILTER RECORDS

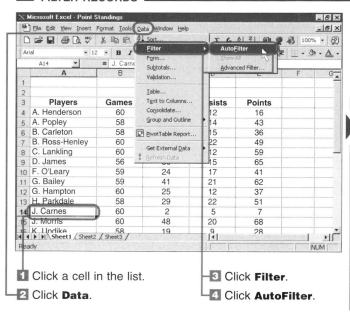

1 Click a cell in the list.

2 Click **Data**.

3 Click **Filter**.

4 Click **AutoFilter**.

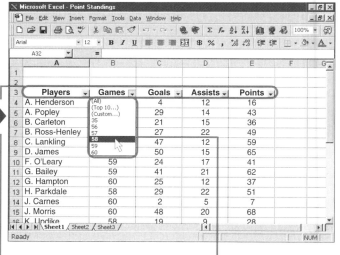

■ An arrow (▼) appears
beside each column label.

5 Click ▼ in the column
containing the data you
want to use to filter the list.

6 Click the data you
want to use to filter
the list.

256

How do I turn off the AutoFilter feature when I no longer want to filter the records in my list?

To turn off the AutoFilter feature, repeat steps **2** to **4** on page 256.

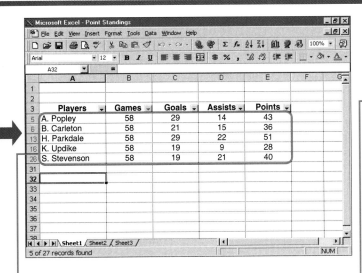

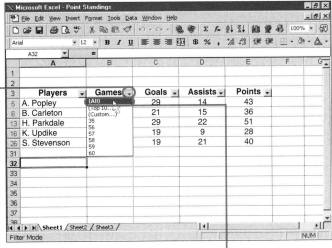

■ The list displays only the records containing the data you specified. The other records are temporarily hidden.

■ In this example, the list displays only the records containing players who have played 58 games.

REDISPLAY ALL RECORDS

1 To once again display all the records, click ▼ in the column containing the data you used to filter the list.

2 Click **(All)**.

FILTER RECORDS IN A LIST

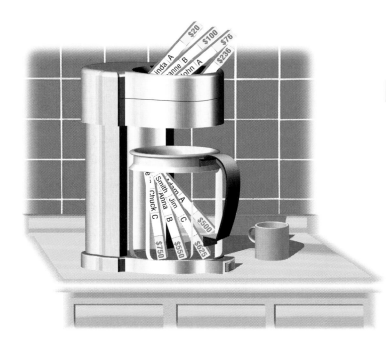

You can filter your list to display only records containing data within a specific range.

For example, you can display records for employees whose sales are greater than or equal to $500.

FILTER RECORDS BY COMPARING VALUES

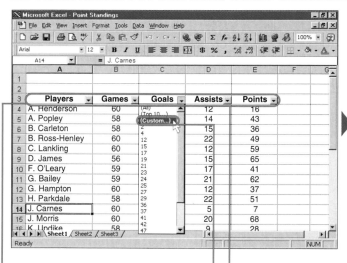

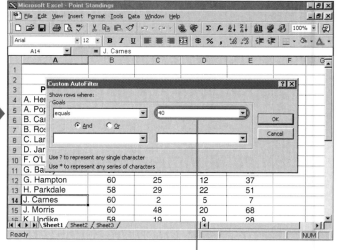

1 To turn on the AutoFilter feature, perform steps 1 to 4 on page 256.

■ An arrow (▼) appears beside each column label.

2 Click ▼ in the column containing the data you want to use to filter the list.

3 Click **(Custom...)**.

■ The Custom AutoFilter dialog box appears.

4 Type the data you want Excel to compare to each record in the list.

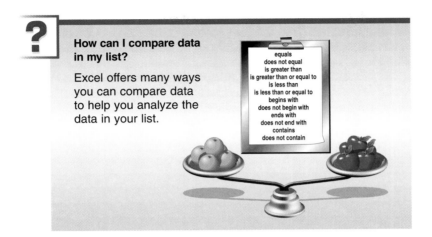

How can I compare data in my list?

Excel offers many ways you can compare data to help you analyze the data in your list.

equals
does not equal
is greater than
is greater than or equal to
is less than
is less than or equal to
begins with
does not begin with
ends with
does not end with
contains
does not contain

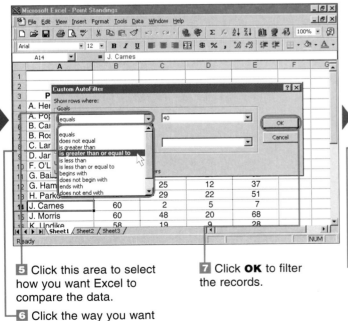

5 Click this area to select how you want Excel to compare the data.

6 Click the way you want Excel to compare the data.

7 Click **OK** to filter the records.

■ The list displays only the records containing the data you specified. The other records are temporarily hidden.

■ In this example, the list displays only the records for players who have scored 40 goals or more.

■ To once again display all the records, perform steps **1** and **2** on page 257.

■ To turn off the AutoFilter feature, perform steps **2** to **4** on page 256.

ADD SUBTOTALS TO A LIST

You can quickly
summarize data by
adding subtotals to
your list.

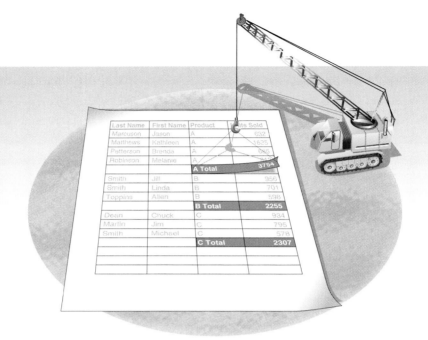

ADD SUBTOTALS TO A LIST

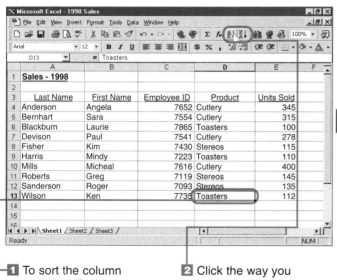

1 To sort the column
you want to display
subtotals for, click
a cell in the column.

2 Click the way you
want to sort the data.

⬆ Sort 0 to 9, A to Z

⬇ Sort 9 to 0, Z to A

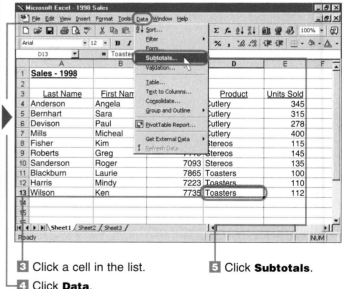

3 Click a cell in the list.

4 Click **Data**.

5 Click **Subtotals**.

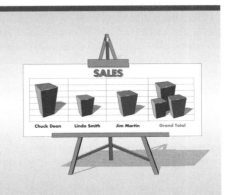

How can subtotals help me?

You can use subtotals to help
analyze the data in your list
and quickly create reports and
charts to summarize the data.
For example, in a list containing
employee names and sales,
you can use subtotals to find
the total sales made by each
employee and the grand total
of all the sales.

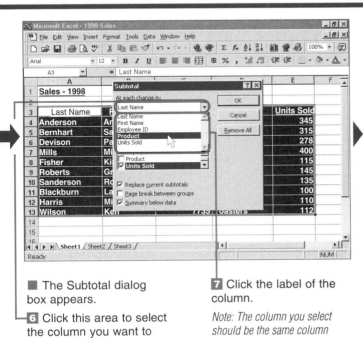

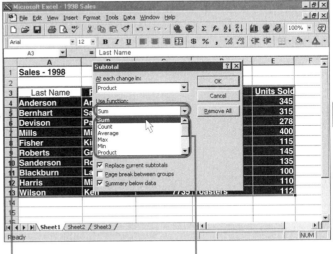

■ The Subtotal dialog
box appears.

6 Click this area to select
the column you want to
display subtotals for.

7 Click the label of the
column.

*Note: The column you select
should be the same column
you sorted in step 1.*

8 Click this area to
select the calculation
you want to perform.

9 Click the calculation.

CONTINUED

ADD SUBTOTALS TO A LIST

After adding subtotals to your list, you can display just the grand total, the grand total and subtotals or all of the data in the list.

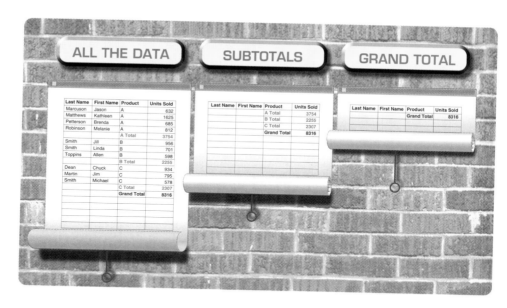

| ALL THE DATA | SUBTOTALS | GRAND TOTAL |

ADD SUBTOTALS TO A LIST (CONTINUED)

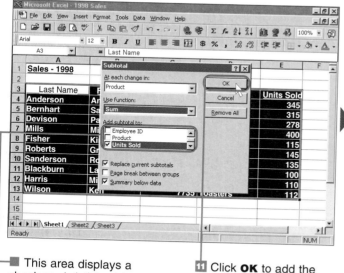

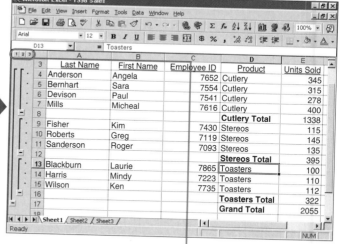

■ This area displays a check mark (✔) beside the label for the column that Excel will subtotal.

■10 To add or remove a check mark, click the box beside the column label.

■11 Click **OK** to add the subtotals to the list.

■ The list displays the subtotals and a grand total.

■ These symbols help you change the display of the data.

? **How do I remove subtotals from my list?**

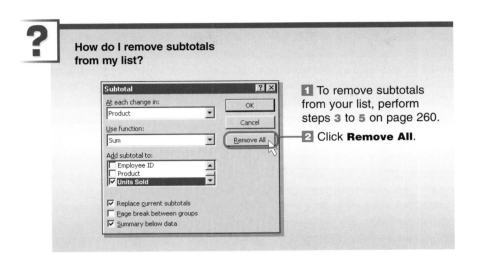

■1 To remove subtotals from your list, perform steps **3** to **5** on page 260.

■2 Click **Remove All**.

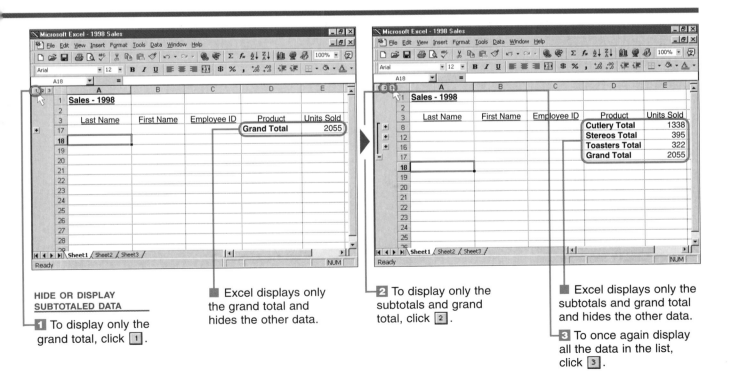

HIDE OR DISPLAY SUBTOTALED DATA

■1 To display only the grand total, click 1.

■ Excel displays only the grand total and hides the other data.

■2 To display only the subtotals and grand total, click 2.

■ Excel displays only the subtotals and grand total and hides the other data.

■3 To once again display all the data in the list, click 3.

CHAPTER 13

Excel and the Internet

Are you wondering how Excel can help you take advantage of the Internet? In this chapter you will learn how to display a Web page, create a hyperlink and save data as a Web page.

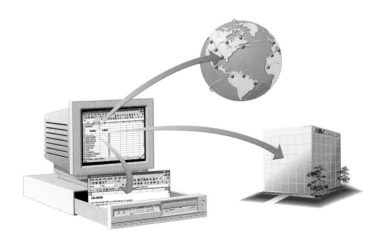

CREATE A HYPERLINK

You can create a
hyperlink to connect
data in a workbook to
another document or
Web page. When you
select the hyperlink,
the other document
will appear.

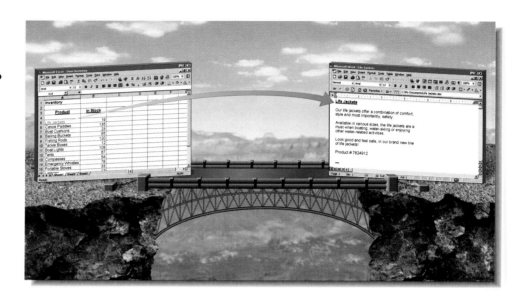

CREATE A HYPERLINK

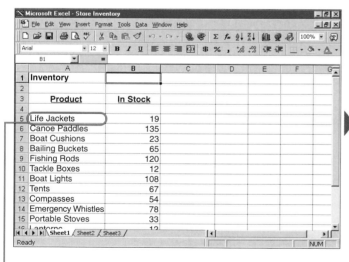

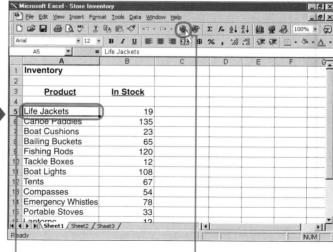

1 Enter the data you
want to link to another
document.

2 Save the workbook.
To save a workbook,
see page 24.

3 Click the cell
containing the data
you entered in step **1**.

4 Click 🔗 to create a
hyperlink.

■ The Insert Hyperlink
dialog box appears.

Where can a hyperlink take me?

You can create a hyperlink that takes you to another document on your computer, network, corporate intranet or the Internet.

Note: An intranet is a small version of the Internet within a company.

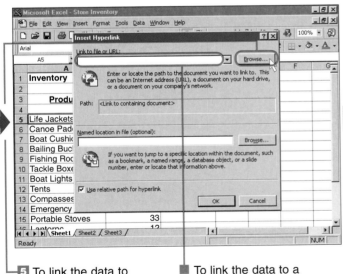

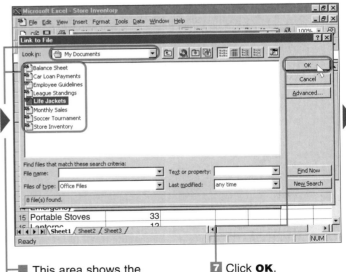

■ **5** To link the data to a document on your computer or network, click **Browse**.

■ The Link to File dialog box appears.

■ To link the data to a Web page, type the address of the Web page (example: **www.maran.com**). Then skip to step **8** on page 268.

■ This area shows the location of the displayed documents. You can click this area to change the location.

■ **6** Click the document you want to link to.

■ **7** Click **OK**.

CONTINUED

CREATE A HYPERLINK

You can easily see the hyperlinks in your workbook. Hyperlinks appear underlined and in color.

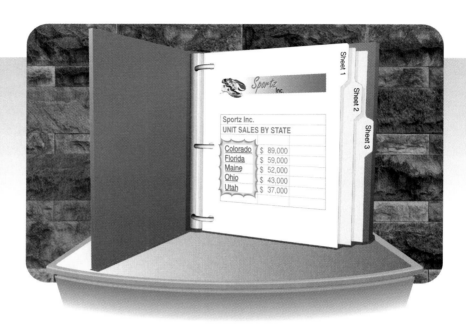

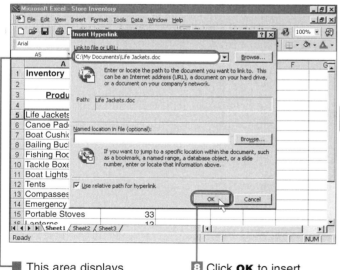

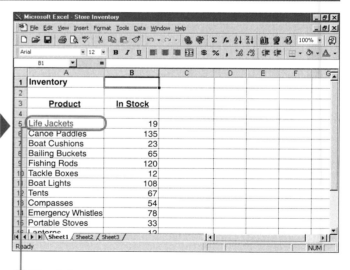

■ This area displays the address of the document.

8 Click **OK** to insert the hyperlink into the workbook.

■ The data you selected in step **3** becomes a hyperlink.

What information can I use as a hyperlink?

You can create a hyperlink using information such as worksheet data, AutoShapes, pictures and maps. Make sure the information you choose clearly indicates where the hyperlink will take you.

DATA   PICTURE   MAP

SELECT A HYPERLINK

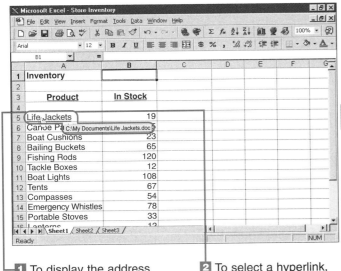

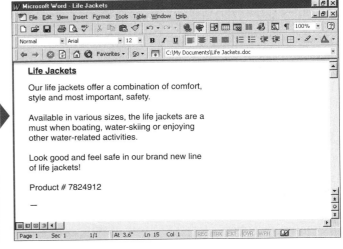

1 To display the address of the document connected to a hyperlink, position the mouse ⟍ over the hyperlink (⟍ changes to ⟨ᕽ⟩). After a few seconds, the address appears.

2 To select a hyperlink, click the hyperlink.

■ The document connected to the hyperlink appears.

■ If the hyperlink is connected to a Web page, your Web browser opens and displays the Web page.

DISPLAY THE WEB TOOLBAR

You can display the Web toolbar at any time. The Web toolbar allows you to access information on the Internet, your company's intranet or your own computer.

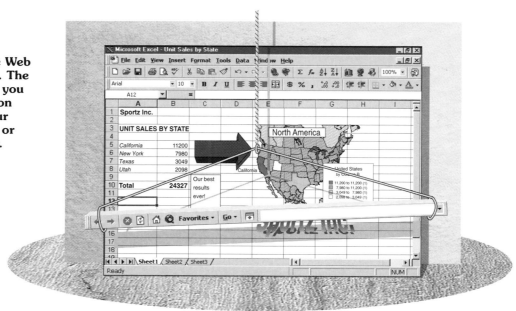

DISPLAY THE WEB TOOLBAR

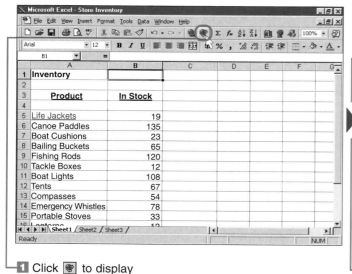

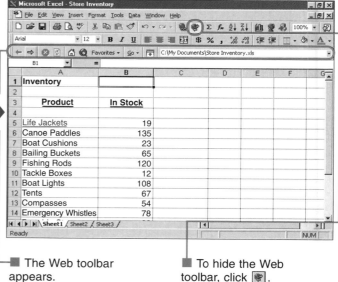

1 Click to display the Web toolbar.

■ The Web toolbar appears.

■ To hide the Web toolbar, click the button.

MOVE BETWEEN DOCUMENTS

You can easily move
back and forth between
documents you have
displayed using
hyperlinks.

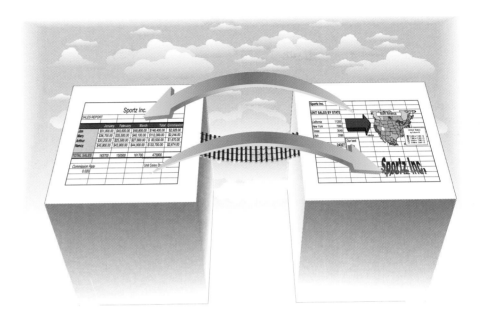

MOVE BETWEEN DOCUMENTS

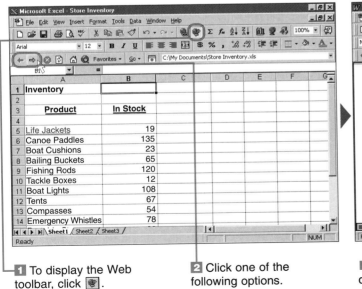

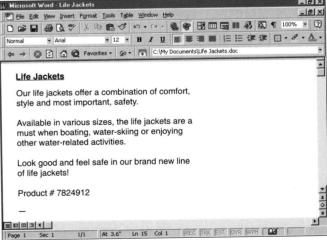

1 To display the Web
toolbar, click 🌐.

2 Click one of the
following options.

⬅ Move back

➡ Move forward

■ The previous or next
document appears.

DISPLAY A WEB PAGE

While working in
Excel, you can
quickly display
a Web page of
interest.

DISPLAY A WEB PAGE

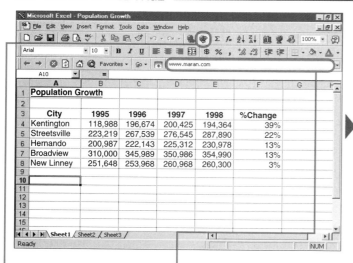

1 To display the
Web toolbar, click 🌐.

2 Click this area and type
the address of the Web
page you want to open
(example: **www.maran.com**).
Then press the **Enter** key.

*Note: A dialog box may appear,
warning you about security issues.
Click **OK** to open the Web page.*

■ Your Web browser
opens and displays
the Web page.

*Note: If you are not currently
connected to the Internet, a
dialog box may appear that
allows you to connect.*

DISPLAY THE START OR SEARCH PAGE

You can quickly
display the start
or search page.

Start page

The start page is the Web
page that appears each
time you start your Web
browser. The start page is
often called the home page.

Search page

The search page is a
Web page that allows
you to search for
information of interest
on the Web.

DISPLAY THE START OR SEARCH PAGE

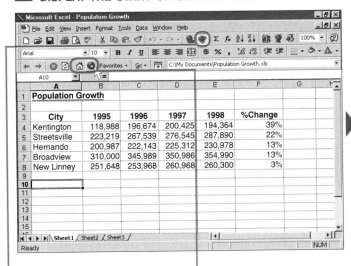

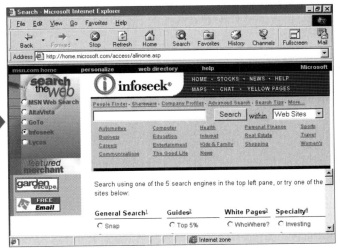

1 To display the
Web toolbar, click 📊.

2 Click one of the
following options.

🏠 Display start page

🔍 Display search page

*Note: A dialog box may appear,
warning you about security
issues. Click **OK** to open the
Web page.*

■ Your Web browser
opens and displays the
Web page you selected.

*Note: If you are not currently
connected to the Internet,
a dialog box may appear
that allows you to connect.*

ADD A WORKBOOK TO FAVORITES FOLDER

You can add a workbook you frequently use to the Favorites folder. This allows you to quickly open the workbook at any time.

ADD A WORKBOOK TO FAVORITES FOLDER

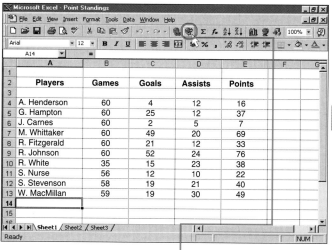

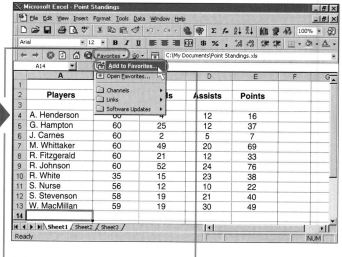

1 Open the workbook you want to add to the Favorites folder. To open a workbook, see page 36.

2 To display the Web toolbar, click 🌐.

3 Click **Favorites**.

4 Click **Add to Favorites**.

■ The Add to Favorites dialog box appears.

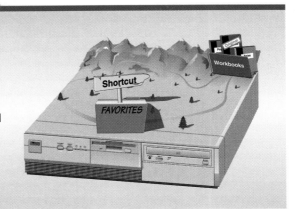

When I add a workbook to the Favorites folder, does the location of the workbook on my computer change?

When you add a workbook to the Favorites folder, Excel places a shortcut to the original workbook in the folder. The original workbook does not change its location on your computer.

OPEN A WORKBOOK IN FAVORITES FOLDER

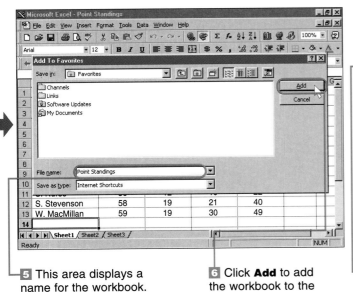

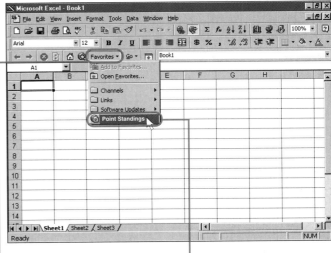

5 This area displays a name for the workbook. To change the name, type a new name.

Note: Changing the name for the workbook in the Favorites folder does not change the name of the original workbook on your computer.

6 Click **Add** to add the workbook to the Favorites folder.

1 Click **Favorites** to display a list of items in the Favorites folder.

2 Click the name of the workbook you want to open.

Note: If your Web browser has a Favorites feature, your favorite Web pages may also appear in the list.

You can save your worksheet data as a Web page. This allows you to later publish the data on the Web or your company's intranet.

Before you can save your data as a Web page, you need to install the Web Page Authoring (HTML) component from the CD-ROM disc you used to install Excel.

SAVE DATA AS A WEB PAGE

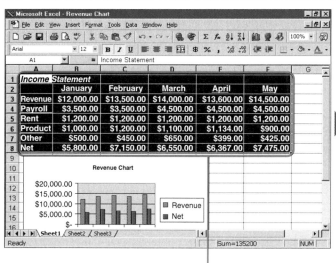

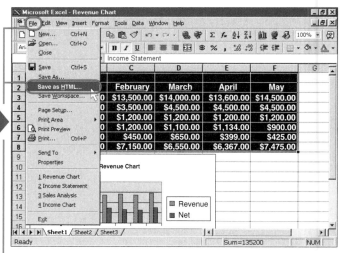

1 Open the workbook containing the data you want to save as a Web page. To open a workbook, see page 36.

2 Select the cells containing the data. To select cells, see page 14.

3 Click **File**.

4 Click **Save as HTML**.

■ The Internet Assistant Wizard appears.

*Note: The first time you save data as a Web page, the Office Assistant may appear. Click **No** to hide the Office Assistant.*

? How do I publish my data on the Web?

After you save your data as a Web page, you can publish the page by transferring the page to a Web server. The company that gives you access to the Internet usually offers space on its Web server where you can publish your Web page.

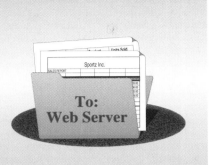

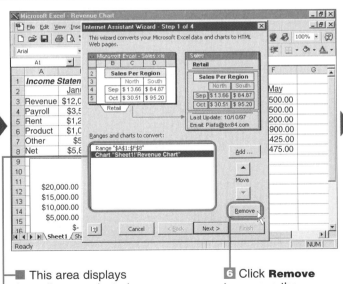

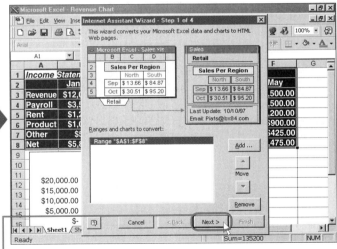

■ This area displays the cells you selected and any charts in the workbook.

5 If you do not want to include a chart on the Web page, click the chart.

6 Click **Remove** to remove the chart from the list.

7 Click **Next** to continue.

CONTINUED

SAVE DATA AS A WEB PAGE

Excel lets you add additional information, such as a title, your name or your e-mail address, to your Web page.

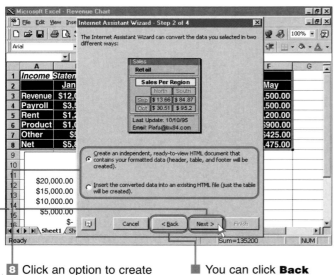

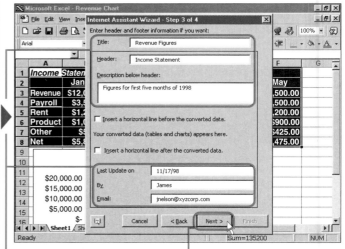

■8 Click an option to create a new Web page or add the data to an existing Web page (○ changes to ⊙).

■9 Click **Next** to continue.

■ You can click **Back** at any time to return to a previous step and change your selections.

■ The options available in the next screens depend on the option you selected in step 8.

■ The information in these areas will appear on the Web page.

■10 To enter information, click each area and then type the appropriate information.

■ If an area contains information you want to delete, drag the mouse I over the text in the area to highlight the text. Then press the Delete key.

■11 Click **Next** to continue.

How can I view the Web page I created?

You can use your Web browser to view the Web page you created. This is useful if you want to preview the Web page on your computer before publishing the page on the Web.

To view the Web page, perform steps **1** and **2** on page 272, except type the location and name of the Web page in step **2** (example: **C:\My Documents\Sales Report.htm**).

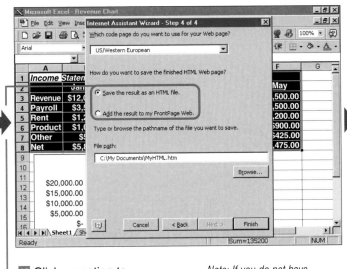

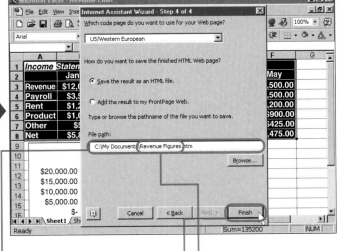

12 Click an option to specify how you want to save the Web page (○ changes to ⊙).

Note: If you do not have FrontPage installed on your computer, save the result as an HTML file.

■ This area displays the location and name of the Web page.

13 To change the name of the Web page, drag the mouse ⌶ over the name to highlight the name. Then type a new name.

14 Click **Finish** to create the Web page.

INDEX

INDEX

INDEX

INDEX

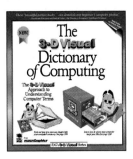
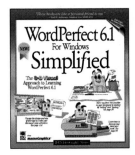

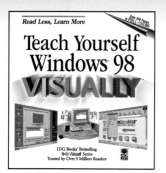
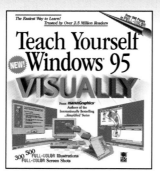

IDG BOOKS ®

TRADE & INDIVIDUAL ORDERS	EDUCATIONAL ORDERS & DISCOUNTS	CORPORATE ORDERS FOR 3-D VISUAL™ SERIES
Phone: **(800) 762-2974** or **(317) 596-5200** (*8 a.m. – 6 p.m., CST, weekdays*) FAX : **(800) 550-2747** or **(317) 596-5692**	Phone: **(800) 434-2086** (*8:30 a.m.–5:00 p.m., CST, weekdays*) FAX : **(317) 596-5499**	Phone: **(800) 469-6616** (*8 a.m.–5 p.m., EST, weekdays*) FAX : **(905) 890-9434**

Qty	ISBN	Title	Price	Total

Shipping & Handling Charges

	Description	First book	Each add'l. book	Total
Domestic	Normal	$4.50	$1.50	$
	Two Day Air	$8.50	$2.50	$
	Overnight	$18.00	$3.00	$
International	Surface	$8.00	$8.00	$
	Airmail	$16.00	$16.00	$
	DHL Air	$17.00	$17.00	$

Subtotal _____

CA residents add applicable sales tax _____

IN, MA and MD residents add 5% sales tax _____

IL residents add 6.25% sales tax _____

RI residents add 7% sales tax _____

TX residents add 8.25% sales tax _____

Shipping _____

Total _____

Ship to:

Name_____

Address_____

Company_____

City/State/Zip_____

Daytime Phone_____

Payment: ☐ Check to IDG Books (US Funds Only)
☐ Visa ☐ Mastercard ☐ American Express

Card # _____ Exp. _____ Signature_____

maranGraphics™